BEING YOU!

Awaken to the Abundance of
Your Natural State of Being

DR SCOTT ZARCINAS

OTHER BOOKS BY SCOTT ZARCINAS

Non-fiction

The Banana Trap
It's Up to YOU!
The Power of YOU!

Fiction

Samantha Honeycomb
The Golden Chalice
DeVille's Contract
Ananda
Roadman

BEING YOU!

Awaken to the Abundance of
Your Natural State of Being

DR SCOTT ZARCINAS

DoctorZed
Publishing
www.doctorzed.com

Copyright © Scott Zarcinas 2023

All rights reserved. No part of this book may be used or reproduced by any means, graphic, electronic, or mechanical, including photocopying, recording, taping or by any information storage retrieval system without the written permission of the publisher except in the case of brief quotations embodied in critical articles and reviews.

First published as Your Natural State of Being.
This revised and updated 3rd edition published 2023 by DoctorZed Publishing.

Copies of this book can be ordered via the author's website at www.scottzarcinas.com, booksellers or by contacting:

DoctorZed Publishing
10 Vista Ave, Skye,
South Australia 5072
www.doctorzed.com

ISBN: 978-0-6456384-7-9 (hc)
ISBN: 978-0-6456384-8-6 (sc)
ISBN: 978-0-6456384-9-3 (e)

A CiP number is available at the National Library of Australia.

Because of the dynamic nature of the Internet, any web addresses or links contained in this book may have changed since publication and may no longer be valid. The views expressed in this work are solely those of the author and do not necessarily reflect the views of the publisher, and the publisher hereby disclaims any responsibility for them.

The author of this book does not dispense medical advice or prescribe the use of any technique as a form of treatment for physical, emotional, or medical problems without the advice of a physician, either directly or indirectly. The intent of the author is only to offer information of a general nature. In the event you use any of the information in this book for yourself, which is your constitutional right, the author and the publisher assume no responsibility for your actions.

DoctorZed Publishing rev. date: 10/02/2023

CONTENTS

Acknowledgements		vii
Signs of the Ink		viii
Introduction		**1**
Part I	**Motivation**	**15**
Chapter 1	Pleasure & Pain	17
Chapter 2	Goodness, Truth & Beauty	51
Chapter 3	Light, Life & Love	65
Chapter 4	The Gateway of Stillness	95
Part II	**Suffering**	**107**
Chapter 5	The Fall into Nothingness	109
Chapter 6	The Cycle of Addiction	135
Chapter 7	Grasping at Source	157
Part III	**Love**	**163**
Chapter 8	The Power of Love	165
Chapter 9	The Manifestation of Love	179
Part IV	**Perception**	**197**
Chapter 10	Big Mind, Small Mind	199
Chapter 11	The Pathway of Perception	215
Chapter 12	Another World	249
The Last Word		259
Bibliography		267

For every seeker—may you awaken to the abundance of your natural state of being.

ACKNOWLEDGEMENTS

To my wife, Martie, for your continual love and support. Paul and Lizzie Bradley, for your continuing friendship over the many years. Last, but never least, my wonderful daughters, Zsa Zsa and Zenya, through you I learn more of the joy of life every day.

Signs of the Ink

The letters are the signs of the ink; there is not one,
Save what the ink hath anointed; their own color is pure illusion.
The ink's color it is that hath come into manifest being.
Yet it cannot be said that the ink hath departed from what it was.
The inwardness of the letters lay in the ink's mystery,
And their outward show is through its self-determination.
They [the letters] are its determinations, its activities,
And naught is there but it. Understand thou the parable!
They are not it; say not, say not that they are it!
To say so were wrong, and to say 'it is they' were raving madness.
For it was before the letters, when no letter was;
And it remaineth, when no letter at all shall be.
Look well at each letter: thou seest it hath already perished
But for the face of the ink, that is, for the Face of His Essence,
Unto Whom All Glory and Majesty Exaltation!
Even thus the letters, for all their outward show, are hidden,
Being overwhelmed by the ink, since their show is none other than its.
The letter addeth naught to the ink, and taketh naught from it,
But revealeth its integrality in various modes,
Without changing the ink. Do ink and letter together make two?
Realize then the truth of my words: no being is there
Save that of the ink, for him whose understanding is sound;
And wheresoe'er be the letter, there with it is always its ink.
Open thine intellect unto these parables and heed them!

—Abd al-Ghani an-Nabulusi
Cairo 1889

INTRODUCTION

THE PROBLEM WITH HUMANITY

THE HISTORY OF humanity is scarred with torment and pain. Suffering is an everyday component of our lives. In our efforts to eradicate the alleged causes of it, such as disease and illness, we have managed to conjure magical medicines and develop tremendous scientific techniques. In our efforts to accrue greater happiness and freedom, we have managed to build marvelous machines and invent terrific technology. We have tried in many ways to increase pleasure and limit pain, all to no avail. Hunger and famine are rife throughout the world. Wars and torture continue unabated. Women are still physically, emotionally and sexually abused. Children die in the thousands every day from preventable illnesses and lack of potable water. Mental illness, alcoholism and drug addiction are at pandemic proportions. Due to the over-exploitation of the planet's resources, the rainforests are dwindling at an alarming rate and the oceans' fish stocks are threatened with extinction. Our efforts to build a better world, one in which every man, woman and child can live in peace and harmony, where everyone has equal rights, has shelter from the elements and food to share, have been a failure.

Thankfully, this is not necessarily the whole truth. It may seem as if what we have is as good as it gets, but there is a path that will lead us out of the mess we have created. Although, it must be said, the path is not an easy one. It is certainly no quick-fix solution, nor is it pleasant or trouble-free. In fact, to the majority it will be repugnant. But it is, as it has always been, our only hope.

Like any disease or illness, two requirements must be fulfilled before a cure to humanity's suffering is even considered a possibility.

First, the presence of the illness or disease must be correctly identified and completely accepted before it can be treated:

The acknowledgment of suffering is a prerequisite to its cure.

Peter G. is a high-flying friend in the corporate world who refuses to accept the notion that he is suffering. In quiet moments, he readily admits to bouts of depression, loneliness and fatigue, but will then claim that these symptoms are nothing in comparison to the "real" suffering in the Third World. It is as if the acknowledgment of suffering is a weakness, and weakness is not something the corporate world looks kindly upon. His ego will not even allow him to consider the possibility that mental torment is as valid as physical torture in regards to suffering. Consequently, his attitude of, "Everything's all right. There's nothing wrong with me," leads to the delay of his healing and prolongation of his symptoms. Denial for Peter, like so many others, merely perpetuates the problem.

The second requirement for healing humanity's problems is desire and intent, or will, to eradicate it. Once the presence of suffering has been fully acknowledged, the next step is to develop the will to do something about it. In the Buddhist tradition, the desire to end human suffering is called compassion, and the desire for others to find happiness is called loving-kindness. It is, in fact, no surprise that will is the beating heart of compassion and loving-kindness. Will opens up pathways that were previously hidden. If there is no desire or intent to change our beliefs or points of views, if there is no will to seek beyond the horizon, we won't even look for alternative paths or routes to lead us out of our suffering.

"Where there's a will, there's a way," as the saying goes. Taking a medical point of view, a sick patient must develop the will to improve his or her state of health before healing can begin: a patient must want to get better. This includes agreeing to the type and course of treatment and any other procedures identified by the health professionals, what is known as compliance.

INTRODUCTION

Wanting to get better may sound like plain common sense, but it is surprising the number of patients that have a vested interest in remaining unwell and that secretly harbor abhorrence of any treatment that might actually improve their condition. Pain and suffering to some, is beneficial. It can provide much needed attention for the lonely. It can provide a sense of bitter joy to those with a masochistic personality, to those that know happiness only through wallowing in misery. Most of all, it can provide a sense of identity, or more precisely, a sense of victim identity to those with a highly developed blame personality.

I know of a man with a particular narcissistic bent who likes nothing more than to regale his guests and fellow bus commuters with stories of malpractice and outrageous indecencies perpetrated by the medical or legal profession. He has become bitter with age but the last thing he wants is to get better and end his suffering. He has invested so much of himself in his pain that to become pain-free would, in effect, be a loss of identity and that, to him, would be like dying.

In finding a cure (do we dare yet call it salvation?) for the suffering on our planet, we must therefore identify and acknowledge what the problem facing humanity actually is and then we, as a collective whole, must want to do something about it. We cannot afford to live in denial of our problems, nor can we afford to have a vested interest in maintaining our suffering.

The fate of humanity and the planet is at stake.

ACKNOWLEDGING THE PROBLEM

Our beliefs are the eyes with which we see the world and ourselves. They are the filtering system of our reality, and if we are to get to the root of humanity's suffering we must first acknowledge that every problem in the world begins with our beliefs. The pandemic error of thought afflicting the human condition, the cause of all our suffering, is the belief that we are born in isolation with nothing. The basic tenet, or assumption, is this: born isolated from our Source and everything else in the universe, we start our life from scratch and must work to accumulate as much as we can to make up for the shortfall. We must fill the void of nothingness we feel inside with material wealth and the one with the most at the end of their life is the winner.

Like a noxious weed, this idea takes root in the nooks and crannies of our psyche where it is nurtured and encouraged in the hothouse of our society. Its roots dig deep and take hold, becoming so entrenched that it is almost impossible to remove and, eventually, maturing to spawn its own seeds and spread them on the winds of time. The next generation believes it without question and passes it onto the next, and the next, and the next, until it is so ingrained it is called "human nature".

Buddhists call this error in belief an illusion, or ignorance of the Nature of Reality, brought about by "grasping at self" (this will be discussed further in Part II, *Suffering*). Christians, Muslims and Jews more commonly describe this error as the Fall from Grace, Adam and Eve's banishment from Eden for eating the fruit of the Tree of Good and Evil. It has other names too: sin, insanity, discrimination, darkness, somnolence, inattention, and even unconsciousness. There are a lot of negative connotations surrounding these words, especially the word sin, so I prefer to call it *forgetfulness*, which is simply a failure to remember who we really are.

At the deepest level of our being, on the other hand, we remember exactly who and what we are, a spiritual being having a human experience, to borrow a phrase from Pierre Teilhard de Chardin (1881–1955), a French scientist, theologian, philosopher, and author. The memory of our connectedness to our Source is still intact but it is a memory lying dormant beneath the veil of forgetfulness.

So what, exactly, is it that humanity seems to have forgotten about its true self? What is it about our self that we believe we are lacking from the moment we are born? What is it that we believe we need

INTRODUCTION

and want? What is it that we think we must accumulate through the lifelong search and pursuit of a career, a house, a partner, or simply a good time? Essentially, the varieties of human conditioning can be pared down to the search for and pursuit of prosperity. We want to flourish and be successful in life. We want to strive through the day with that winning feeling, of being on top of the world. But what is it about that winning feeling we find so desirable? In the end, it seems that what we are really seeking comes down to five things:

1. Joy
2. Security
3. Acceptance
4. Peace
5. Freedom

These five states of being are what I call The Five Pillars of Love. They are what we think are missing from birth, what we believe we need more of. At all levels of body, mind and spirit, The Five Pillars of Love are the embodiment of wholeness and completeness. As will be discussed, the attainment of these pillars, in varying degrees, is the very motivation for doing what we do. Every single one of us has sought, or is in the process of seeking, happiness, safety and acceptance. We have all striven for peace and freedom in our life. We have all done this because, in our forgetfulness, we believe we don't have enough love in our hearts. The desperate lack of joy, security, acceptance, peace and freedom entering our lives makes us hungry. We are literally starving for love.

The problem is that most of us don't know, or have failed to remember, that we have already been given everything that we are searching for, in abundance. Most of us have forgotten that we don't need a fancy car or house to be happy; the Joy of Being already exists within us. Most of us have forgotten that we don't need a husband or wife or partner to feel safe now or when we retire; the Security of Being is already assured within us. Most of us have forgotten that we don't need a high-powered career to feel accepted by our friends or family or community; the Acceptance of Being is already affirmed within us. Most of us have forgotten that we don't need to be in control of everything and everyone to feel at ease with the world; the Peace of Being is already within us. Most of us have forgotten that we don't need to own nine houses and a portfolio of stocks to liberate ourselves from the rat race; the Freedom of Being already exists within us.

This, therefore, is one of the greatest secrets of all:

You are already where you want to be.

Your life is already supported by The Five Pillars. Nothing is required to get them.

Why, then, is this knowledge confined to just a few? Why does the majority of the world continue to suffer with pain and torment?

The answer comes back to belief and the nature of free will.

Your Natural State of Connectedness

When we forget, or reject, the notion that we are connected to our Source of joy, security, acceptance, peace and freedom, when we cling to the belief that we are born with nothing and must spend a lifetime acquiring material wealth to make up the shortfall, we invariably end up living a life of despair.

Says Eckhart Tolle in his book, *The Power Of Now*:[1]

> *Your natural state of felt oneness with Being [Source] . . . is a state of connectedness with something immeasurable and indestructible, something that, almost paradoxically, is you and yet is much greater than you. It is finding your true nature beyond name and form. The inability to feel*

---

[1] *The Power of Now*, Eckhart Tolle, Namaste Publishing, 1997

INTRODUCTION

this connectedness gives rise to the illusion of separation, from yourself and the world around you. You then perceive yourself . . . as an isolated fragment. Fear arises, and conflict within and without becomes the norm.

The despair we have all felt at some point in our life stems from the continual, never-ending "conflict within and without" that accompanies the belief of disconnection from our Source. When we, the letters of the Book of Life, believe we are independent of the Ink that is our essence, our constitution, when we believe ourselves to be our own writer and creator, isolation is the inevitable and predominant experience. Moreover, if the initial belief of separation from our Source—forgetfulness—is maintained and reinforced over our lifetime through our thoughts, words and actions, the isolation we feel becomes deeper and deeper until it is a bottomless pit of emptiness. We look inside our hearts and see a horrifying abyss of dark nothingness. We know instinctively that this insatiable void cannot be satisfied with worldly things, yet in fear we still try to fill it with money, power and positions of authority because we do not know how to achieve wholeness by any other means.

Within time, the need to fill the hollowness inside becomes our reason for existing. Life becomes nothing more than a quest to kill the terrible feelings that arise from the pit of that dark void: unhappiness, insecurity, rejection, turmoil and limitation. In order to nullify our sufferings, the human personality compensates with what psychiatrists refer to as coping mechanisms. Laughter, sex, drugs, sport, relationships, and work are just some examples that can, and are, used to cope with life's difficulties. Some of us cope by spending money, what the media likes to refer to as "retail therapy". We buy anything and everything to smother the horridness of our suffering; cars, houses, diamonds, chocolates, the list is endless.

Others cope with their inner emptiness by throwing themselves into work and career, often at the expense of meaningful relationships with their family and friends. Even fantasizing is a coping mechanism. To create a fantasy out of our lives—the romantic prince we wish to marry, the sporting hero we want to be, the multi-million dollar lottery we hope to win—is a common method of coping with our daily pain.

The problem, without diminishing their importance in our life, is that coping mechanisms do not deal with the cause of the suffering; they only plaster over the surface and offer only short-term relief. They can even add to the problem they are trying to cope with. The delight of a new TV, or the thrill of sporting achievement, eventually passes us all and we are left with the feeling of emptiness once again, often worse than before. The fleeting joy of a new career lasts longer in some, shorter in others, but it never lasts until retirement. Relationships soon lose their romance and it isn't long before our eyes start to wander.

Because that is the nature of addiction: *it gets worse*.

It escalates. Like drug addicts, we need more of what we think we need to get a high. We seek it out. We chase it. Individually and collectively, the pace of our life rapidly increases. Before we know what's happened, we find that we have no time for anything except to chase more wealth to be happy and content, bigger houses to be safe and secure, more promotions to be important and accepted.

We spend so much time chasing these things because what we have accumulated isn't achieving the results we want—permanency—to feel happy, secure, accepted, peaceful and free all the time. The void is still there, if not bigger and darker than ever. Sooner or later, we come to the dreaded realization that the abyss inside will never be satisfied. We get worn down with the attempt, tired with the chase. Life becomes pointless. Despair sets in. Like Peter G., my corporate friend, we become

INTRODUCTION

cynical, cranky and depressed. Shrugging our shoulders, we say to ourselves, "That's life. You take the ups with the downs. It's as good as it gets."

There is a way out of our despair, however. By dispelling disbelief and opening the doors to the possibilities that we are not born isolated and separated from our Source of joy, security, acceptance, peace and freedom, we can begin to acknowledge the real causes of our suffering and pain—forgetfulness. By ridding ourselves of the belief that we must start from scratch and then spend a lifetime accumulating material wealth to make up for the shortfall, we can begin to acknowledge the denial of our suffering and develop the will to do something about it, to remember our connection to our Source.

We can and we must, if we truly care about this life.

DEVELOPING THE WILL

Developing the will to end our suffering and pain on a permanent basis, developing compassion and loving-kindness for ourselves and others, cannot occur without the acknowledgment that we are still connected to our Source. The relationship is like that of ice and water. If we consider humans as living icebergs, then water, the vast ocean, is our Source (excluding, for the sake of this analogy, that the ocean's icebergs are freshwater and the sea is saltwater). The same molecules of H_2O that constitute our being are the frozen, solid, or physical materialization, of the non-solid, watery essence from which we have arisen. Although we exist on a different phase or vibration from our Source, our Source is in us, as us, and not something separate or severed from whom and what we are. Essentially, we are created, or "frozen," in the image or likeness of our Source, as it were, disturbed crystallizations of perfect fluidity.

Similarly, to use the analogy of ink and letters described in the poem at the beginning of this book, "wheresoe'er be the letter, there with it is always its ink." The Ink, our Essence, is that which we cannot exist without. It is, if you like, our Being, our Life, our unseen Energy. As such, we, the words, can consider ourselves as written with invisible ink.

There is also another analogy to consider in regards to the relationship we share with our Source. As ice crystallizes from water, as letters are written from ink, the real-life images populating our dreams are fashioned from our own consciousness. In dreams, people and places may look and feel very real, even seem independent and separate from you and everything else in the dream, but they are only illusions of the intelligent source that creates and energizes them, your mind. Dream images are not real. They come and go. The only constant is the creative mind that sustains these images within the context of their own particular time and place.

Likewise, this universe is created and energized by an invisible intelligence, a "Big Mind", to coin a Buddhist phrase, which sustains everything contained within it in the flow of time and space.

It follows, then, that the act of dismissing the possibility of a Higher Intelligence is somewhat like a person in your dreams dismissing the existence or reality of your mind, the very thing from which that dream person is being created. It is also to assume that the human mind is the highest form of consciousness in the universe, which is to believe that humanity has already achieved its evolutionary goal and that what we see is all there is, that this is as good as it gets. If this were so, then there is no possibility to end or cure our individual and collective suffering.

Without a Bigger Mind, there simply is no hope for us, or indeed the planet.

Breaking the Spell

There is a suspicion that the human mind is not the pinnacle of evolution, however. Those that reserve judgment on this are generally those who, at some point in their life, have doubted

INTRODUCTION

that what they see is all there is, that this is as good as it gets. They have an intuitive knowledge that the cause of humanity's suffering is linked to the severance of human consciousness from the human spirit. They, therefore, realize that a spiritual bridging or reconnection is required to establish any sort of a permanent cure for our suffering.

Unfortunately, the belief in God, or a Higher Intelligence, often lumped together under the term "Religion," has often been scorned as hypocritical and superstitious and disregarded as a valid means of healing the world's problems. To many, religion is the cause of the world's problems. Granted, the double standards of religious institutions and the violence of religious fanatics over the centuries have not done themselves or their faith any favors, but this says more about humanity than it does about the true nature of the spiritual path that religions call us to follow.

God, our Source, doesn't cause hunger or start wars, humans do. God, our Source, doesn't rape women or abuse children, humans do. Humanity has a long history of ignoring the needs of its fellow beings, just as it has a long history of using any justification—famine, over population, oil, water, and the favorite of all time, God—to go to war and commit untold atrocities on one another. Humanity has always found an excuse not to feed a hungry family. Humanity has always found it easier to blame the gun rather than the finger that pulled the trigger.

Despite the doubts surrounding its validity, the spiritual path has always been, and thus remains, the only viable and permanent means to ending suffering and pain on the planet.

The spiritual path is the only solution that gets to the root of the problem.

How many more women need to be raped, how many more children need to die of preventable illnesses, how much more of our rainforests do we have to destroy, to realize that the materialistic methods we are employing to fix the problems of the world, although important, simply cannot provide the complete solution?

The world as we see it—hunger, rape, mental illness, wars, torture, environmental exploitation—are but symptoms of a far greater suffering that exists in the hearts of every man, woman and child. The world is groaning with humanity's pain and everything we have done so far to remedy the situation—the impressive feats of science, technology and medicine—has only bandaged our suffering. It hasn't provided a cure. Nor will it, because, although science and medicine is very good at interfering with and manipulating the physical mechanics of suffering, it cannot get to the root of the problem, which is spiritual.

Yet, even if we don't believe in an omnipotent Source, or an Eternal Spirit, or a Higher Intelligence, a momentary willingness to dispel disbelief of the spiritual realm still has beneficial consequences to the individual brave enough to dispel that disbelief and to the lives of those with whom that individual is involved. Surface reality may seem otherwise, but that doesn't detract from Ultimate Reality. We may feel a huge void of sadness, insecurity, rejection, turmoil and limitation, but under this surface illusion, beneath this veil of forgetfulness, there is a Vast Stillness that transforms any darkness into light, that quells any chaos into serenity. Inside each and every one of us remains a connection to the alchemic Source, which transmutes our leaden pain into golden peace. The problem is that most people simply don't believe it. It's a promise too good to be true.

Part of the process of developing the will to do something about our problems, therefore, involves coming to terms with a reality that is somewhat different to what we consider it to be. It involves disregarding the popular belief that we are born with nothing. It involves acknowledging that we are actually born with everything we need, that we only have to remember and access the abundant joy, security, acceptance, peace and freedom we already have through our connection to our Source.

INTRODUCTION

Alas, when push comes to shove, whatever our sex, age, race, or religion, most of us have greater faith in the power of money than in the power of Being. Despite our great technological feats in the last three centuries, humanity's essential beliefs haven't changed all that much since our ancestors emerged from the jungles of Africa. When Jesus turned the tables of money at the Temple, he was frustrated at such complicity. The love of money, as the Bible says, is a root of all kinds of evil.[2] Not money itself, but the love of it, and it is this that competes for the love of God. That is why the Bible has more references to money than heaven and hell combined.

The spell of Mammon is certainly dazzling. Money hypnotizes you with the promise of providing everything you need and want. The ultimate seductress, it lures you into its embrace. But its promises are covetous and false—they never last—and what keeps you, me and everyone else under its spell is our own desires, our own self-interests, the weeds of need that grow in the fertile soil of our beliefs and fears. Why do we want a car, a house, a wine cellar, or a trip to Europe? Invariably, to have the things we think we need to be happy, secure and accepted. We want to have peace and freedom. We want to feel loved. It's what we all want.

What remains for each and every one of us to experience the abundance of our Natural State of joy, security, acceptance, peace and freedom on a permanent basis, to sever the never-ending cycle of suffering, is a change in will or intent to reconnect with our Source, that "something immeasurable and indestructible" residing in the center of our being. What remains is to identify and change our motivations for seeking worldly cures for our spiritual sufferings, a change that begins by taking the path we, that en-masse as a race of people, have not yet truly explored.

What remains is to step forth, individually and collectively, upon the spiritual path back home.

---

[2] *The NIV Student Bible*, Revised. Zondervan, 2002. First published 1986.

POINTS OF REMEMBRANCE #1

- Suffering is an everyday component of our lives.

- Your acknowledgment of suffering, and the will to eradicate it, are two prerequisites to its cure.

- Beliefs are the eyes with which you see the world and yourself.

- The cause of suffering is forgetfulness: the belief that you are born with nothing in isolation from your Source and must accumulate material possessions to make up for the shortfall.

- The varieties of human conditioning can be pared down to the search and pursuit of Joy, Security, Acceptance, Peace and Freedom—the Five Pillars of Love.

- You are already where you want to be.

- Although helpful, coping mechanisms do not deal with the cause of suffering.

- Like people and places in a dream, this universe is created and energized by an invisible intelligence, a Big Mind.

- The spiritual path remains the only viable and permanent means of ending suffering and pain on the planet.

PART I

MOTIVATION

*There is a force within that gives you life—Seek that.
In your body there lies a priceless jewel—Seek that.
. . . If you are in search of the greatest treasure,
don't look outside, look inside, and seek That.*

Jalaladdin Rumi

1 PLEASURE & PAIN

FEAR

VERY FEW PEOPLE sit down and seriously ask themselves why they do what they do. Most of us tend to breeze over the questions, "What is the motivating force behind my actions?" "What am I doing with my life?" "Why do I go to work?" "Why do I get drunk every weekend?" "Why did I buy that dress?"

Of those who actually do ask the serious questions, many don't scratch past the surface and get beyond the obvious. "I go to work to earn money so that I can do what I want to do. I work to live, not live to work." Others come to the conclusion: "I get drunk because it's fun. Besides, all my friends do it." Some say, "I bought the dress on credit because I don't have the ready cash at the moment. It's so nice, I just had to have it."

The few that actually do scratch past the surface may even come to the realization that their behavior falls into two categories; pleasure seeking or pain avoiding (behavior that is motivated by what is known as "the pleasure principle," which is non-other than the psychological equivalent of the body's "fight or flight" response). They may realize that they run into the arms of whatever or whoever makes them feel good, or flee from whatever or whoever makes them feel bad.

"I go to the cinema so that I can forget everything and escape for a while," says Julie P., a friend.

But, when the credits roll and she steps outside into the street, what has she actually achieved besides a fleeting sense of relief or liberation? Instead of enjoying the movie for what it is, a story, she has sought from it something that it cannot give, abiding freedom. Back she steps into the "real world", possibly with a sense of dread that she has to return to her daily life, maybe slightly more relaxed than when she went inside but almost certainly knowing that she hasn't escaped her troubles at all. What she has sought to flee is herself. So, like a pinball, she voluntarily ricochets from pleasure to pain, pain to pleasure, a self-confessed victim of her environment.

Those that have a deeper insight into their seeking behavior may yet realize that the pleasure they crave is happiness, security and acceptance. They may come to acknowledge that all they want is peace and freedom. Fewer still, in avoiding the pain in their life, may admit that they are fleeing sadness, insecurity and rejection. They may even admit that they can no longer cope with the turmoil of daily existence and the social conditions in which they feel trapped. They may recognize their needs but are confused as to the origins of them, and even more confused as to finding a cure for them.

For many, fear is the main motivating factor of their lives. There are few who do not live under its control and there are three basic types:

1. Fear of darkness (vulnerability)
2. Fear of death (loss/annihilation)
3. Fear of desertion (abandonment)

Our fear of darkness, death and desertion can manifest and exert its influence in many ways—anxiety, dread, horror, terror—and acknowledging its origins and role in our suffering goes a long way to diminishing its power and hold over our sense of being. The sense of vulnerability, loss and abandonment can strike suddenly like a sledgehammer, as with the terror of panic, or sometimes less obviously, but no less harmfully, as a pervasive and insidious anxiety that wreaks havoc on our lives for years. The phobias are classical examples, such as the fear of flying or heights, the fear of spiders or snakes, as well as the fear of open or closed spaces. In most circumstances, however, fear is subtle and covert. It can fly beneath our radar and influence our day-to-day existence and behavior in ways we are completely unaware of. Its stealth comes from within, by intensifying our forgetfulness—the belief that we are born with nothing—and, fear of all fears, that we will have nothing when we are old and infirm unless we accumulate material wealth and prosperity to indemnify against it.

To our detriment, the habit of fear is so ingrained that we have become desensitized to it, so much so that we consider it a normal part of human existence:

> *We have absorbed fear for so long it has become who we are.*

But this is not true. Fear is, in fact, an integral part of the cycle of suffering (which will be discussed in greater detail later). Fear arises from the pit of isolation that occurs when the connection to our Source has been lost, when we no longer feel the essential joy, security, acceptance, peace and freedom of Being. It provides the motivation, the impetus, the energy, for our everyday behavior by cultivating and nurturing every sense of need that is felt, namely, the need or want to gain something, or the need or want to rid our self of something:

> *Fear stokes our need to run toward that which we think will be our salvation (pleasure), or it stokes our need to flee from that which we think will be the cause of our suffering (pain).*

But the need, or want, to gain pleasure and the need, or want, to avoid pain are inseparable. Need is a coin with two sides. What side is flipped over depends only on the passing of time. Embracing one side and rejecting the other is therefore ultimately futile; there's no such thing as a one-sided coin. Sooner or later the other side will be flipped over: heads it's pleasure, tails it's pain.

Although desirable, it is impossible to always land on the side of heads, pleasure. We refuse to admit that life is difficult, that it has its ups and downs, its good times and its bad times. We want life to always be plain sailing. We want things to be easy-peasy all the time. We want the ups, not the downs and we certainly don't want to expend too much energy in getting what we desire. Yet, as the age-old African saying goes, smooth seas never make a good sailor. It's the challenges in life that hone our skills.

Still, who of us actually want life's difficulties and obstacles? Who of us actually dares to say, "Bring it on!" to the challenges and hardships that life can throw at us? How many actually spend most of the day fighting the challenges that confront us, making mountains out of molehills and end up wasting vital energy that could have been spent finding solutions to our problems?

Most of us are aware of the futile longing for easy street on some level, yet we still cling to the hope that we can flip the coin throughout our life and have it land, every time, on the pleasure side. In an average lifetime of seventy-five years, at one flip of the coin per second, that's the equivalent of 2,365,200,000 heads in a row. We seek the impossible and, when it doesn't happen, we get frustrated. Yet, paradoxically, the impossible has already happened.

We are already where we want to be. We just don't remember.

NOT AS THE WORLD GIVES

Before his crucifixion, Jesus said to his followers, "Peace I leave with you; my peace I give you. I do not give to you as the world gives."[2]

He also left instructions to be in this world but not of it.[2] In both circumstances, he was hinting at the differentiation between the world in which we live, the relative world of duality—subject and object, up and down, hot and cold, left and right, good and bad—and the world of Absolute Reality, the Formless Realm of Spirit that is beyond time and space and has no opposite.

PLEASURE & PAIN

In contemporary language, the dualistic nature of this world is to express and reveal itself in form. "Form is emptiness, and emptiness is form," as the Buddhist saying goes. Form is everything objective we observe, such as money, our body, trees, clouds, and even includes our mental abstractions or concepts such as happiness, justice and liberty. In other words, form is that which has a polar opposite, of this and that, of right and wrong, of you and me. It is anything and everything from which we can create an object separate and distinct from our self, either imaginary or physically. Even understanding and knowledge are shadowed by naivety and ignorance.

Kahlil Gibran writes in his book, *The Prophet*,[3] poetically describing the duality of this world:

> *Your joy is your sorrow unmasked, and the selfsame well from which your laughter rises was oftentimes filled with your tears.*

In accordance with this dualistic nature of form, the peace of this world, that Jesus spoke of, is intimately tied to its opposite—confusion and turmoil. This form of peace cannot exist without a context in which to express itself: there is no peace without war, and no war without peace. Peace and turmoil, as this world gives it, go hand-in-hand, and what separates one from the other is only the passing of time. Why, then, do we expend so much energy in attaining that which will cause pain and suffering in the future?

Consider a thorn stuck in our foot. Where do we feel pain?

Contrary to what we might think, the pain is not felt in the foot but in the brain, in an area called the pain center. When we tread on a thorn, it triggers pain receptors in the skin of the foot, which then send electrical impulses up the leg and spinal cord to the pain center of the brain. The mind then analyzes the sensation and locates it to the area from which the pain impulses are being

---

[3] *The Prophet*, Kahlil Gibran, Penguin Arkana, 1998. First published 1923.

transmitted. This is not to imply that pain is made up and a fantasy because it is located in the mind, or that we should dismiss it as not real, only that the causes of bodily pain and the experiences of it are different processes:

The cause of pain may be physical, but it is always experienced mentally.

We know this because of the phenomenon of phantom limb pain. In the effort to re-grow and re-organize, the severed nerve endings of an amputated limb often send erratic and misleading signals to the brain's pain center, which the mind can misinterpret as originating from the limb that no longer exists. Although illusory, amputees can be driven crazy trying to scratch an itch on a leg that has long been severed.

Hypnosis also supports the notion that pain is an experience of the mind. There are numerous examples in medical literature of patients under self-hypnosis tolerating all types of invasive surgery, including thyroidectomy, breast augmentation, skin grafting, and even maxillofacial reconstruction, without the need for anesthesia. Psychiatrists are also well aware that a patient's mental state directly influences the ability to withstand painful events: depressed or neurotic patients do not cope nearly so well with pain as do those with a positive or healthy attitude to life.

On the flip side, the same mental activities involved with the experience of pain also exert an influence over our more pleasing sensations, like tickling and caressing. Indeed, this is true for the whole range of our emotions:

Pain and happiness are mind experiences.

All of life, in fact, is experienced in some way or another within a spectrum of consciousness.

This is an extremely important point, for when we accept that happiness and suffering are dependent upon the mind, we begin to seek happiness and solutions to our suffering in the mind itself. When we understand and acknowledge that the causes of joy, security, acceptance, peace and freedom are entirely within us, we release our dependence on external sources for them. Happiness is not a state of your bank account but a state of your being.

George Fowler writes in *Learning to Dance Inside*:[4]

> *Your highest bliss and eternal fulfillment already exist within you, as you. Your sole and simple task—so simple as to be elusive—is to recognize this inner Reality and no longer imagine that you are a spiritual pauper required to embark on a lengthy search to find your wholeness and happiness elsewhere.*

The peace that Jesus would have us seek is in this world but not of it. Stemming beyond duality from the realm of Absolute Reality, it is Formless and has no opposite. It is Pure, Infinite and Eternal. It is Abiding, Unchanging and Indestructible. It is not as the world gives it. More so, it is free of pain and suffering.

Jesus could just as well have said, "My joy I give you. I do not give to you as the world gives." He could also have said, "My strength and security I give you. I do not give to you as the world gives." He could yet have spoken about acceptance and freedom.

These remaining four states we have thus far been discussing—joy, security, acceptance, and freedom—are similar to Jesus' peace in that they are not of this world. Unlike what would be expected from this relative world of duality, all five states of Being are not dependent upon or tied to their opposites—sadness, insecurity, rejection, turmoil and subjugation—but instead exist in the world of Absolute Reality. Being Formless, they are Pure, Infinite and Eternal. They are Abiding, Unchanging and Indestructible.

They are not as the world gives.

---
[4] *Learning to Dance Inside: Getting to the Heart of Meditation*, George Fowler, Perseus Books, 1996.

Who You Really Are

An important point to note, and one of the main tenets of this book, is that the five states of joy, security, acceptance, peace and freedom are not states of emotion: they are your Natural State of Being. They are who you really are, your essential human nature. Inside each and every human being is an eternal flame which cannot be doused by water, or extinguished by wind. Your Natural State of Being is the jewel that Rumi would have you seek. It is your "natural state of felt oneness with [Source]"[1] but which has been forgotten or denied.

Emotions are constructs of the mind and body and are therefore subject to the world of duality. As with all things of form, they are tied to their opposite positive or negative emotion. Happiness is tied to sadness. Comfort is tied to anxiety. Respect is tied to rejection. Serenity is tied to turmoil. Liberty is tied to subjugation. To crave the pleasurable emotion of happiness is to also crave its shadow emotion, the pain of sadness; they are inseparable. To crave the relief of liberty is to also crave repression and subordination; they are inseparable.

Your Natural State of Being, on the other hand, lies beyond duality and has no opposite. Joy, security, acceptance, peace and freedom—The Five Pillars of Love—naturally arise from the state of union with our Source.

The need to seek out and understand our Higher Self, to commune with Spirit, to experience Oneness, is a greatly motivating and noble force. Yet, paradoxically, it is only when our needs and cravings are relinquished that the abundance of our Source is made apparent. The need to be happy, unfortunately, pushes happiness away and, like a carrot on a stick dangling in front of a donkey, it remains tantalizingly out of reach. On the other hand, the desire for others to be happy brings happiness our way. This is because the biggest problem that arises from desiring the fruits of our Natural State of Being is the reinforcement of isolation, of forgetfulness.

PLEASURE & PAIN

The need to feel joy, security, acceptance, peace and freedom strengthens and solidifies the image of a self, or ego, that is separated from our Source, a subconscious admission that we actually don't possess what we want. In instances like this, it is easy to forget that the larder is full.

The truth is, we already have what we desire or want. There is no need to need. There is nothing we need understand. Our Natural State of Being is the state of union with Spirit. Our Natural State of Existence is the state of Oneness with our Source. We are not required to do anything to "get" it, only to recognize and acknowledge our True Self for what it is, to recognize and acknowledge that we already have all the joy, security, acceptance, peace and freedom we could ever want, then cultivate the will to seek it out. Recognition (remembrance), therefore, not need, is the key to unlocking your Natural State of Being.

Remembrance brings dimensional awareness of our Formless Source into this world of form, of duality.

Take, for instance, the city of London. Think of it as a state of existence. If, for some reason, you are currently living in a small, windowless apartment in the West End, the four walls that impede your view of the outer world make it easy to forget that you are still residing in the UK capital. If you never left your tiny room, you would soon begin to yearn for the experience of what the state of London has to offer. Despite no longer perceiving the sights, sounds and smells outside, you would feel a deep irritation, an uncomfortable itch, in your memory that there is something more to your life. Time goes by, and yet you find yourself continuing to sit in your little room unaware that you are already where you want to be, that you are already in the heart of the action. You have fallen into the realm of forgetfulness, failing to remember that London is not something to "get," that it is a state of existence you are already in, your current address.

To experience London in all its fullness, however, you must connect with it. This you do by first acknowledging and recognizing (remembering) where you already are (which is non-other than a leap of faith, to believe in something you can't actually perceive at the present moment) and then, secondly, work to break down your walls and step outside.

The same is true with your Natural State of Being. It is the state of existence in which you already reside, your natural self, who you really are, and not a commodity you are required to "get." You are already where you want to be. As Kahlil Gibran writes:

> *Say not that God is in your heart, but that you are in God's Heart.*

God's Heart (Spirit) is where the action is and you are already there. But a point of note: although our heart may be the organ that registers the perception of Spirit, and this also provides a useful definition for the soul as being "that entity or point of consciousness which perceives Spirit," this doesn't mean that Spirit is limited to our individual awareness or inner felt sense, only that our heart, being rooted in our Source, is the place where Spirit is made real and tangible for us.

Rumi, the Persian poet and mystic, asks:[5]

> *How could the rays of God's light fit into the heart? Yet, when you search, you will find it there, not from the point of view of containment such that it could be said that the light is in that place. You will find it through that place...*

In another sense, Spirit is like air, in as much as the air we breathe is not limited to the bronchi and alveoli of our lungs, but replenished and renewed from a greater body or source with every

---

[5] *Signs of the Unseen: The Discourses of Jalaluddin Rumi*, W. M. Jr Thackston, Shambhala Publications Inc., 1994

respiration. Although we feel the air move in and out of our chest, it is by no means limited or restricted to its fleshy walls: the air knows no boundaries between inside and outside.

Once we realize and acknowledge, therefore, that we are already in union with our Source (and discarded once and for all the idea that God is some old man in the sky looking down over His creation), once we have taken the leap of faith and realized, as in the state of London, we are already in that State of Existence, we can then work to break down the walls of forgetfulness and ignorance impeding our view of the Infinite Universe.

The walls, in fact, are the walls we use to describe our self, the images and ideas built up over time of who we think we are. Once these wall-like images have been broken down, what remains is that part of us which is boundless and unlimited, the Soul of Spirit. To our surprise, we come to realize that what was standing in our way all the time was our self. Thus we come to experience the fullness and abundance of living in the Heart of joy, security, acceptance, peace and freedom.

We come to see that we are the beneficiaries of everything we could ever want, even before we have asked.

JOY

Everyone wants to be happy, but to search for happiness in the outside world is to do things inside out.

In all forms of media—print, radio, television, the internet—we are inundated with the message that identity, happiness and gratification can be found external to us, that everything we are searching for can be purchased in a bottle or cardboard box. This consumer philosophy has been traded under many different brands in the past—standard of living, way of life, cultural tradition—but the contemporary name for it is lifestyle. There are many different types of lifestyle to choose from (just look in any homemaker magazine), all of them for sale at the right price. There are even businesses and companies that specialize in servicing their own particular brand of lifestyle: contemporary, rustic, urban, eco-friendly, self-funded, the list goes on and on.

In fact, our fear of not having the lifestyle we think we need or deserve, now or in the future, drives the capitalist market system and perpetuates the falsehood that we are born with nothing and must accumulate material wealth to make up for the shortfall. Politicians and economists also have a vested interest in maintaining this back-to-front, inside-out consumer philosophy because that's how they get re-elected and stay employed. But this philosophy is not true. It is forgetfulness, and suffering is its child.

As the quote in one of my Christmas cards once read,

> *We don't have things so that we might enjoy life, we have life so that we might enjoy things.*

The key to finding joy is like a personalized passport: it is the discovery of your true identity. Says Eckhart Tolle in his book, *The Power of Now*:[1]

> *Nothing can give you joy. Joy is uncaused and arises from within as the joy of Being. It is an essential part of the inner state of peace . . . It is your natural state, not something that you need to work hard for or struggle to attain.*

Although I have previously interchanged the words joy and happiness, I would now like to draw a distinction between them. Joy and happiness are not the same. Happiness, as a thing of this world, is tied to sadness, its opposite. It has a cost. Take, for example, the pleasure of smoking a cigarette, in which the future cost is disease and pain—cardiac arrest, brain infarction, lung and throat cancer, micro-vascular disease, and many other illnesses.

PLEASURE & PAIN

Likewise, when an individual seeks pleasure for pleasure's sake, there is a price to be paid, usually discomfort or pain of some kind. Furthermore, when it is a cultural norm to seek fulfillment through pleasure or entertainment on a mass scale, the price is magnified accordingly, and the price is mass suffering. In Western society, this is evidenced by the rising statistics of divorce, suicide, child abuse, drug and alcohol addiction, gambling, and other dysfunctional behaviors. Is it to our benefit as individuals and as a culture to keep denying the cost of seeking pleasure for pleasure's sake? Is it to anyone's benefit to pretend or hope that we will not have to pay the price for our addictive pleasure seeking one day?

Joy on the other hand, arising from the realm of Absolute Reality, has no opposite. It is without form. It is Abiding, Unchanging and Indestructible. Joy is not as the world gives it. It is not happiness and it has no cost.

To continue from *The Power of Now*:[1]

> *In the unenlightened, mind-identified condition, what is sometimes wrongly called joy is the usually short lived pleasure side of the continuously alternating pain/pleasure cycle. Pleasure is always derived from something outside you, whereas Joy arises from within you.*

There is nothing you need to do or buy for enjoyment. You need only to recognize and acknowledge that Joy already exists in abundance as your Natural State of Being, through your connection to your Source, and then develop the will to seek it out.

SECURITY

Like joy, everybody desires to feel safe and secure. We desire the security of our mind and body (sanity and health), of our own and our children's future (finances and education), along with security from the forces of nature (shelter and protection), from famine and drought (food and water), and from external threats (violence and war). Our goal is to seek greater safety and to flee or minimize its painful opposite, insecurity—worry, anxiety, fretfulness, dread.

More often than not, the methods employed in the hunt for safety and the avoidance of insecurity generally involve the accumulation of material things or the taking of worldly actions. Both attitudes can be lumped collectively as the desire for one thing, power—political, economic, sexual, cultural, familial, social, to name a few. Power can be thought of as the ability to control our inner and outer environments and the ultimate power is that over life and death. The common belief is that the more power we have, as an individual or culture, the more we can control our ability to attract the things we desire—money, health services, education, food, oil—which will ultimately ensure the security we crave.

Somehow, though, the inability to control our future is viewed as a guaranteed formula for failure. In our individual hunt for power, we work longer and longer hours to earn higher wages and end-of-year bonuses in order to accumulate a greater portfolio of property and stocks (ironically called "securities"), driven by the belief that the more cashed-up we are, the more secure our future will be. We hang onto jobs and careers we don't really like, or even hate, because it pays the mortgage and the university fees. We elect governments that send our sons and daughters to war with near or distant neighbors that have allegedly threatened our lifestyle. We do many things to increase our power to control the environment and ensure our safety in this world. But the promises of worldly power are false. They cannot deliver on their word. They cannot provide permanent security.

This does not mean that we should not consider seeking shelter from the storm or fleeing an abusive relationship. Nor does it mean that we should not take measures to prevent bankruptcy, famine or drought. As children of the earth, we are outwardly bound to the natural cycles of birth and decay, of life and death, of duality. We are contracted to live with the knowledge of good and evil and needs must take evasive action when lightning strikes. As the Sufis say, "What's the point in having Wisdom if you're dead?"

But to put our faith and trust in this world to provide permanent security is to court disaster. In accordance with its dualistic nature, any security we may get in our efforts for greater power is only fleeting and temporary. Worldly security has a price and the price is insecurity and fear. What gives us security today does not guarantee security tomorrow. Companies go bust, or the stock market crashes and we lose all our savings and pensions. Our jobs are made redundant and we can no longer pay the mortgage or health insurance premiums. Our sons and daughters return from the battlefields in wheelchairs or coffins.

The security we seek in this world is therefore no security at all: it is fraught with worry and fear.

As such, there's no such thing as financial freedom. If you don't have money, you worry that you will never have it; and if you do have money, you worry that you're going to lose it. Does this really provide the freedom and security you think you need?

Driving to the gym one day, I approached a car at the traffic lights that had the insignia of my old high school stuck to its rear window. A spark of memory flashed across my mind. It was the school's Latin motto, which had been drummed into me nearly every day for five years as a teenager: *Ex Unitate Vires*—in unity comes strength. It occurred to me, as the lights changed to green, that this was an appropriate motto for remembering Unity with Spirit—there is great strength in Oneness.

This little incident emphasizes the point that we have been making, that Real Strength and Security arises from reconnecting with our Source in Unity and Oneness, where, beyond duality, our dependency on the outside world, on form, is relinquished. Where our fears of darkness, death and desertion—vulnerability, annihilation and abandonment—are washed away. In the deepest part of our Natural State of Being, we are secure in the knowledge that we cannot not exist. We are secure in the knowledge that we have not been born with nothing and do not need to start from scratch to make up for the shortfall; we already have all the joy, security, acceptance, peace and freedom we need.

There is no greater security than this. In Unity comes Strength, for without opposites, there are no hidden costs. There are no worries or doubts or insecurities. There is freedom from the false promises of worldly power. "Though I walk through the Valley of the Shadow of Death," we may rightly say, "I shall not fear."

This kind of security cannot come from external sources. You need only to recognize and acknowledge that Real Security already exists in abundance as your Natural State of Being, through your connection to your Source, and then develop the will to seek it out.

ACCEPTANCE

One of the most basic urges in humanity is the desire to be accepted or approved by others—we want to be affirmed. We want our existence to be valid and important. We want to belong and to be worthy. As M. Scott Peck writes in *People of the Lie*:[6]

> *We humans are so constituted that we need a sense of our own social significance. Nothing can give us more pleasure than the sense that we are wanted and useful. Conversely, nothing is more productive of despair than the feeling that we are useless and unwanted [worthless].*

---

[6] *People of the Lie*, M. Scott Peck, Arrow Books, 1990. First published 1983

Human beings are social animals. A lot of epidemiological evidence exists in the medical, psychological and sociological journals to suggest that social isolation is linked to significant morbidity and mortality. According to the keynote speakers at the Spirituality & Health conference in Adelaide, 2007, most cultures view isolation as a form of punishment. Some prisoners even consider solitary confinement worse than torture. Closer to home, in regards to family dynamics, the reason such psychological illnesses as autism, Asperger's Disease and psychopathic personality disorders are so devastating, particularly for the parents of those individuals with the disorder, is because of the chronic and irreversible failure of human attachment that these individuals exhibit. In contrast, family members caring for Down's Syndrome children do not suffer nearly as much, as these children are very sociable and have a high capacity to bond to others.

The inherent need of each individual to feel part of a larger group or family of other human beings could almost be described as instinctual. In fact, belonging is such a pre-eminent human requirement that Abraham Maslow, the American psychologist considered the father of humanistic psychology in the 1950s, felt justified in listing it amongst his "Hierarchy of Human Needs". Of late, contemporary psychologists have even developed a "Law of Belonging" to describe their observations of it.

Humans need to belong, of that there is little doubt, and although it seems we feel this need most strongly in our teenage years, when all aspects of who we think we are is most vulnerable — our body image, our cultural image, our peer image, our sexual image, and so forth — the desire for belonging and acceptance is by no means exclusive to this age group. Our need for acceptance and worthiness evolves as we pass through the various stages of life. Throughout childhood, young adulthood, parenthood, and retirement, we wear our need for belonging and acceptance like a second skin, sometimes as a need for friendship, sometimes as a need for comfort, sometimes as a need for physical gratification. The need for acceptance is a constant companion, and not only does it change throughout the years but it also changes in reaction to our moods, often many times in a single day.

One of the most common forms that our need for acceptance takes is respect, usually from friends, family and colleagues. Sometimes our need for respect is so desperate we even demand it from complete strangers. Some feel the need to drive the biggest, fastest or loudest car to win respect on the road. Some feel the need to keep vicious dogs or an armory of guns to enforce the respect of others. Some feel the need to be always right in order to secure another's respectful impression of them.

No matter who we are, almost all of us derive a great deal of satisfaction when people show us respect, but this need for respect is more often than not a sign of underlying weakness, a cover to hide our deeper insecurities and fears of rejection. Our world can so easily crumble around our ears at the slightest hint of another's disrespect. Sometimes something as minor as a friend or colleague differing from our point of view is taken as a personal affront, a lack of respect for our beliefs. On a subconscious or minimally conscious level, we interpret the failure to receive respect or understanding as a failure to be affirmed and validated. We see it as a failure to feel important and worthy. We get upset. We slam the phone down. "Nobody understands me!" we cry out in our hurt.

Unfortunately, to our detriment, the need for acceptance and approval is often subtle and veiled. The craving for respect is just one mask it wears but no matter what clever disguise it dons, the need to feel important or to belong follows the same two behavior patterns of pleasure seeking and pain avoidance we are now familiar with: the need to run toward whoever or whatever wants and appreciates us, or the need to flee whoever or whatever rejects us.

But, as with every kind of seeking behavior, the quest for acceptance goes hand-in-hand with rejection, and what separates one from the other is only the passing of time. What gives us acceptance today will reject us tomorrow. What treats us as important this morning will despise us before nightfall.

The Need to Be Needed

Laura is one of those friends that will do anything for anybody. Call her up in the middle of the night and she will lend a listening ear. Ask her to mind your children for an hour or so while you have a doctor's appointment and she will do it. Moving house? No problem either. She will help lug the boxes, clean and stack the shelves, and wash the floor until it sparkles. Like a super hero flying here, there and everywhere, she will go out of her way to help anyone and everyone, even to her own disadvantage. And this is the major cause of her suffering.

I do not know what traumas Laura suffered in the past, or what pain she carries from her childhood, all I know is that she has a crying need to be needed. In her efforts to help the whole world, she dons her Wonder Woman suit in the belief that she will become invulnerable to rejection. Rejection is her archenemy, her Cheetah, and her fight to save everyone on the planet is a fight against the evils of dismissiveness and rebuff.

That is why her help has a hidden cost—you must pay her with acceptance, and God help you if you fail to do so. The slightest hint of rejection—forgetting to return her call or SMS, cancelling a visit at the last minute, failing to thank her for holding the door open as you pass—will unlock the gates of hell. Her fragile ego is so dependent upon others for acceptance and worth that even the simplest act of forgetfulness is like a dagger thrust into the heart of her sense of wellbeing. There are days and weeks when friends of ours simply do not hear from her, presumably because they have overlooked to give the appropriate acceptance for some act of kindness she has performed for them. Her impregnable suit, it seems, is riddled with rips and tears.

Like many of us, Laura hasn't fully comprehended the link between pleasure and pain. She hasn't yet observed that her need to be needed and accepted is directly responsible for the pain of rejection she constantly suffers. She hasn't yet realized that it is impossible to go through life without rejection, to be always accepted by others. The goal of constant approval and continuous validation is futile. Even the greatest man that ever lived couldn't achieve this. Hated and rejected, he was crucified for nothing more than preaching love for one another.

How, then, can we mere mortals possibly hope to avoid rejection in this world?

We can't. We can try to use our career as a shield against the arrows of rejection from friends and family. We can strive at all costs for monetary success in order to build a future fund of self-acceptance and approval. We can accumulate university degrees and PhDs in our struggle up the erudite ladder toward academic importance. We can be right and logically sound in every argument we make, but like joy and security, the search for acceptance in worldly institutions or people—to feel a sense of affirmation, worth, belonging, validation, importance, acknowledgment, and respect—can, and will, ultimately lead us down the path toward pain and rejection.

Reconnecting with our Source is the key to unlocking the permanent and abiding acceptance each of us seeks. Your Natural State of Being is a state of Universal Belonging, of Oneness. Is Life not affirming your existence, your being, right at this moment? Is Love not validating your presence right now? Is Consciousness not acknowledging your awareness this very minute?

Indeed, there is no threat to the stream of affirmation, validation and respect flowing from the Eternal Fount. Spirit's acceptance is beyond duality and rejection; it has no opposite. In its Oneness, it is all encompassing, all embracing.

This kind of affirmation is not as the world gives. You need only to recognize and acknowledge that Total Acceptance already exists in abundance as your Natural State of Being, through your connection to your Source, and then develop the will to seek it out.

PEACE

Peace has long been the desire of humanity. The collective dreams of every man, woman and child is for peace in this world. Songs and ballads have been sung about peace. Laws have been written to establish it. Wars have been fought to enforce it. Politicians have even tried to buy peace. We have all, at some time in our life, striven for peace of mind.

Yet peace is so often confused with the temporary relief from turmoil. As long as there is no turmoil, we think, we have peace. Minimize disharmony, the reasoning goes, and we maximize peace. But peace, as this world gives it, is continually alternating with its opposite, chaos. They go hand-in-hand and what separates one from the other is only the passing of time.

To better understand the peace that is "not of this world," consider the Buddhist analogy of the ocean.

On the surface there exists waves, a metaphor for the duality of this universe; we have moments of ups and downs, sometimes large, sometimes small, and sometimes moments of tranquil calm. The natural cycle of the ocean surface flows from calmness to storminess and back to calmness again.

The vast depths below the waves, however, are not subject to the ravages of the surface. Here it is eternally still, unaffected by the cycle of tranquility and chaos. The deep of the sea is a metaphor for the Realm of Spirit, where Deep Peace reigns.

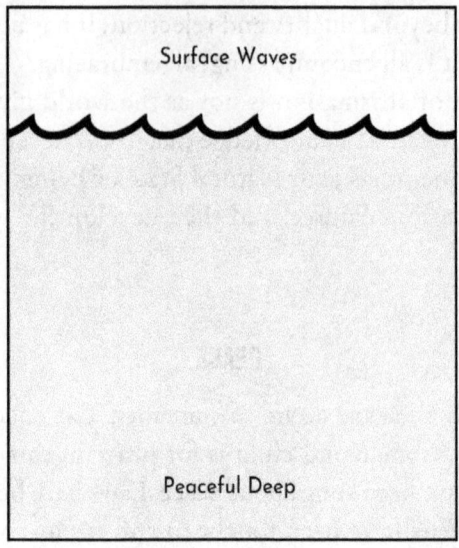

FIGURE 1: The Peaceful Deep

In the above diagram, note how the surface and its activities—the crests and troughs of the waves—are entirely dependent upon the depths below to exist. The Vast Deep, however, exists beyond the waves of duality and has no such dependence upon the surface. The Vast Deep is the Timeless Immensity of Absolute Reality that masters speak of. The relative world of time and space are ripples, or disturbances, of this Perfection: when Perfection is disturbed, the universe is created.

> *For it was before the letters, when no letter was; and it remaineth, when no letter at all shall be.*

Thus the paradox of mutual compatibility between Deep Peace and outer turmoil is resolved: even though the world may collapse around our ears, even though wild storms may thrash the surface of our life, there is still a Vast and Infinite Peace deep within, our Natural State of Being. The Deep Peace remains unaffected irrespective of what is happening on the surface: it is omnipresent.

Likewise, Inner Joy co-exists with outer sadness; we may suffer loss and grief on an untold scale, but the Inner Joy of our Natural State of Being remains deep within. Real Security, too, co-exists with outer fear and anxiety; our journey may lead us through the Valley of Death, but the Real Strength and Security of our Natural State of Being remains.

You Are Not Alone

Part of the process of reconnecting with our Source is to become comfortable with the paradox of stormy waters and Deep Stillness. To continually focus on the surface undulations of our existence, the crests and troughs of the waves, is to do our self a continual disservice. There is no salvation surrendering to the mercy of the waves, just a lifetime of repeated highs and lows, of periodic relief from the seemingly never-ending chaos.

This point came home to me one day as I was standing in front of the TV. After a few seconds of flicking through the channels, my finger suddenly froze on the remote control at the image of a malnourished baby dying in his mother's arms. A news reporter was telling the world of the famine ravaging the West African nation of Niger. After another dry summer, more than fifty percent of the population was dying of starvation and little aid was getting through. What struck me though, bad enough as it was, was not the scale of the disaster but the helplessness, the picture of the mother's face as she watched her baby die.

It begged the question why, with modern technology and billions of dollars at our disposal, does a significant proportion of Africa and the world go without shelter, food and medicine? Why do we allow so many human beings to die prematurely?

With my finger still frozen over the remote, I began to reflect on my own daughter. Although privileged to live in an affluent country, she was still a vulnerable child. Cancer, infection, accidents and pedophiles, to name but a few, could assault her at any moment. Some were preventable. Some were not. It was the "were not" that slid an icy finger down my spine. I shuddered at the thought of so many things beyond my sphere of influence, so many things that I had no control over. I felt completely helpless.

Then something strange and mysterious happened. While I looked at the dying baby on the TV screen, a voice inside, gentle and kind, yet firm, whispered to me:

He Is Not Alone.

Instantly, with those quiet words, the void of helplessness was filled with an overwhelming sense of peace. Somehow, I had been touched with the ineffable understanding, the utter surety, that nobody dies alone. No matter who or where we are, God is always with us. No matter what we do, what trials and tribulations the future holds, the Great Peace will forever be with us.

This experience of watching the death of the baby, sad and distressing as it was, taught me a valuable and lifelong lesson:

A lifebuoy has been thrown within everyone's reach to save us from drowning in the stormy waters.

Not floating on top of the water, as we might think, but below it. Grabbing hold of the lifebuoy, finding refuge, therefore required a redirecting of my focus. Reconnecting with the Deep Peace is to reach beneath the stormy waters and take hold of something that has no opposite, something that is Abiding, Unchanging and Indestructible. It is to hear the reassuring Voice of Wisdom whisper that we are not alone. It is to connect with "The peace of God, which passes all understanding,"[2] the kind of peace that is not as the world gives.

It also made me think, as it still does, of the immense repercussions for life on earth should every man, woman and child dive beneath the waves of our surface consciousness and experience the Vast Peace that is waiting to be known.

What wondrous potential exists for a world in which everyone makes these mysterious depths a permanent abode? What amazing opportunities await humanity if everybody recognizes and acknowledges that Deep Peace already exists in abundance as our Natural State of Being, through our connection to our Source, and then develops the will to seek it out?

FREEDOM

As much as the search for peace has shaped the course of human history, individually and collectively, so too has the quest for freedom. The human spirit detests any form of limitation or constraint. Its very nature is free. It needs to fly. It cannot be caged. Like peace, songs and ballads have been sung about freedom (the most stirring I know is Verdi's 'Va Pensiero', the yearning of the enslaved Jews in Babylon for their homeland). Laws have been written to establish it. Wars have been fought to enforce it. Politicians have even tried to buy freedom. We have all at some point in our life striven to be free.

Yet, as with the misunderstanding of peace, freedom is often confused with the temporary liberation from oppression. As long as we are not under anyone's, or anything's, control, we think we have freedom. Remove the prison bars, the reasoning goes, and we liberate ourselves. But freedom as this world gives it is continually alternating with its opposite, tyranny. They go hand-in-hand and what separates one from the other is only the passing of time.

To quote the enduring wisdom of Kahlil Gibran once more from *The Prophet*:[3]

> *At the city gate and by your fireside, I have seen you prostrate yourself and worship your own freedom. Even as slaves humble themselves before a tyrant and praise him though he slays them. Ay, in the grove of the temple and in the shadow of the citadel, I have seen the freest among you wear their freedom as a yoke and a handcuff.*

The human condition is subject to the influence of two kinds of freedom, relative and Absolute. We are outwardly bound and inwardly free, as the Sufis say. Outwardly, our relative freedom is bound by the chains of duality and subjectivity: like an eagle soaring in the sky, what appears on the surface to be free is still subject to the laws of gravity. The eagle has seemingly moments of blissful freedom—soaring high, gliding on the wind, escaping the monotony of the ground—but it cannot truly escape the chains of duality and fly for ever; eventually it must obey the limitations of its tether and return to earth. Even the birds, the freest amongst us, cannot avoid wearing their freedom as a "yoke and a handcuff".

Inwardly, in contrast, our Higher Consciousness is beyond the limitations of duality and relativity. In its natural state, the inward flight of our Being soars on the wind of freedom blowing from the Realm of Absolute Reality, our Source.

It is here, in Paradise, that we learn the truth of Absolute Freedom: it is freedom from fear and need.

Beyond Thought

After much worrying about my financial affairs, one night, I glimpsed through a dream the essence of Absolute Freedom. I remember wishing, in my dream, that I could escape my problems, especially the problem of my empty bank account. Finding the money to cover the utility bills, to buy presents for friends and family, to afford food and pay the rent, was a load that was becoming too heavy for me. The need for money was pressing on my shoulders. I felt crushed beneath the weight of worry. I didn't know how to proceed. I was stuck. My mind was whirring with despair.

Suddenly, in an instantaneous flash of understanding, I was aware of one simple fact of life:

> *I cannot run away from my problems. There is no escaping them; they are a part of me and I am a part of them.*

In that split, satori-like second, I knew that I had been trying to do the impossible—I had been trying to run away from myself—and the profoundness of this insight instantly lifted every burden from my shoulders. My whirring mind had spun so fast that it crunched to a halt like an over-revved engine blowing its pistons. I suddenly stopped worrying. I stopped thinking. Somehow, through the mind's self-destruction, I transcended thought into the gap before thinking occurs, before form is created, the state of Unity Consciousness. I was no longer trapped in the chaos of constant thinking but simply aware, and in the pristine silence and stillness I felt light and weightless, infinite and unbounded, truly free. The sensation was like a submarine floating deep in the vast and undisturbed waters of the Pacific Ocean, a speck of consciousness submersed in Immense Awareness. Never had I felt or imagined anything so beautiful, but a moment later, when I began to think and analyze this dark, blissful nothingness, this Glorious Infinity, in which I was floating and I asked myself, "What is this? Is this God?" the feeling was gone and the heavy weight of my problems bore down on me again.

Later the following morning, while reflecting on the dream, I saw the depth of truth to which I had been graced. First, True Freedom emerges from the space and silence when thinking stops, the Formless Source that exists before created form. Although I had known this truth on a mental level, a level of intellect, I had, as yet, not known it on a level of real experience, ineffably, until now. Theoretical knowledge, although very important, is no substitute for experience, and that sublime feeling of peace and freedom that came from direct communion with my Source still lingers with me to this day.

Second, my dream had revealed that no matter how much I wanted to, I cannot escape my problems because I created them.

I created my problems? Me?

This second point took a while to sink in. Then, I realized that although I might not create the actual situation (for example, the loss of money or job or spouse), I created the experience of the situation as being a problem: I have labelled it as problematic. The situation is just a situation. It just is. Labeling it as a problem is in fact a greater reflection of the extent to which my consciousness is disconnected from my Natural State of Being, that state of being which is free of problems, than it is of the actual situation itself.

For example, when I cling to my money or my job or my spouse like a drowning man to a plank of wood in fear of what would happen should he let go, and then, suddenly, I am faced with the situation in which they have been taken away or lost, my mind labels it as a problem because the situation is in direct conflict with the outcome I wanted or desired.

Yet, my dream had taught me that I cannot run away from my problems. I cannot escape them because I have created them inside my own consciousness. They have not happened to me. Rather, my problems have come through me and are therefore attributable to the entity that is myself.

In a sense, I am my own worst enemy, my own nemesis, and hence there is nothing to escape from except the ghosts of my own mind. The means of escaping my problems, therefore, is not to escape them at all (I cannot escape my consciousness or myself) but to change the experience of them being troublesome.

PLEASURE & PAIN

As Jesus said to his followers:[2]

Therefore I tell you, do not worry about . . . what you will eat or drink; or . . . what you will wear. Is life not more important than food, and the body more important than clothes? . . . Do not store up for yourselves treasures on earth, where moth and rust destroy, and where thieves can break in and steal.

What stands between how we are now and the achievement of our true potential is the way we think. The barriers to Absolute Freedom (Spirit) are cemented with the gravel of our worrisome thoughts and the sand of our subjective wants and desires. Creating problems out of life is like building dam-like obstructions to the flow of our Natural State of Being, the natural consequences of which, to our downstream consciousness, is aridity and suffering—sadness, insecurity, rejection, turmoil and limitation—and all that has been achieved is a self-imposed drought of all the abundant goodness that life has to offer. Therefore, as Jesus advised, do not worry.

The lesson here is to take responsibility for the creation of your problems, as emphasized from Shakespeare's Hamlet, that there is nothing either good or bad, "but thinking makes it so".

Taking responsibility is an act of empowerment. Accepting and acknowledging that your own consciousness attaches problem-labels to things and situations empowers you to completely detach from them and let them go (or give them to God, as a Christian would say). It allows the heavy weight of suffering to slide from your shoulders. The situation that has been judged and labelled as a problem may not have changed, it may still persist as vigorously and unchangeably as before, but the problem is no longer there. The solution is to develop sufficient awareness to dissolve your problems, your pain, when they arise. Here, in attentive consciousness, the cause of suffering can be eliminated at its very root and the ground cleared for the seeds of True Freedom to take hold and grow, which is non-other than the Presence of Spirit, that which is Abiding, Unchanging and Indestructible.

This kind of freedom is not as the world gives. You need only recognize and acknowledge that Absolute Freedom already exists in abundance, as your Natural State of Being, through your connection to your Source, and develop the will to seek it out.

THE SEARCH

The search for joy, security, acceptance, peace and freedom is non-other than the search for our true self. It is the search for our Natural State of Being, that state we seem to have lost somewhere in our forgetfulness. We yearn to reconnect with what is Real. We yearn to reconnect with what is Right. In other words, what is True.

Little is it realized, however, that what is Real, Right and True is not lost at all but covered up.

> *Like a childhood toy stored in the attic and forgotten, our Natural State of Oneness with our Source—joy, security, acceptance, peace and freedom—is a treasure simply waiting to be found under the dusty layers of time.*

The ego, our falsely independent, separate sense of self, created from the belief that we are born with nothing, knows what is missing but knows not how or where to look for true salvation. The ego knows and understands the world of duality and it knows all too well the corollary of its belief of isolation and separation from its Source, fear—fear of darkness, death and desertion. It then expends all its energy in finding a solution to its intolerable vulnerability and inevitable annihilation and abandonment in the only manner it knows, pleasure seeking and pain avoidance.

PLEASURE & PAIN

This solution, however, is no solution at all. It is simply one that progressively and invariably leads to a marked decrease or waning of consciousness. In other words, numbing.

The ego, in its never-ending quest to eradicate fear and pain, inevitably comes to the conclusion that what it is trying to achieve is impossible. In its despair, it turns to the only things that can numb the pain—alcohol, drugs, sex, entertainment, careers, real estate, cars, travel, and so forth—if only for a short while. In its extreme, it is nothing short of hedonism.

Alas, the self-administered anesthetic wears off after time and the pain returns, usually worse than before. Once again we inject our self with society-condoned painkillers—a splash more alcohol, a higher dose of diazepam, another senseless video, needy sex, a new job, a bigger house—until we can no longer live without them. Instead of seeking to transcend our pain and suffering, we actively and purposefully take measures to suppress our awareness, steps that tend to descend into lower, not higher, consciousness.

This is why the entertainment industry has become such a huge moneymaking machine, why we are so eager to throw every cent we have at those who entertain us, even if all they do is kick a football or juggle a basketball. We want to forget our suffering so much that we have become addicted to the painkillers of life and every day is viewed through the foggy lens of numbed awareness.

This is because the ego has overextended its contextual role as a foil by which you can know your True Self, possessing you. With this in mind, you may now begin to see that what you really desire in life simply cannot come from the world outside, the relative world of duality.

You may now begin to see that your efforts to increase happiness, security, acceptance, peace and freedom in your life has always come at a painful cost—sadness, insecurity, rejection, turmoil and subjugation.

You may now begin to see that true joy, security, acceptance, peace and freedom, permanent and without opposite, exist only in the Absolute Realm, the realm beyond time and space that is intimate with all created form but experienced only with the inner awareness of your heart, your soul.

Hopefully, you may now also begin to develop sufficient willingness to seek out and connect with that which has been the most elusive of all things, that which is Real, Right and True—your Natural State of Being.

POINTS OF REMEMBRANCE #2

- Fear has become the main motivating force of our life: Fear of darkness (vulnerability); Fear of death (loss/annihilation); Fear of desertion (abandonment)

- The dualistic nature of this world is to express and reveal itself in form.

- Life is experienced within a spectrum of consciousness.

- The Five Pillars of Love—joy, security, acceptance, peace and freedom—are not states of emotion: they are your Natural State of Being.

- Recognition (remembrance) is the key to unlocking your Natural State of Being.

- Your soul is that point of consciousness which perceives Spirit.

- Finding your joy is like a personalized passport: the discovery of your true identity.

- There's no such thing as financial freedom.

- In the deepest part of your Natural State of Being you are secure in the knowledge that you cannot not exist.

- Your Natural State of Being is a state of Universal Belonging.

- Even though wild storms may thrash the surface of your life, there is still a Vast and Infinite Peace deep within.

- You Are Not Alone.

- The human spirit detests any form of limitations or constraints: your very nature is free.

- You cannot run away from your problems; they are a part of you and you are a part of them.

- The barriers to Absolute Freedom (Spirit) are cemented with the gravel of your worrisome thoughts and the sand of your subjective wants and desires.

- Your Natural State of Oneness with your Source—joy, security, acceptance, peace and freedom—is a treasure waiting to be found under the dusty layers of time.

2 GOODNESS, TRUTH & BEAUTY

REAL, RIGHT & TRUE

PEOPLE HAVE CRAVED the salvation of joy, security, acceptance, peace and freedom since time immemorial. Religions have arisen in the quest for it. Entire cultures and civilizations have been created around it. Political factions, philosophical principles, scientific endeavors, and artistic trends have all been devoted to its pursuit. People have even sacrificed their life for it. There is something in the human spirit that simply will not rest until salvation has been attained, something inside all of us that will not give up until we find paradise.

Like beauty, however, paradise is in the eye of the beholder. To me, paradise is mile after mile of golf courses, an endless vista of fairways, bunkers and putting greens. Yet, this is the very definition of hell to those who can't stand golf. Likewise, somebody else's definition of paradise will be my definition of hell. So this leaves us with a dilemma. If paradise is dependent on our perception of it, how can we be sure that what we perceive is genuine? Does our mind distort everything it receives through the five senses? Can we trust our perception of paradise, our experience of Being? Are we not just creating what we want to see, a delusional world stemming from our wants and desires? What, in heaven's name, is Real, Right and True?

Over two millennia ago in ancient Greece, before the New Testament was even written, Plato was plagued by the same kind of questions. After much contemplation, he came to the conclusion that Absolute Reality (as opposed to the relative reality of our senses, what he called the subjective world of "shadows" we perceive outside us) can be experienced and expressed as Goodness, Truth and Beauty.

Later, at the beginning of the Twentieth Century in her book *Mysticism*,[7] Evelyn Underhill extrapolated Plato's philosophy to include the three noble principles of humanity: Philanthropy (Goodness), Science (Truth) and Art (Beauty). Society, she says, has divided itself along these three lines—Religion, Science and Art—in its quest to experience and describe what is Real, Right and True. Those in whom goodness is a virtue are naturally drawn to charitable and philanthropic deeds and in particular to the church (or that individual's cultural religion). For those in whom the truth is of prime importance, the sciences are the fields in which they choose to explore. For those over whom beauty casts its spell, the artistic realms (poetry, painting, sculpting, dancing, singing, and music) hold supreme sovereignty in their thoughts and actions.

In her chapter on *Introversion and Contemplation*, she writes:

> *This final, satisfying knowledge of reality—this understanding of Truth by Truth—is, at bottom, that which all men desire. The saint's thirst for God, the philosopher's passion for the Absolute; these are nothing else than the crying need of the spirit, variously expressed by the intellect and by the heart. The guesses of science, the diagrams of metaphysics, the intuitions of artists; all are pressing towards this.*

To those pilgrims drawn to religion, the Goodness of Mercy is the candle of hope lighting the way to paradise and salvation. The Inner Mystery of Life, the metaphysical Ink, appears to them as Divine Goodness and at its heart is the experience of abiding joy, security, acceptance, peace and freedom.

---

[7] *Mysticism: A Study in the Nature and Development of Spiritual Consciousness*, Evelyn Underhill. Dover Publications, 2002. Unabridged, unaltered republication of the twelfth edition (1930) by Dutton and Co.

GOODNESS, TRUTH & BEAUTY

Likewise those adventurers exploring the objective fields of reason and logic. Consciously or unconsciously, scientists, philosophers and doctors are attracted to the principle that Truth holds the key to the gates of paradise and humanity's salvation. The Light of Consciousness (the Ink) appears to their methodological gaze as the vision of Absolute Truth and only through its rigorous and systematic extraction will they find the absolute joy, security, acceptance, peace and freedom that comes from the experience of knowing what is Right and Real. For what other reason do they search for it?

Likewise, it is the power of Beauty that delivers artists their sense of paradise and salvation. The Perfume of Love (the Ink) appears to them as Utopian Beauty, electrifying their impression of the Divine in an ecstasy of joy, security, acceptance, peace and freedom.

For do we not recognize in our own constitution a little of the religious pilgrim, a measure of the scientific adventurer, and a splash of the dreaming artist? Do not our very own scientific guesses, religious diagrams and artistic intuitions all press towards the salvation of Goodness, Truth and Beauty?

As Underhill writes in her chapter on *Mysticism and Symbolism:*[7]

> *The three great classes of [Goodness, Truth and Beauty] . . . appeal to the three deep cravings of the self, three great expressions of man's restlessness. The first is the craving [for Truth] which makes him a pilgrim, a wanderer. It is the longing to go out from his normal world in search of a lost home, a 'better country'; an Eldorado, a Sarras, a Heavenly Syon. The next is that craving of heart for heart [for Beauty], of the soul for its perfect mate, which makes him a lover. The third is the craving for inward purity and perfection [for Goodness], which makes him an ascetic, and in the last resort a saint.*

In some, the religious light may outshine our scientific and artistic qualities. In others, reason and logic may subordinate our charitable and creative needs. In yet others, the expression of beauty may hold dominion over our religious and scientific beliefs.

But, in our hearts, are we not all in some degree or another restless with "deep cravings" for Goodness, Truth or Beauty as a means of salvation? Do we not crave Goodness, Truth or Beauty as immunization against the malady of sadness, insecurity, rejection, tragedy and subjugation?

GOODNESS

Any seeker of Goodness is an "ascetic," someone who follows their inward craving "for inward purity and perfection." It is the act of seeking the merciful and cleansing nature of Goodness that defines the ascetic on her pilgrimage. She is the pilgrim's pilgrim, grasping life in the living of it, surrendering everything to the natural state of Goodness.

Goodness, however, is not a concept an ascetic can consider to be defined or dictated by morals or ethics. Morals change with the whims of our moods and the vagaries of the weather. Just as unstable, ethics have a habit of changing throughout history; what is championed in one century is vilified in another. Morals and ethics also vary from culture to culture and even intra-culturally, village to village, town to town, city to city. Not to mention the divergent religious values and beliefs that exist around the world. From the ascetic's point of view, Goodness is the essential quality of Spirit, her Source: it lies beyond community, religious and cultural definitions, even, like the state of Nirvana, beyond the duality of heaven and hell. Goodness, being the pure and perfect heart of Being, is without opposite.

The winter of 2005 was unusually cold and wet in my part of the world. It was also the time when I was struggling unusually with the concept of good and evil, in particular the goodness of God. If God was infinite and eternal, I had begun to theorize on those rainy days, then there was nothing in life that was not God. God, our Source, is Everything There Is, and if there was something that existed that God is not, then God cannot, by definition, be Infinite or Eternal. The very existence of something other than God refuted the Infinite Nature of God: you cannot have infinite + 1. Therefore, I reasoned, because good and evil existed, God, or Being, was both. The conclusion didn't sit well in my stomach, but it was there. Irrefutable. Then I had a dream.

It was a moonless night, the kind of night that made you wish you were safe and sound behind locked doors, tucked beneath the bed sheets. Lost and tired, I was stumbling through thick scrub looking for a shortcut back to the road from which I had deviated. Branches scratched my face and arms. Mosquitoes attacked me from every angle. Then, suddenly, I stepped through the scrub onto a long, narrow driveway lined with tall trees, the end of which to my right terminated at a small, yellow-brick cottage. Looking at it, I was immediately filled with fear. The cottage belonged to an infamous criminal and I knew I had to get away before he discovered that I was on his property. If he caught me, I was as good as dead.

The gate to the road was at the furthest end of the driveway to my left. With my heart now beating at double speed, I hurried into a trot. I shouldn't have. A motion sensor detected my movements, triggering a bank of floodlights along the driveway, blinding me. Like a rabbit that had stumbled out of the bushes into the path of an oncoming car, I froze in terror. Although, as yet, I could hear no barking dogs or shouting guards, I had no doubt the criminal had seen me on his electronic surveillance system. I knew it was just a matter of seconds before he set them on me.

Still frozen to the spot, wide-eyed, mouth agape, I said a quick prayer. "God, you have to help me," but I was secretly thinking that if I was taken prisoner then it was something that I would have to deal with on my own. God was trying to show me that I had to take the good with the bad.

God obviously wants me to suffer, I thought.

Then suddenly, the entire pitch-black vault above my head boomed like some kind of cosmic speaker system. A thundering voice shook me to my knees:

"NO! GOD IS ALWAYS GOOD."

Instantly, in half a heartbeat, bright white light filled the sky. Surprisingly, even though the light was as blinding as the floodlights, I could still see everything around me; the tall trees, the long driveway, the yellow-brick cottage. I stopped quivering. There was no pain, just lightness, and then, as if it were the most natural thing in the world, my feet began to levitate off the ground. I ascended horizontally toward the stars, lying on an invisible bed of air. I felt electric and alive, with blissful waves of ecstasy surging through my body. I could hear music, like a church organ, and choral voices, as though the angels were singing.

Then I woke up, totally alert, my mind and body buzzing with adrenaline. The transition from dream-state to wakefulness was so quick and smooth it was as if I had never been asleep, and I knew deep in my heart that it was more than just a dream.

I had had a vision.

Two Sides of a Coin

This "peak experience," to use Maslow's terminology, gives useful insight into my previously mistaken logic of good and evil. In the world in which we live, the temporal world of duality, good and evil exist as polar opposites. The relative nature of the universe, in fact, demands their mutual co-existence. As discussed before, good and bad, or pleasure and pain, are two opposing sides of a coin called intent (or need).

For example, the intent to seek pleasure is also the wish to avoid pain—what we want is the visible side of our intent and what we don't want is the hidden side. Usually, our intent or need for a particular outcome is called right or good. The flipside of our intent, the very outcome we don't want, is its natural and mutually inclusive partner, its opposite or negative form, and is usually labeled wrong or evil. In other words, anything that aids our intent (pleasure) is deemed good, and anything that is detrimental to it (pain) is deemed evil. For instance, in regards to the intentions of my golf game, a birdie putt is good and a bogy putt is evil.

Alas, the duality of this world also dictates that my heavenly Golf Land Paradise is a subjective desire of need and therefore a pure fantasy—it is not the Real Thing, and there are no golf courses in heaven, or in hell, for that matter.

Despite this, there is no need to lose hope in whatever visions of heaven you believe in. Heaven is simply God's Joy revealed to you and it can be experienced during this lifetime as well as after it (along with hell). What is being revealed—the revelation—is unique and relative to you. It is a relative appearance of what is, a metaphor for the Absolute Universe of Spirit, the Infinite Ink. As such, within the context of duality, any goodness we experience is just a symbolic expression or revelation of the Greater Good. Any evil, for that matter, is a reminder that goodness is just that, a symbol not to be mistaken for, or worshipped as, the Real Thing, a reminder that it is only in the Timeless Realm of the Absolute, the Realm before space and time, that True Good exists.

As potently explained in Martin Lings' book, *A Sufi Saint of the Twentieth Century*:[8]

> *All imperfections, all decay, all sufferings, all evils . . . are simply phases of a gradual demonstration that there is no he but He [that naught is there but it].*

---

[8] *A Sufi Saint of the Twentieth Century*, Martin Lings, George Allen & Unwin Ltd, 1971, second edition. First published 1961.

It is therefore a trap to idolize the good of this world and make of it our savior, for it is merely a label that comes at a cost: what it gives with one hand it will take with the other. Real Goodness, in comparison, has no opposite. As Jesus has already reminded us:

No one is good—except God alone.[2]

Which simply means that in the Kingdom of Heaven there is only Goodness: the lions lie down with the lambs; light dispels darkness; evil has been vanquished.

This is where I had made my error of judgment. I had assumed that the relative subjects of good and evil equated to the very Goodness that exists without opposite. I had turned the Formless into a concept, a form.

They [the letters] are its determinations, its activities . . . They are not it; say not, say not that they are it! To say so were wrong, and to say 'it is they' were raving madness.

My vision was a wakeup call. It revealed in no uncertain terms where I had gone off track, my raving madness, as it were. In our world, good and evil are two sides of the same coin.

God, however, is Always Good.

TRUTH

Any seeker of Truth is a scientist, whether he be a doctor, physicist, chemist, philosopher, teacher, IT consultant, or bus driver. Just as the search for Goodness defines the ascetic, the act of seeking the Truth defines the scientist.

But where the ascetic is searching for a perfect state of Goodness and pureness, the scientist is searching for a perfect place of Truth, an idyllic paradise. His lifelong quest is to go "out from his normal world in search of a lost home, a 'better country.'" In this sense, he too is a pilgrim, "a wanderer," testing theories along the way, digging up facts, investigating the unknown. He is a truth finder.

The Truth, however, in the context of Absolute Reality, is not an objective fact that can be collected, documented and placed on a museum shelf like a stuffed animal brought back from an exotic island as proof of its existence. To the ontological scientist, the Land of Truth lies beyond the duality of objectiveness and subjectiveness, a place bathed in perpetual sunshine.

If he has directed his search in the right areas, the relentless scientist eventually discovers what he is looking for and is rewarded for his efforts. In a moment of profound insight, the Truth reveals itself as an unshakeable sense of certitude; the scientist, the objective observer, merges with the object he is observing and becomes One with the eternal, non-dimensional nothingness from which the universe is created. His knowing is like no other. It is the ultimate a-ha! moment. Stepping foot upon the ladder of Universal Truth, the scientist's consciousness ascends to the level of Unity Consciousness, the level of his Source, where he can now take in the purified, heady smell of rarefied air. He suddenly has clarity, recognizing, perhaps for the first time, the Truth of existence through direct experience. It has set him free. No theories and nobody can tell him the Truth: he knows because, having delved into what is Real, Right and True, he has been imbued with an unshakable sense of joy, security, acceptance, peace and freedom. He has experienced the ineffable awareness of his Natural State of Being, a state of conscious knowing. He has found his "better country."

He has, in fact, found his paradise, his Land of Abundance. He has joined the learned community of pilgrims, saints and explorers that have successfully returned from their journey of illumination with the blissful knowledge of Truth:

Only God exists.

"My me is God,"[7] says St. Teresa, the enlightened medieval Spanish nun famed for her dedication to the Unitive Life. "He is the First and the Last and the Outwardly Manifest and the Inwardly Hidden,"[8] says the Prophet Mohammed. "I tell you the truth," says Jesus of the King in the parable of *The Sheep and the Goats*, "whatever you did for one of the least of these brothers of mine, you did for me."[2]

All these great teachers of Truth aim to raise our conscious awareness to the level of our Source, the level of Unity Consciousness. In our society, the general belief is that thinking and reasoning are the pinnacle of human consciousness, but it isn't so. Thoughts are the results, the activities, of consciousness, the pre-material images visualized on the screen of awareness. Knowing is not the Knower. Form is not the Formless. Words are not the Speaker. If we consider consciousness as a river, then thoughts (and emotions and feelings) are "down-stream", or sub-conscious, in relation to our Source. Our Higher Intelligence, or Big Mind, is where the action really is, which is higher "upstream" at the supra-conscious level of pure awareness, where inspiration, insight and love have greatest clarity. From this ultimate high ground, spiritual masters speak of the same thing:

> *At the deepest level of our Being, we are all One. There is only Consciousness, only Life, only Love. All else is illusion; all else is forgetfulness.*

The same message is repeated over and over again throughout millennia—separateness is an illusion, a misperception based on a mistaken identity. What we do unto others, we do unto our self.

> *Look well at each letter: thou seest it hath already perished but for the face of the ink, that is, for the Face of His Essence.*

In recognizing and acknowledging this, recognizing and acknowledging that he is born with everything he is searching for, that he need not start from scratch to make up for the shortfall, the adventurous scientist paves the way to his "better country."

In developing sufficient willingness to break his obsession with the false truths of this world, developing sufficient willingness to explore new worlds, the scientist steps forth and begins the long trek toward the land of abundant joy, security, acceptance, peace and freedom—the land of permanent and abiding Truth.

BEAUTY

Just as the search for Goodness defines the ascetic, just as the search for Truth defines the scientist, the act of seeking Beauty defines the artist. But where the ascetic is searching for a perfect state of Goodness and pureness, where the scientist is searching for a perfect place of Truth, an idyllic paradise, the artist is searching for the perfect personality, his partner for life. The artist is consumed by the "craving of heart for heart, of the soul for its perfect mate, which makes him a lover." If it is the Truth that sets the scientist free, it is Beauty that lifts the artist to the dizzying heights of love.

As an infatuated lover, the artist submits himself totally and utterly to the Will of the Everlasting Ink, his Beloved's Essence. Real Beauty, the artist knows, is not in the eye of the beholder at all; it is not a subjective interpretation conditional upon the needs and desires of an independent, objective observer. Real Beauty lies beyond duality. In a sense, it is Perfect Being.

On a family trip to Sydney in 2006 I witnessed an amazing event, probably a once-in-a-lifetime event, that caused me to think of the context between ugliness and beauty, or more precisely, between imperfection and perfection. Through the window of a friend's apartment, seven stories high, I was watching the wind and rain sweeping across the adjacent parklands. The treetops bent and swayed erratically with each gust of cold wind. Large pools of water were collecting on the grassy fields. Mothers with strollers were fighting to hold onto their umbrellas, scurrying for cover.

"Is it ever going to end?" I grumbled to myself, wanting nothing more than to get out and do some sightseeing before nightfall.

Then, on the far horizon, I caught a glimpse of the first colorful rays of a forming rainbow. It emerged from the grey clouds and stretched toward the suburban rooftops like a slippery-dip for giants, half an arch of red and yellow and green and blue. Over the next few minutes, the remaining half of the rainbow materialized out of the heavens, completing the bow. It was like watching a magic pyrotechnic show from the best seat in the stadium.

But as I watched, the most amazing thing began to happen—the rainbow started to move. "Look at it!" I said to my wife. "It's coming toward us."

Sure enough, to our disbelief, the arch of color had shrunk. It barely extended across the parklands, each end diving into a grassy patch of field not much more than a kilometer apart.

"I've never seen anything like it," she said, and neither had I.

Two minutes later it was even closer, less than fifty meters away. Its ends were now plunging into two rooftops separated by a distance of no more than nine or ten houses. Did the neighbors know what was happening above them? Looking down, I could almost reach out of the window and dip my fingers into its colors.

Half expecting the rainbow to now move over us, the most amazing thing of all (as if this wasn't enough) suddenly happened—the rainbow stopped moving. The rain pelted down and the wind howled through the trees, but the rainbow stayed planted in the neighbors' attics. It was as if it was saying to Martie and me, "Do you see? Even in the storm there is color. You just have to remember to look." And there it stayed for the next five minutes, with all the wildness happening around it, peaceful and serene, until it slowly faded into thin air.

Eventually, the rain paused long enough to allow us to get out of the apartment and do some sightseeing, but my thoughts were focused upon the deeper meaning of what I had seen earlier. On one level, even a child knew that rainbows needed rain, which, interpreted into the language of duality, simply meant that rain provided the context in which rainbows can exist, just as sadness provided the context in which happiness can exist, insecurity for security, rejection for acceptance, turmoil for peace, and so forth. Like good and evil, beauty and ugliness (rainbows and rain) existed in this world where everything is tied to its polar opposite. But on another level—the level of our Source—the colors of this relative world were entirely dependent upon the Eternal Rainbow for their existence. Without it, they were simply nothing.

The message was as clear as the gaps of blue sky parting the clouds overhead: although storms may gust through my life, although rain may persist for days before blowing over, the Rainbow of Perfection shines come what may. All we have to do is remember to look.

Thus it is with the loving eyes of an artist. The Essence of Beauty inherent in all created life is clear and visible, even in the shadow of imperfection.

> *Even thus the letters, for all their outward show, are hidden, being overwhelmed by the ink, since their show is none other than its.*

POINTS OF REMEMBRANCE #3

- People have craved the salvation of joy, security, acceptance, peace and freedom since time immemorial.

- Society is divided along three lines—Religion, Science and Art—in its quest to experience what is Real, Right and True.

- Humanity is restless with deep cravings for Goodness, Truth and Beauty.

- The ascetic is searching for a perfect state of Goodness and pureness.

- GOD IS ALWAYS GOOD.

- It is a trap to idolize the good of this world and make of it our savior.

- The scientist is searching for a perfect place of Truth, an idyllic paradise bathed in perpetual sunshine, a place beyond the duality of objectiveness and subjectiveness.

- We are all One.

- The artist is searching for the perfect personality, his partner for life.

- The Rainbow of Perfection shines come what may.

3 LIGHT, LIFE & LOVE

PRESENCE

INVARIABLY, ALL ENDEAVORS at salvation through religion, science and art, all quests to find joy, security, acceptance, peace and freedom through Goodness, Truth and Beauty, are simply the attempts to fill the void that stems from forgetfulness—the belief that we are born separate from our Source, that we are born with nothing and must start from scratch. The disciple's spiritual pilgrimage toward Goodness, the scientist's relentless march toward Truth, and the artist's pursuit of Beauty, will ultimately come to a dead end, either as a spectacular crash of disillusionment or as an insidious demise of hope and faith, if the very Source of Life is ignored. Any pilgrim, any scientist, any artist, is ultimately doomed to fail in their quest for salvation if the Spirit of Goodness, Truth and Beauty is dismissed as irrelevant.

Most people probably know, or have been aware of, someone approaching the dead end of faith. The aloof Samaritan who thinks he is the only one in the community who does good works, who helps feed the hungry and house the homeless but has silently begun to doubt the meaning of his life. The arrogant scientist who thinks she knows it all, who thinks she has an open mind but, in her failure to recognize the limited sphere within which the human mind has been conditioned to operate, refuses to acknowledge any possibility of a universe beyond her laboratory. The depressed artist who sees only ugliness in the world and has tossed the scraps of her creative passion to the dogs of futility and disdain.

Some of us may even be that aloof Samaritan, that arrogant scientist or depressed artist. Some of us know all too well, from our own personal experience, the despairing cries of Isaiah, laboring for no purpose, spending his strength in vain and suffering.[2]

But what are we to make of this pain and suffering that seems such an inevitable component of our quest for Goodness, Truth and Beauty?

Evelyn Underhill gives us a clue, again from her book, *Mysticism*.[7]

> *Pain, however we may look at it, indicates a profound disharmony between the sense-world and the human self. If it is to be vanquished, either the disharmony must be resolved by a deliberate and careful adjustment of the self to the world of the sense, or, that self must turn from the sense-world to some other with which it is in tune.*

Whenever a pilgrim's quest for Goodness, Truth and Beauty has waned and she has succumbed to the futility of it all, the cause of this pain is more often than not over-attentiveness toward the things of this "sense-world"—things that by their very nature come and go and have no permanency—and the consequent inattentiveness of Source.

As Deepak Chopra reminds us in *How To Know God*:[9]

> *When a person forgets that . . . his source is rooted in eternal Being, separation results, and from separation all other pain and suffering follows.*

Whenever the letter pays little or no attention to the Ink, its Source, whenever the pilgrim refuses to "turn from the sense-world to some other", suffering exists. There is profound disharmony, "pain and suffering follows". Conflict occurs within and without. Fear arises.

---

[9] *How To Know God*, Deepak Chopra, Rider (Ebury Press imprint), 2000

In the later part of the 1990s, during my tenure as a pediatric resident in the Neonatal Intensive Care Unit of The Royal London Hospital, I was pleasantly surprised to learn of a study in which it was revealed that premature babies who were routinely stroked and caressed by their parents or nursing staff fared much better than babies whose physical contact was minimal and restricted to the times of feeding and nappy changing. The babies who were caressed and touched were healthier, gained weight faster, and suffered fewer infections than the babies who had much less contact. Somehow, the felt presence of another has a beneficial and quantifiable impact on a baby's physical wellbeing. In contrast, the absence of physical contact has a detrimental influence on a baby's health.

It is similar for older children, adolescents and adults. Pain and suffering is magnified when we believe we are on our own, and it is greatly reduced by the presence of another, even if they do nothing more than sit next to us and hold our hand. Pain has to be released. Its continuing build up, physical or psychological, can cause untold hardship and suffering. The loving presence of a partner, a family member, or a friend can act as an outlet for the release of pain. They can help us to open our pressure valve and let go of the worry, to get things off our chest, to soothe our hurt. People who live in isolation—those in remote countries, in nursing homes, even those who live alone in a busy city—know all too well the value of another's presence, a kindly word, a gentle touch.

The felt presence of Being, the felt connectedness of our mind, body and soul to our Source, provides the same kindly word, the same gentle touch, to ease our pain. Unlike people, however, who are prone to leave or abandon us, Being is permanent and abiding. The Stillness of our Source is an enduring, continuously anointing balm for those feelings of sadness, insecurity, worthlessness, turmoil and limitation we are unable to alleviate. Through the

Silence of Being we are connected to the whole and, as such, made wholesome: we are healed. Spirit's Presence is cathartic.

Conversely, the inability to see our Source, the failure to feel Spirit physically, mentally and spiritually in our day-to-day life, has a detrimental impact on our sense of wellbeing. The absence of felt connectedness to our Source magnifies the inner feelings of vulnerability and abandonment, which we automatically seek to control and nullify. In our misguided desperation, we snatch and scrounge for Goodness, Truth and Beauty in the things we see around us in the "sense-world", little realizing that the continual dismissal of the Source of Everything infects the wounds of our suffering and prevents them from healing.

Like Isaiah, we cry out in our despair, laboring for no purpose, spending our strength in vain and suffering.

Where the Money Is

To end suffering and to feel whole requires a humble acknowledgement that what we are in fact looking for is Spirit, to feel connectedness on all levels of being to our Higher Self. The search for Spirit, in turn, is the search for the underlying invisible order of the universe, the Plan behind every action, every coincidence, every living moment. In other words, the organization beneath the outward chaos.

I remember watching an American football game for the first time on television. Nothing I had ever seen on a sporting field resembled so much chaos. Players were running this way and that, jumping on each other, dodging and fleeing one another, throwing the ball backwards and forwards, sometimes kicking it, sometimes pretending to kick it and then doing it all over again for three more quarters. Yardage was prime, I gathered, and measured by the ten, but sometimes an inch was more valuable than thirty yards.

Worse, just when I thought I had gained some comprehension of what was going on, the teams ran off the field and were replaced by another team. There were two teams for each team!

As time passed, however, and I watched each weekly game beamed in from the US, I began to learn the basics of the game and understand what the players were trying to achieve. My quality of awareness of American football was rising. I was beginning to see that there was actually something else going on behind the scenes. There was a hidden and invisible organizational body of rules underpinning the chaos on the football field, a kind of "spirit of the game" that all the players were obeying. Slowly but surely, with this knowledge, the madness no longer seemed so mad. Where once before I had seen only chaos, there was now order, even though the game itself had not changed.

On one level, Spirit is like the rules of a football game. What appears in this world of duality as chaotic and random on the surface is actually following the plan or rules of some hidden organizing consciousness. There is something else going on behind the scenes. Yet for the majority of us, the quality of our awareness remains on the level of physicality. There is certainly no order to the madness. The Spirit of the Game of Life remains invisible and irrelevant and, every day, seems to follow no set plan or rules of any kind.

But what is Spirit? Can its invisible Presence really be felt or experienced? What is this organizing Consciousness really like?

Spiritual masters tell us that Spirit is the incomprehensible nothingness from which the universe is created, the infinite Source of everything, including our own body, mind and soul. Once you have acknowledged this point, they advise, and if it is still your desire to feel Spirit as a real and living Presence, you need simply to begin with your own felt sense of presence, your own awareness of being, which is directly connected to Spirit's Presence, your Higher Being, as part of its continuum. Tap into your own presence, your own sense of being, spiritual masters say, and there you will find your Source.

"Because that's where the money is," the thief said to the policeman when asked why he kept re-offending and holding up banks. Your presence is where your spiritual money, your Natural State of Being, is safeguarded. You are present right now, are you not? Can you feel what your own sense of being is like? Is it awareness of being alive, awareness of being here and now? Is it awareness of awareness? Or is it something else, something still, something silent, like the space between the words on this page, or the gap between your thoughts?

Your presence is actually the tip of a greater iceberg, one tiny drop in an infinite sea. In truth, it is not your presence at all, but Spirit's. But, putting this to one side for the moment, tapping into your own felt presence is actually the real embarkation point of the spiritual journey. Felt being is the very beginning of direct communion with Spirit. Although, spiritual masters warn, Unity Consciousness may, at first, appear to the seeking mind as invisible, formless and dark, an immense nothingness or vast emptiness.

Yet, despite these dark beginnings, there is light at the end of the tunnel. Through persistent determination on behalf of the seeker, Spirit eventually emerges like rays of dawn from beyond the horizon of the limited human mindset. When it does, it reveals itself in three main ways:[7]

1. The Substance of Truth.
2. The Energy of Goodness.
3. The Essence of Beauty.

As such, underlying our quest for all things True, Good and Beautiful is non-other than the quest for their original Source—their Substance, Energy and Essence, which I have given the acronym "SEE"—which is also the quest for Spirit's Presence.

All quests therefore end up at the same point. They have to;

there is nothing else other than what is, only one Source. (Although some interpretations of religious texts may interpret the universe as having two sources of power, good and evil, this is ultimately shown to be false: evil is like cancer, a mutation, a grotesque distortion of what power or energy already exists, not an independent, creative source unto itself; evil cannot create, only recreate, and it is ultimately self-destructive.)

This ultimately leads us to ask what actually is being observed when our one, single Source appears on the horizon, when we finally get to feel Spirit's Presence? What does the Substance of Truth look like? What does the Energy of Goodness feel like? What does the Essence of Beauty taste like?

In other words, what is it that we actually SEE when we lift the veil of Goodness, Truth and Beauty and behold the Face of our Beloved?

According to spiritual and religious texts, we see three things:[7]

1. Light
2. Life
3. Love

That is to say, the Source (Substance, Energy, Essence) of Truth, Goodness and Beauty, appears to the seeking pilgrim as either a manifestation of Light, a manifestation of Life, or a manifestation of Love, or a combination of the three. Time after time, those who have been closest to Spirit have come down from their lofty heights and related to us what they have seen in these terms. No matter what religion we are aligned to—Islam, Christianity, Judaism, Buddhism, Hinduism, Paganism—we find a consistent history of terminological reference to God (Spirit, Being, Higher Self, Big Mind, Source), as a Light that is Uncreated, a Life that is Infinite, and a Love that is Eternal.

They are describing, no less, visions of the Divine Faces of Being.

THE DIVINE FACES OF BEING

The trinity of Light, Life and Love appears again and again throughout spiritual and religious texts around the world and in the personal writings of spiritual masters. Take, for instance, the most popular text of all, the Bible. The pages of the Old and New Testaments are saturated with the "Love of God". Jesus speaks of "the light and the way". Even the Holy Trinity itself embodies the very essence of Light (Heavenly Father), Life (The Christ) and Love (the Holy Spirit).

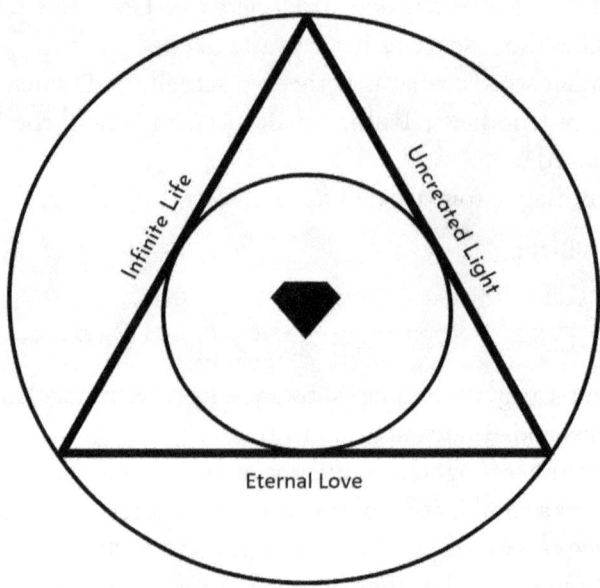

FIGURE 2:   The Triune of Being

But such terminology of our Source is not solely confined to Christian doctrine. In Buddhism, Zen Masters talk of "grasping the Essence of Life in the living of it".[10] Muslims too profess to the

---

[10] *An Introduction to Zen Buddhism*, T. S. Suzuki, 1st Grove Weidenfeld edition, 1991

reality of God's Love, Light and Life. The Islamic insistence that there is no god but God, is not, contrary to some interpretations, an arrogant proclamation of spiritual supremacy over all other religions and cultural deities, but a profound statement on the Nature of Infinite Life. It is, in fact, a proclamation of the essential truth that there is nothing other than One Thing, that

There is not one, save what the ink hath anointed.

Each religion uses its own unique blend of language and symbolism to describe the imagery of Absolute Reality or Transcendent Oneness within the vernacular that is most understood by the culture which that religion is addressing. More often than not, century after century, religious thinkers have tended to fall back on the same imagery of Light, Life and Love. These concepts are cross-cultural. They have stood the test of time. They are the best we have, within the limitations of language, to try and describe that which cannot be described, only experienced.

Furthermore, the imagery of Light, Life and Love is not just the sole property or monopoly of the world's religions. It is pervasive throughout the arts and sciences. Poets have surrendered to the catharsis of love in odes and ballads for thousands of years. Fairytales yearn to enlighten us about the truth of Eternal Love, if only we scratch beneath the surface turmoil of daily existence, if only we read between the lines and penetrate the heart of the letter to the Mysteries of the Ink. Likewise, scientists and mathematicians have long been comfortable with the universal concepts of infinity and eternity. Physicists openly admit to the reality of an infinite "nothingness" from which everything was created, a timeless eternity of non-dimensional emptiness that existed before the universe was thrust forth in an explosion of unimaginable proportions as four-dimensional time and space (or eleven dimensions, depending on which theory is in vogue).

The mistake, of course, is to assume that this nothingness is a relic of the distant past with no relevance to the present rather than an ever-present Source that continues to sustain and carry us through time and space. Nonetheless, think about the implications of what physicists are saying with their theories and get to the heart of their complicated mathematical equations: the universe is actually a thing that has arisen from nothing. But what faith! Something created from nothing. A miracle, no less, whether it is discussed in the language of gospel or the language of mathematics.

Yet, no matter what language we are comfortable with, life shows us again and again that all roads lead to the same place. Followed to their absolute end point, all religious, all scientific, and all artistic pathways lead, in fact, not to Rome but to the New Jerusalem—the Uncreated Light, the Infinite Life and the Eternal Love. Light, Life and Love are one and the same City. The Substance of Truth, the Energy of Goodness, and the Essence of Beauty are one and the same Source. They are the Ink or Inner Mystery of God. They are David's "Rock".[2]

How that Ink or Mystery or Rock is experienced, however, is largely dependent on the personality of the seeking pilgrim. What Face of the Divine Being is revealed beneath the veil is determined by which eye is scanning the Infinite Horizon. Just as quantum physics has shown us that the universe waits for the observer to make his or her intentions known before revealing itself, the actual intent of the seeker is what is important when it comes to seeing Spirit.

Our intent, as observers, determines what is seen or experienced of our Source as it flows from its Formless Realm. Or more precisely, our state of *readiness* determines what we are capable of seeing. As the quote on one of my bookmarks reads:

> God says, 'I will be whatever you need me to be, and when you are ready, I will be more.'

This more or less reflects the deeper insight from Deepak Chopra: "God is as we are."[9] At the highest level, God, our Source, is our conscious awareness, our being, our love—the Divine Being is as we are here and now. The point is: God is as our needs dictate.

Divine Being unveils its face in a form that is palatable to our state of mind.

This, in turn, is a reflection of the quality of awareness we have evolved to, namely our current level of consciousness, being and love. An atheist sees a black void. A saint sees the Light, Life and Love of Spirit. Neither is right or wrong. One just sees more wonder and glory of the Infinite and Eternal All than the other. One just has a greater quality of awareness, a greater clarity of what is. Like a mirror, the universe reflects back to both atheist and saint who they are and what they want to see:

The universe simply confirms the beliefs we hold deep in our heart.

At the highest level, spiritual masters know that everything begins with the metaphysical Ink, our Source. Apart from years of hard toil along the spiritual path, the difference between what a spiritual master knows and what we in the general population know, or think we know, has its beginnings in belief. Spiritual masters are children at heart. They are not trying to be anything other than what they are right now. They do not resist anything that is. As such, they are joyous, spontaneous, energetic, playful, but, most of all, completely trusting of their Higher Self. God is such a given fact of life that it is beyond any doubt, even beyond consideration. Their quality of awareness is sharp and crystal clear. They are aware of and experience firsthand the Presence of Light, Life and Love in every moment of the day. Consciousness fills their sense of awareness, which is attentive and alert. Life abounds in everything, from the mountains to the seas to the trees to their own sense of being. Love embraces them everywhere they go, even, or especially, in the midst of disaster.

To a spiritual master, only the Light, Life and Love of our Source exists. All else is transitory. All else is forgetfulness. "Why," they ask, "is there any need to look anywhere else? It is all here in this moment."

This is what having the faith of children means, to have so much trust in God that it goes beyond the realms of belief and into the realms of everyday reality.

To our benefit, we too can come to know what spiritual masters know, we too can share the same quality of awareness. The Divine Mystery is always revealing its secrets. Our Source holds nothing back from anybody, saints and sinners alike. The Beloved is continually wooing his lover (you), an Eternal Romeo forever serenading his Juliet with the Song of Life. For whenever we, as letters of the alphabet, believe and acknowledge that we and all other letters are nothing less than the activities of the Ink, we too, like spiritual masters, open our self to the influx of all the Majesty and Beauty of Divine Mystery, bringing it into our conscious reality.

Like them, we come to know something more, a great secret:

There is nothing else.

"I am that I am. You are that you are," we come to confess. "And that is all there is."

We also know that Light, Life and Love are the only things we take with us when we die, because that is all we really are.

Yet, what Face of Romeo Juliet sees, what Features of the Infinite Eternal All she beholds—Light, Life or Love—is determined by what virtues or path she aspires to—Truth, Goodness or Beauty. That is to say, deep at heart, the requited yearnings of Juliet for her Romeo, the desires of the seeking pilgrim for her Eternal Fountain, are nothing less than the deeper longings of every man, woman and child for joy, security, acceptance, peace and freedom.

Most importantly, given the will and the determination, each scientist, pilgrim and artist will eventually find what they are seeking. The treasure of your Natural State of Being is assured. Your efforts will not go unrewarded. Seek and you will find; knock and the door will be opened for you. For everyone who asks receives.

But will you be attentive enough to recognize the Light, Life and Love—your Source—for what it really is?

THE UNCREATED LIGHT

For our purposes, the Uncreated Light, as the Substance of Truth, is synonymous with our Higher Intelligence or Ultimate Awareness. It is the Conscious Source—That Which Knows—conscious awareness in its purest state of being.

In the book, *A Sufi Saint of the Twentieth Century* by Martin Lings,[8] the deeper meaning of Light and Consciousness has been beautifully captured in Shaik Al-Buzidi's explanation of what remains of a person stripped of his peripheral senses—sight, hearing, taste, touch and smell. What is left of such a denuded person, the Shaik says, is a

> *... faint gleam which appears to him as the lucidity of his consciousness ... There is perfect continuity between this gleam and the Great Light of the Infinite World, and once this continuity has been grasped our consciousness can (by means of prayer) flow forth and spread out as it were into the Infinite and become One with It, so that man comes to realize that the Infinite Alone is, and that he, the humanly conscious, exists only as a veil. Once this state has been realized, all the Lights of Infinite Life may penetrate the soul of the [seeker], and make him participate in the Divine Life ...*

The "Great Light of the Infinite World" is uncreated and formless. It exists before and after the creation of time and space, the very Thing that requires no-thing to exist but from which no-thing can exist without.

For it was before the letters, when no letter was; and it remaineth, when no letter at all shall be.

Without it, there simply is no Truth. In the Absolute Universe, there is nothing else other than the Uncreated Light, the Godhead, and it is this Eternal Substance that determines what Truth is and how it is perceived.

The Truth is what happens when Spirit breathes.

In short, Consciousness is Truth and Truth is Consciousness. Just as the sun is the source and substance of sunlight, the Light of Consciousness is the Source and Substance of Truth. In other words, when the Conscious Light shines forth from the depths of the Silent Stillness, the Truth radiates in our mind: it is as the shadow-soaked land greets the rising sun, a dawning of awareness. For when the Conscious Light rises from beyond the dark horizon, you are illuminated with Reality as it truly is. You understand the Way of Things with utter surety, beyond any doubt.

"I was blind and now I can see," the awakening pilgrim cries as he stumbles out of the dark cave of unconsciousness and into the Light of Consciousness. After years of fumbling for a way out of the illusion, he suddenly has clarity, and clarity is seeing the Uncreated Light in its purest form, a pristine quality of awareness. It is nothing less than a revelation of Truth.

But what Truth is being revealed and clarified to the awakening pilgrim? The Awareness of Big Mind. The "I" in "I am." The Knower within.

Clarity—the awareness or conscious sense of Truth—is the mechanism by which Consciousness (Formless Self) knows itself through consciousness (formed self). Just as the study of sunlight invariably leads us back to its source, the sun, so too the study of Truth leads us back to the Conscious Light. Delve deep into a spark of light, and there you will discover the Great Fire from which it emerged. In terms of Unity Consciousness, this is how the loop of Oneness closes, how we, the highest evolution of physical form, come to know That Which Knows, the Knower within, the Invisible Ink.

Actually, your degree of clarity is directly proportional to the depth to which you, the seeker, has delved into the mysterious process of how you are aware you are aware. For instance, in keeping with what has already been discussed, things in this duality-created universe, objects of form, even thoughts, are only knowable through the division of "me" and "something other than me," through subjective polarization. But who, you may well ask, is the Knower behind the whole process of knowing? Who is it that is able to know and experience the things of form?

Alternatively, it may help to put it another way and ask this Zen-like question: Who is the "I" that is aware of my thoughts when I say, "I am thinking"? This is where clarity steps in. Either the answer is clear and true, or it isn't.

All these questions, however, are just one variation or another of the age-old question that has been plaguing humanity since time immemorial: Who am I? When stripped of everything I know about myself—my age, my sex, my thoughts, my likes, my possessions, my personal history, and so forth—who is the knower, the remaining, permanent, essential self that knows these things about me?

Who am I?
I Am That.
Who are you?
You Are That.
Is there anything more than That?

At the Speed of Light

Although the natural instinct of the human mind is to manipulate the Conscious Light into a convenient concept amenable to reason and logic, that is the last thing the Substance of Truth will let us do. It cannot be captured, framed and hung on the wall like a family portrait.

> *The Formless cannot be turned into a thing of form, a concept, a picture in our mind, only allowed to be.*

Consider for a minute the physical speed of the fastest known thing in the universe, a photon of light. At a mind-boggling three hundred thousand kilometers per second (300,000 km/s), light speed is a constant physical barrier, according to the laws of physics, beyond which nothing in the universe can penetrate and cross. Indeed, it cannot even be reached. Physicists in Switzerland at the European Council for Nuclear Research, CERN, regularly use powerful electromagnets to propel beams of protons, inside a gigantic particle accelerator beneath the ground, to speeds in excess of ninety-nine percent (almost 99.99%, in fact) the speed of light. They do this in order to smash opposing beams of protons together to examine the sub-atomic particles released from the collision and thus attempt to gain a better understanding of the building blocks of the universe.

Interestingly, however, no matter how fast the beams of protons are propelled, physicists cannot accelerate the protons to the full, one hundred percent speed of light. It is unattainable, a bridge too far, in part due to the slippery nature of light itself.

Now imagine riding at the vanguard of one of the beams of protons beneath the Alps at CERN. Imagine, also, a photon of light just ahead of you as the powerful electromagnets begin to whirl you around and around the particle accelerator. Even as you increase your velocity, however, you will begin to notice that the distance between you and the photon of light is not diminishing.

Still quirkier, as your velocity approaches the speed of light, the photon you are chasing is still dancing in front of your eyes and teasing you to reach out and grab hold of it.

But it is a hopeless quest. You will never be able to grab hold of the slippery photon, no matter how fast or how hard you try. This is because the speed of light is relative to your position and speed, which means that whatever speed you have reached—slow, medium, fast, close-to-light-speed, stationary—the speed of the photon will always be three hundred thousand kilometers per second relative to you, forever out of reach.

As discovered by Einstein, the laws of the universe strictly forbid you to cross the light barrier. Even time will be bent to prevent you from doing so: the faster one travels, the more time slows down. Through this science-fiction-like temporal distortion, the photon of light is thus able to maintain its relative speed ahead of the chasing proton. (More will be said on the interesting effects of temporal distortion on perception in Part IV.)

When it comes to being grasped, the Light of Consciousness has an equally slippery and relative nature as a photon of light. No matter how close we get, the Light will always dance in front of our eyes and remain tantalizingly out of our reach. At some point in the evolution of our awareness, however, there comes a realization that the effort of trying to grasp the Light stems from a heightened confusion as to our true nature. Trying to grasp Consciousness is a silent admission that we don't believe we are already that which we want to be and are therefore striving to be it. As such, lost in thought (formed consciousness), we try to grasp onto Formless Consciousness (Source) by turning it into an object to be examined. From this polarity, when we try to enter into the Light—the silence, the gap, the stillness—it's as though we've put our self in one corner and the Light in the other, then tried to move over and into it, which, on a quantum level, is like a proton trying to crack the speed of light. Not surprisingly, our efforts become thwarted, not too unlike forcing a square peg into a round hole.

That is, until we realize that our true nature is the Uncreated Light itself and that all we have to do to bring the Light into this world—which is our purpose in life, to refrain from hiding our light under a bushel—is a simple process of being who we really are, not resisting our Natural State of Being. As long as we maintain a position of duality, the Truth will never be grasped and our Light will be kept hidden. The issue, technically, is therefore not to align one's self with the Light, but to realize and remember that you *already are* the Light. Only when we finally realize that we are the very thing we are chasing, that we are the round hole and not the square peg, that there is no "me" and "something other than me", will the Light of Consciousness reveal the true nature of Itself and open our eyes to all the abundance of glory and wonder that the universe has to offer.

Thus, paradoxically, to capture the Light we must release it from our rational and logical grasp and refrain from boxing it within the confines of duality. Practically, this means cleaning all reflections of egoic selfhood ("me") from the perceptive window through which we view life (that is, clearing the mental cobwebs of our belief systems, wiping away the smudges of our unconscious thoughts) by being silent and still, then simply observing the rays of Truth that shoot our way from our Source. Go to where the money is, your presence, your sense of being, because only the Knower within knows. Only Consciousness can sense the Truth. Only Awareness can have clarity and, through clarity, through the pristine quality of attentiveness, we eventually come to know the Light. In a sense,

Clarity is how you know you know the Truth.

Clarity and Truth are therefore signposts of Consciousness, or Knowing. In every aspect of life, the degree of clarity and truth we behold is a reliable indication of our nearness to Spirit, or the strength of our communion with our Source. The greater the lucidity of Truth, the greater the luminosity and quality of our awareness, the closer we are to our Source—That Which Knows.

Conversely, the more turbid and foggier our sense of Truth, the dimmer and darker our conscious reality seems to be, the further we have to travel to commune with our Source.

But your Source, the Uncreated Light, is closer than you think; you are already where you want to be. Knowing the Truth comes down to knowing the Truth of the Knower within, your Natural State of Being. This Truth will not only set you free, it will also set you on the path to the place of abundant joy, security, acceptance and peace that is not of this world.

THE INFINITE LIFE

On the other hand, the Infinite Life is that which we can consider to be our Higher Self or Universal Being—That Which Is. The Infinite Life is the Source that has always been, always is, and always will be. It is the Infinite and Omnipresent Word, whose spoken power is the Energy of Goodness that revitalizes and animates every known thing.

The Infinite Life is what remains after all else is stripped away. Look closely outside your window to the nearest bush or tree. Its branches and leaves are constantly renewing over the days, months and years. A branch dies while another is growing. A leaf withers and falls to the ground while another is sprouting. But when a branch or leaf dies, what remains of the tree? Is it any less of a tree for having lost a part of itself? Has it lost any of its essence? After several seasons, all of its branches and leaves will eventually die and be replaced by new ones. Is it a different tree then? Is it, in fact, a different tree than when it was a sapling, or even a seed? Will it be a different tree in the future?

If we just take into consideration its physical components, then we would have to say yes, it is a different tree. Like a hammer that has had its head replaced three times and its shaft replaced twice, it is not the same hammer as when it was bought (although, to the carpenter, it's still the same, trusty old hammer he's used for forty years!). But, unlike a hammer, a tree is alive. It is infused with life-energy, with Goodness.

This life-energy is the "spirit", or essence, of the tree, the one constant presence throughout its life cycle as a seed, sapling, mature, and old tree, the one constant living presence that exists while all the decay, death, re-birth, and growth of its branches and leaves are happening. This spirit, this renewing blueprint, is, in truth, the real tree, not the one that is appearing in front of your eyes at this moment. Said Jesus: [2]

> *See how the lilies of the field grow ... Yet I tell you that not even Solomon in all his splendor was dressed like one of these. If that is how God clothes the grass of the field, which is here today and tomorrow thrown into the fire, will he not much more clothe you?*

Indeed, as with the trees and the lilies, so it is with you. If you are old enough to read this book, your body has died at least twice without you knowing it since you were born. Doctors estimate that every cell in the body is replaced on average every seven years. Some cells die and are renewed even more quickly. The liver you have today is not the same liver that cleared the alcohol from your bloodstream after that dinner party two months ago. The lining of your stomach is not the same stomach that digested lunch several days ago, nor are the cells in your mouth that ate it.

Even taking into consideration the atoms and subatomic particles from which every cell is built, the body you have now is not the same one you had several years ago. Using the seven-year estimate of complete bodily renewal, some readers have died nine, ten, eleven, or even more, times.

But how could this be? How could you have died even once and still be here flicking through these pages?

Because you are not your body. Nor are you your mind. You are bigger, much bigger, than either. In truth, you have not died at all. You cannot die. You are eternal. Only the physical apparatus has died and been replaced, the conduit through which you are present in this particular space-time event.

As a spiritual being having a human experience, you are a soul with a body and mind. Your true nature, your essence, is the life-energy that animates your constantly changing body, the renewing vitality that transcends the duality of life and death. As such, you are not clothed "in" your body but, just as your heart is inside your chest, your body is "in" you. You are not trapped inside your head, within the confusing psychological network of your mind. Rather, your mind is one strand of a greater tapestry of consciousness.

Because your body and mind are small, to be caught in the body's emotions and the mind's thoughts, and thus to identify completely with your form, is to shrink yourself down and make yourself as small as they are. This, in fact, is what the ego does: it shrinks you (Formless Self) down and traps you inside your physicality (formed self) by making you believe you are small, limited and isolated.

But you are not small. You are big, so big in fact that you are even bigger than this moment, because this moment comes and goes and you do not. Your body dies and is renewed, but you remain when all your atoms, cells and organs have disappeared. Your thoughts come and go, but you persist when all your ideas, memories and thoughts have all been forgotten.

Being Formless, your true nature is embedded within Infinite Life itself and infused with the energy of its eternal Goodness.

Look well at each letter: thou seest it hath already perished, but for the face of the ink, that is, for the Face of His Essence.

The Leap of Faith

At the most fundamental level, the Infinite Life is the powerful Source or Energy that determines what Real Goodness is and how it manifests. The Goodness of the Infinite Life is its creative and life-giving nature. It is a wholesome, cathartic force. Consciously connecting with it physically, mentally and spiritually heals all levels of our being; our mind, body and soul.

Just as the Nile emerges from its source and meanders as a mighty river toward its Mediterranean delta, so, too, do the waters of life flow from the Eternal Fount. To drink its waters is to be invigorated with its Goodness, that life-energy which is merciful and kind, that force which is benevolent and caring and self-sustaining.

However, without first having faith (belief and trust) in the Infinite Life, without first having faith in the Goodness of its Being, it is nigh impossible to be enlivened or cleansed by its waters. If we do not trust the stream to dip in and scoop our cup, how can we be revitalized or healed by its freshness? If we do not trust the well from which we drink, how can our thirst be sated?

The channel, or means, by which we consciously receive the revitalizing force of the Energy of Life, therefore, is the belief and trust in the power of Goodness, the belief and trust in the power of our Source. To extrapolate the recent discussion on spiritual masters and their childlike belief in God, this means that the manner in which we are invigorated and rejuvenated by That Which Is, is our faith. Through the strength of our belief and trust in our Source, we are flooded with the Goodness of its Being. (Remembering, of course, that Goodness is not defined as the fulfillment of our wishes and desires, like a cure for cancer, instantaneous riches, popularity or fame, or a new career opportunity, but that which lies beyond duality in the Heart of Life.)

Faith, it can be argued, is the manner in which Life energizes and sustains itself through life. By believing and trusting his Higher Self to direct his thoughts, words and actions—allowing the Lord to be his Shepherd—the devoted pilgrim learns that Goodness is the hand that always catches his fall when he takes the leap of faith. In time, with experience, his faith is solidified into the tangible and practical reality that Spirit always provides what he needs when he needs it, his daily bread.

Through faith, he comes to live with the certitude that there is no life but Life, the Abundant Waters from which flow the currents of joy, security, acceptance, peace and freedom.

THE ETERNAL LOVE

If the Uncreated Light is the Intelligence (Mind) of Being and, if the Infinite Life is the Power (Body) of Being, then Eternal Love is that which we can consider to be the Personality (Soul) of Being.

Says the Bible:[2]

> *God is love. Whoever lives in love lives in union with God, and God in him.*

Love is Spirit—That Which Unifies—the invisible force that unites the universe as One. Love dissolves all barriers, all resistance, that separate the lover from the Beloved.

Melting into the Soul of the Beloved has recognizable effects on our state of being:

> *Love clarifies the mind and purifies the heart.*

Remember the first person you ever fell in love with? When held in the embrace of love, we feel the blissful infusion of true happiness. When in the presence of a loved one, we feel invincible and strong, we lose our self-consciousness and we feel totally validated in who we are. When we experience love we feel at ease with our self and connected to the world; we feel a sense of lightness, as though we can walk on water. We feel liberated.

At its core, Love is the Essence of Beauty.[7] Without Love, there would simply be no Beauty (just as there would be no Truth without the illuminating rays of Consciousness, and no Goodness without the rejuvenating waters of Life) and, because God is Being and Being is Love, the word Beauty or Being can readily be substituted for the word Love in any situation we choose. For instance, when applied in the above paragraph, it now reads like this:

> When held in the embrace of Being [Beauty], we feel the blissful infusion of true happiness (joy). When in the Presence of Being [Beauty], we feel invincible and strong (secure), we lose our self-consciousness and we feel totally validated (accepted) in who we are. When we experience Being [Beauty] we feel at ease (peace) with our self and connected to the world; we feel a sense of lightness, as though we can walk on water. We feel liberated (free).

In a sense, we are locked in an eternal embrace with Spirit through a power or force of attraction not too unlike gravity. Love's power, its modus operandi, is Beauty, drawing us ever closer to its heart, much as the planet earth keeps us firmly fixed to the ground through the invisible pull of its gravitational field. Love unifies and its presence is known through the felt sense of Beauty. In other words, the felt sense of Beauty (for example, feeling the Timeless Perfection beneath the veil of everyday reality, seeing the Formless Face of the universe in every created thing) is your indication of

Love's omnipotent presence in your life, in the same way as the felt sense of gravity is your indication of the earth's global presence.

The Beauty of life is how you know Love is here, holding you in its embrace.

There is a saying, "Birds of a feather flock together," which simply means that like attracts like. In some circles it is also known as the Law of Attraction. Similarly, love attracts love, and it is through Love's persistent tug of attraction that the seeker first becomes aware of her desire, her heaviness, for her Beloved.

She, too, becomes aware that it is not her love attracting her to life's Beauty at all, but that it is, and always has been, Love's gravity dragging her inevitably toward union with itself. She now knows that there is no love but Love, that Spirit's Love is her weight, and the closer she is to her Source, the greater the G-force or pull of gravity she feels; the nearer to communion with Being she is, the faster her desire accelerates and the heavier is her weight.

In time, the seeker comes to know Love's gravity as the holy Face of Spirit—they are one and the same thing—and that she will never stop "falling" for her Beautiful Beloved. She is like a parachutist in perpetual freefall and at the point of terminal velocity (when her acceleration is One, or in union, with the gravity of Spirit) she becomes weightless, en-lightened, completing the circle of Eternal Love—Love loving itself through love.

The seeker is also aware that the opposite holds true: without Love's gravity, she would simply float away into isolation, the inevitable repercussions of which she knows all too well, sadness, insecurity, rejection, turmoil and limitation. If only for this she is grateful for the existence of Love in her life. For it is the very attraction of its gravity, the persistent desire of the Beloved, its Grace, which captures and embraces her heart in the Unifying Beauty of abiding joy, security, acceptance, peace and freedom.

Love, she knows, is her true Inner Beauty.

THE VISION OF BELIEF

Some years back, I took my wife and, then, two-year-old daughter to watch the annual Christmas pageant whistle and sing through the streets of my hometown. We arrived to find another three hundred and fifty thousand or so spectators cheering the colorful and vibrant floats passing by. It was my wife and daughter's first time. For me, over thirty years had rolled on since I had last sat on the pavement and watched the carnival-like procession. Memories came flashing back as if it were only a week ago—the giant Christmas stocking, the silly clowns, the beautiful Pageant Queen and, of course, the reason everyone was there, Father Christmas. Life had come full circle, I mused. Now it was my daughter smiling and laughing with the crowd and waving to the performers.

An hour or so later, at the end of the pageant, I left my wife and daughter and dispersed with the bustling crowd to collect the car. As I weaved through the alleys and streets toward the car park, I came across several floats that had been at the vanguard of the procession. They were now parked in a line along an empty side street: the Toy Train laden with Christmas presents in its carriage, the Nativity float with Joseph, Mary and baby Jesus, as well as the giant mouse of The Night Before Christmas. At first I was amused to see them, but then I was struck with how drab and depressing they suddenly looked. They had literally reached a dead-end and only when I got to my car and started the engine did I realize what the problem was: there were no people.

Without participants giving them animation, the floats had lost their vibrancy. They looked lifeless and without soul. It made me think, is each one of us not a float meandering through the streets in the pageant of life, watched on the pavement by our family and friends and the people we meet? How many of us, though, have already disembarked from The Toy Train? How many are going through the motions of everyday existence lifeless and without soul?

It occurred to me that when the Presence of Light, Life and Love was missing, when the Source that enlivened and animated our float was absent, how easy it was to become lifeless and without soul, just meandering.

It also occurred to me that therein lay the means or process of how to transform the pain and suffering of life's own pageant into abundant joy, security, acceptance, peace and freedom—to resurrect our "dead-end" float into a "living beginning" of Goodness, Truth and Beauty, the vibrant Presence of our Source is mandatory.

Fundamentally, the quest to SEE our Source—to SEE the Substance, Energy and Essence of All That Is—is the real objective of any religious, scientific or artistic endeavor. It is to end suffering and bring salvation, and it is to the benefit of those for whom the thick smog of despair is choking their lungs and blurring their vision to start believing now, this very minute, that salvation is possible. It is not a hopeless cause. The air can be cleared, the mind enlightened, the body purified. Our Source is not hiding. Being wants to be known. Spirit wants to commune.

For one thing is certain, if Spirit didn't want to be known, no-one would get within a light-year of communing with it. Yet we have a veritable history of everyday folk of all races, ages and sexes who have known Spirit most intimately. The writings of Saint Teresa, Saint John of the Cross, Meister Eckhart, and Rumi, to name a mere handful, give us hope that one day, if we desire it with all our hearts and devote our self to its attainment with a sacrificial passion, we too can get to know the Light, Life and Love of Spirit on a deep and personal level.

This, in fact, must be done if we are ever to find the Promised Land and know the true meaning of eternal joy, security, acceptance, peace and freedom.

Figure 3 below highlights the ways in which Spirit, the Infinite Eternal All, is revealed to us. Following the paths upstream, we can see that our quest for joy, security, acceptance, peace and freedom leads one of three ways toward Goodness, Truth and Beauty in accordance with our personality or disposition.

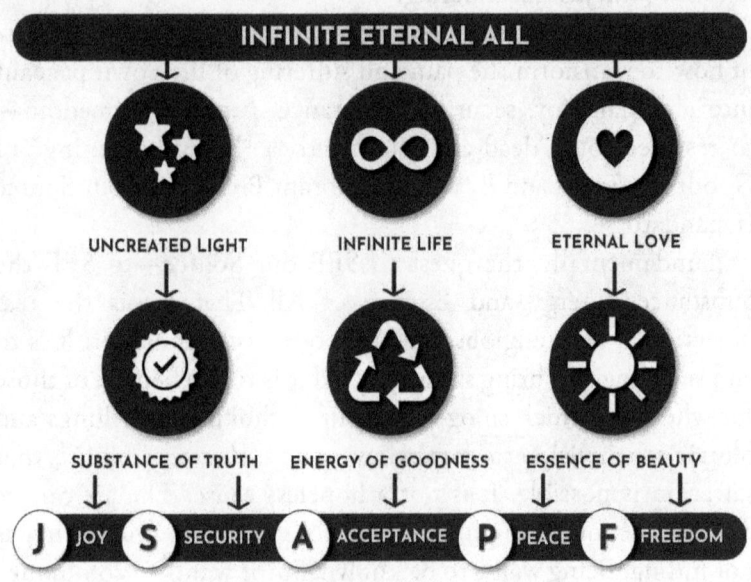

FIGURE 3:   The Paths of Being

Of course each pathway is available to us, and in reality they often overlap and intercourse but, for the purposes of our discussion, I have simplified them as flowing in one direction. In time, after much devotion and discipline, one (or all) of the three Divine Faces of Being, the Infinite Eternal All, is revealed as either:

-> The Uncreated Light (the Substance of Truth).

-> The Infinite Life (the Energy of Goodness). Or,

-> The Eternal Love (the Essence of Beauty).

All pathways are open. None are closed. The most important and primary step is to suspend disbelief and acknowledge that we are always in Spirit's Presence, that we are always connected to our Source of joy, security, acceptance, peace and freedom.

This simple act of recognition and acknowledgment opens the door to the experience of Goodness, Truth and Beauty for the simple reason that accepting Spirit's Presence creates a space into which belief can flow, and we SEE what we believe. This is because beliefs set the boundaries and borders, or conditions, of what we want to see. For example, when we invest in atheistic nihilism, we invariably close our self in and shut out the Light, just like a prisoner holed up in solitary confinement, and thus see nothing around us but a meaningless black void of emptiness.

Conversely, when we truly believe, like a saint, that we are born connected to the Source of Light, Life and Love, we actively set our boundaries upon the infinite horizon (which basically means that we set no boundaries or limitations upon Spirit, nor how its Presence is revealed to us) and thus begin to SEE Goodness, Truth and Beauty imbued in every created thing, which is nothing short of wonder and glory.

The next important step, as we have previously discussed, is to develop the will to SEE more of it. The desire to SEE more then leads us to the method of how to SEE more, a method accessible to everyone on the face of the planet.

Stillness.

POINTS OF REMEMBRANCE #4

- The cause of suffering is over-attentiveness toward the things of this sense-world.

- The absence of felt connectedness to Spirit magnifies your inner feelings of vulnerability and abandonment.

- Your own felt sense of presence is the tip of the iceberg of Spirit's Presence.

- The Source of Truth, Goodness and Beauty appears to the seeking pilgrim as Light, Life or Love.

- The Face of Being is determined by which eye is scanning the Infinite Horizon.

- The Uncreated Light is the Intelligence (Mind) of Being—That Which Knows—the Substance of Truth.

- Clarity is the conscious sense of Truth.

- The Infinite Life is the Power (Body) of Being—That Which Is—the Energy of Goodness.

- Emotions and thoughts make you small, but you are bigger than you think you are.

- Love is the Personality (Soul) of Being—That Which Unifies—the Essence of Beauty.

- Beliefs set the boundaries of what we want to see—we SEE what we believe.

4 THE GATEWAY OF STILLNESS

INNER TREASURE

A GREAT TRUTH that I will never tire of repeating is that through the Grace of Spirit we have already been given what we are looking for. Because separation from Spirit is an illusion, forgetfulness, we are, and have been since birth, connected to the Infinite Source of all joy, security, acceptance, peace and freedom.

Meister Eckhart, an enlightened medieval Christian monk, is believed to have once commented that when he was searching for God, he was like a man riding on an ox looking for an ox. Likewise, we need look no further than our Inner Self for everything we need. Whether you are a Hindu or Buddhist and believe that the connection to God was never broken, only the illusion that it was, or you are a Christian, Muslim or Jew that believes the connection was broken through sin and can only be healed through Christ, Mohammed or the future Messiah, respectively, the fact remains that the connection to our Source exists through our spiritual center, our heart, our sixth organ of perception. Just as the five bodily organs of sight, hearing, taste, touch, and smell connect us to the outside world through our mind, our heart, often unused and withered through inactivity, connects us to the inner world of abiding joy, security, acceptance, peace and freedom.

But how, to expand a previous discussion, do we consciously reconnect with our Source? How do we find Presence? How do we get to where the money is?

Psalm 46 gives us a clue when it says:

Be still, and know that I am God.[2]

Although it sounds easy, the underlying message has been lost in the confusion of our contemporary existence. There is a great deal of misunderstanding as to what it really means. Be still and know what? What is stillness? How do we achieve it?

Fortunately, the inner secrets of the Psalm may be uncovered with a more flexible interpretation of the words. Adding the definitive article "the" into the sentence can actually reveal its greater meaning. Instead of "Be still and know," the commandment now gains a whole new perspective: "Be the still," or more precisely, "Be the stillness and know that I am God." (A Buddhist would most likely say, be the silent witness.)

This minor grammatical change has the potential to release the profoundness within us that the Psalm was hinting at. Be the silence and wait for the magic of Love to come to you. Be the space and be alert for the treasures of Life to be revealed. Be the gap and let the joy of Being flow as it will into your heart.

Through Spirit, through our Source of Being, that vast empty nothingness which is no-where, no-when and no-thing, our deepest, innermost core is the silent stillness, the very essence of Peace, Tranquility and Serenity.

> *The inwardness of the letters lay in the ink's mystery, and their outward show is through its self-determination.*

This Deep Peace is invulnerable and indestructible, the eternal flame that water cannot douse and wind cannot blow out. No matter what happens to us on the outside, no matter what storms ravage our life—illness, tragedy, bankruptcy, divorce, indeed any type of loss we might suffer—nothing can afflict in any way, shape or form the Infinite Peace that is always there (see *Figure 1: The Peaceful Deep*).

To recap a previous analogy, Stillness is the bank vault safeguarding our spiritual money. It is the gateway to our Source. The blockages to experiencing the Inner Treasure of Stillness, however, is psychological, or more precisely, egotistical. A mental gap, a wedge, between Spirit and ourselves is normally established sometime around the age when we become self-conscious of our nudity and stop running naked around the house and garden, usually around the age of five or six. In our minds, we begin to imagine our self in one place (on earth) and God in another (somewhere else, up in the sky). This is a normal part of our psychological development. We need to develop a strong sense of independence and self-identity, or ego, to survive into adulthood.

However, like the clothes we eventually outgrow as we pass from primary to secondary school, we must also outgrow the ego if we are to graduate through the School of Life. Wearing clothes or shoes that are too small for us is inhibiting, and even painful; they must be shed. Likewise, the psychological encumbrances of our ego must also be shed once we have reached adulthood. It is too small for the soul to keep wearing. It is too inhibiting, even painful.

In order for its survival, however, the ego must maintain its sense of individuality. Its greatest fear is to lose itself in the Vast Immensity, for to do so, it reasons, would be to die. Thus separation and isolation are essential for the ego's survival, and all things that maintain this sense of individuality are highly valued—winning, power, positions of importance, fame, fortune, success, and so forth. The ego will even take on board unhealthy, self-defeating attributes—chronic negativity, misery indulgence, a victimization complex, a pessimistic mindset—as long as it maintains the sense of identity. Which is all the ego wants and it doesn't care how it gets it.

But the ego is a servant that has become our master and in order to end our suffering we must overcome its power.

Let Go & Surrender

To reclaim our life and our freedom, we first must understand how the ego asserts its control over us and this we already know. The ego will have us believe that we have forgotten nothing at all, that we really are born with nothing, that we really must start from scratch and accumulate material things in order to make up for the shortfall.

Simply put, the ego controls us with fear, fear of the past, fear of the future and fear of the present. Joy, security, acceptance, peace and freedom, it says, can only come from the pursuit of pleasurable activities, high profile careers, property development, stock market portfolios, and plastic surgery. If we don't spend our life striving for this, then we won't have anything and we're extremely vulnerable; we're as good as dead.

Consequently, we are a race suffering under the continual terror of our own ego. But the ego has no power other than what we give it. As long as we believe its philosophy of isolation and separation from our Source—forgetfulness—we empower it. As long as we believe its philosophy that we are born with nothing, we will spend a lifetime chasing material things in order to make up for the shortfall.

For the ego knows no other way. Being a child of the mind, it asserts its power the only way it can—through the capture of our awareness. Like a magician, it distracts us from what is really happening with the glitter and glamour of material things. Through our five senses of sight, sound, smell, touch, and taste, it keeps us focused on the visible world of form and away from the underlying invisible Realm of the Formless, making us appear small, limited and isolated, which invariably leads to suffering. It works tirelessly in its deception, night and day, week after week, year after year. We get so caught up in it we mistake the magical illusion for the Real Thing.

But its veil is imaginary and therefore extremely fragile. The ego's spell can be exorcised by the insertion of the single definitive article "the" into "Be still and know." Being the stillness—the silent witness, the silence, the space, the gap—is an act of acknowledging the ego's essential non-existence and recognizing our Natural State of Being. It is an act of silencing the voices of our isolated and separate existence from our Source, of surrendering the ego's idea of who we think we are and then allowing Spirit to fill the void with its Peace and Joy. Like a key opening the bank vault of our immeasurable wealth, stillness gives us the power to know and to be who we really are, timeless and infinite.

Only the stillness within can hear the Silence. Only the depth within can perceive the Vastness. Only the gap within can feel the Space. Only the god within can know God.

Sacrificing our self upon the cross of our false image is therefore a requirement that must occur, an absolute prerequisite, before Spirit can resuscitate us with its Breath of Life. Deep Peace can only fill us when we let go of our illusions and false images and allow what is to be as it is.

As Krishnamurti once said of the secret to his inner peace, "I don't mind what happens."

Through being still and silent, he had the ability to see the whole movement of life as one thing, to see its beauty and immense possibilities. It is a great lesson for all seekers of Goodness, Truth and Beauty. Being the silent witness is to detach, to let go, to be non-resistant—to be still and not try to be anything or want to be anywhere other than here and now.

In other words, to use yet another analogy:

> *Deep Peace fills our sense of being when we are still enough to be a speck of attentiveness carried on the tide of Consciousness, a floating buoy on the Sea of Awareness.*

An interesting natural phenomenon on Australia's most famous beach, Bondi Beach, helps to clarify this point. In certain conditions, a strong rip, or current, carries unsuspecting swimmers out to sea, where they often require rescuing by surf lifesavers. Some even drown. Usually they are tourists unfamiliar with the dangers of the local waters, who, in panic, try to swim against the tide, get tired and then sink beneath the waves.

However, according to my surfer friend, who knows the rips and currents of Bondi well, the trick to surviving this frightening journey out to sea is not to fight the current but to flow with it. Apparently, this particular tide is a curious phenomenon: after a while, it brings you around the headland and back to shore, usually at the neighboring beach. Surviving, therefore, depends on trust: letting yourself be carried by the current and calmly accepting where it's taking you. Fighting the current risks injury and even death.

I find this a pertinent metaphor for everyday life. How often do we behave like panicked swimmers, fighting the Current of Consciousness, our Source, until we tire and feel as though we're slipping beneath the waves.

Yes, it is sometimes scary to *let go* and allow some other force to take control of our destiny.

Yes, this force often *sweeps us* into deep and frightening waters, where sharks and other dangers lurk.

Yes, it is difficult to *calmly accept* where it is finally taking us and not want for anything other, to "not mind what happens".

Yes, it asks us to be *completely trusting*.

But to be a still and silent witness, to be a speck of attentiveness and flow with the tide of Consciousness, is the surest way to be at One with the Peaceful Realm of our Source and rediscover our Natural State of Being.

METAMORPHOSIS

The revelation of our Source is a unique and personal experience. As we have seen, it is shaped by the personality of the seeker—the inquisitive scientist, the ascetic pilgrim, the infatuated artist—in particular those qualities to which she holds most dear, Goodness, Truth or Beauty. There is, however, much to be shared with the experience of others.

Invariably, the seeker will know her Source through the Truthful Light, she will trust her Source through the Goodness of Being, and she will love her Source through the Unifying Spirit. In the stillness and silence, she will come to live with the Source of abundant joy, security, acceptance, peace and freedom—she will grasp life in the living of it. Eventually, through the experience of re-connectedness to her Source, she will come to know that the assumption that she is born isolated and separate from everything, that she is born with nothing, that she must start from scratch and accumulate material wealth to make up for the shortfall, is an illusion. She will know that it is not true. It is forgetfulness.

She will know that the main motivating factor in her life, fear—fear of darkness, fear of death and fear of desertion—is a natural repercussion of the belief that she is born with nothing, and that it is the ego's most highly effective tool in maintaining its illusion of isolation and separation. She will also know that fear leads to need and want, the need to gain pleasure and the need to avoid pain, and she will know it for what it really is, an illusion. She will know that it is not true. It is forgetfulness.

She will come to recognize and acknowledge that the quest for the Goodness, Truth and Beauty of her Source is the only motivating factor that really counts and has any genuine meaning. When the desire and intent to SEE the Substance, Energy and Essence of Truth, Goodness and Beauty becomes her main motivation for living, she will notice that her behavior changes. No longer will she seek joy, security, acceptance, peace and freedom in worldly things, things that can only fulfill her desires in limited quantities, things that eventually lead to addictive cravings and desperate, fearful behavior. No longer will she ask of the world what it cannot give—permanency. She will renounce and forgive the world as the source of her salvation, understanding, finally, that suffering can only end when she relinquishes her dependence on temporal form and begins to search within for the connection to her Eternal Formless Source.

For when she knows that through Grace she already has The Five Pillars of Love in her heart, an amazing metamorphosis occurs: she sheds the junkyard-dog mentality and stops snatching and hording anything and everything she thinks she needs to fill the void in her life.

She stops growling, "What can I get? What's in it for me?" She stops whining that the world owes her for all the suffering in her life, the egocentric delusion that everyone and everything exists to serve her needs and desires. In short, she stops seeking affirmation of her ego, her sense of self-identity.

Instead, she gives herself unconditionally to her Source, surrendering her entire being to her Beloved. She knows that with each day that passes she will experience more joy, security, acceptance, peace and freedom. She feels prosperous and flourishing: she has found that winning feeling.

As such, she acquires the "How can I help? What can I do?" mentality and becomes more generous and benevolent, more compassionate and kind, more gracious and grateful, because she knows that within she has an infinite source of Goodness, Truth and Beauty at her disposal. She finally quashes the feeling of dread that she has been born with nothing and no longer sees the future with doom and gloom. In short, she no longer holds any fears that she will have nothing but infirmity, loneliness and poverty in her old age if she doesn't acquire the material wealth necessary to ensure her future wellbeing.

She loses the fear because she knows the well is always full. Nobody can take it away. Nobody can touch it. Through direct experience of her Natural State of Being, she knows that she already has what she is looking for—she is no longer riding on an ox looking for an ox. In doing so, she uncovers a great secret, a universal truth:

> *Spirit reveals more and more of itself through the commitment to giving, forgiving, and thanksgiving.*

These three attitudes, which I have called the three major Attitudes of Abundant Living, effect an awareness of life's wholeness and perfection by diverting our attention away from the fears, desires, needs, and wants of our ego, thereby minimizing any resistance or reactive violence to what is now, and focusing our attention onto the will of the present moment.

These attitudes are self-perpetuating. Giving, forgiving and thanksgiving dissolve the mental chaos of our ego and realign us with the silent stillness of our Source, which in turn makes us more giving, forgiving, and thankful by imbuing us with its own nature.

Giving

In the first major Attitude of Abundant Living, the seeker learns that life's greatest fulfillment comes not from excessive accumulation of material wealth (that is, taking from life anything and everything that she can), but from simply giving.

She also learns through direct experience this universal and fundamental truth:

> *You cannot give what you do not have, and you cannot have what you does not give.*

The more joy she gives, the more joy she experiences; the more peace she gives, the more peace she feels; the more of her self she gives, the more of her Natural State of Being is revealed.

For now she understands directly why it is better to give than to receive—love is its own reward. Thus her giving becomes a joyous celebration of her abundant nature. Her very presence brings to every situation everything she wishes to arouse in others.

She cannot help but give; it has become her worship.

Forgiving

Likewise forgiveness. The second major Attitude of Abundant Living means she finally brings to a halt the blame game she has been playing for most of her life. She forgives others, she forgives herself, and she forgives any events or happenings for any injury, pain or suffering she feels, thereby taking responsibility for her life-situation and sense of self.

In refusing to blame others, herself, or events, she allows the moment to be as it is. There is freedom here and through lack of resistance and restriction, her Natural State of Being bursts forth in all its magnificence.

Furthermore, her forgiveness cuts through other people's façade to their inner core. No matter what frustrations, anger, sadness, or fears they express in her presence, forgiveness reveals their natural self hidden behind the ego, the silent self behind all the noise.

"Forgive them, Father," she may rightly say, "for they know not what they do."

Forgiveness, therefore, is perhaps her greatest gift to humanity:

To see others as they truly are—Good, True, and Beautiful.

Thanksgiving

The third major Attitude of Abundant Living, thanksgiving, is non-other than the attitude of gratitude.

Gratitude puts a break on the mechanical fears, desires, needs, and wants of the seeker's ego, which, in the silence, opens a space in her heart to the unconditional acceptance of what is, to not mind what is happening, and the consequent understanding of the Perfection hidden behind the chaos.

She knows that The Five Pillars of Love do not come from having everything she wants, but from wanting everything she has—she is simply grateful for the way she is, grateful for her Natural State of Being. She sings praise and thanksgiving to her Source, knowing that the more she sings and the more she gives thanks, the more Goodness, Truth and Beauty she receives.

> *She sings not because she is happy, she is happy because she sings.*

Her gratitude is her awe.

One Giant Leap

As a seeker, it is important to know the underlying motivations for doing what you do, to know why you seek pleasure or why you avoid pain. It is important to know why you seek Goodness, why you search for Truth, and why you are so attracted to Beauty. Is it to cover the void inside, the void that is actually an illusion created by the belief that you are born with nothing and need to start from scratch? Is it to maintain a sense of identity, an identity that, upon close inspection, disappears into thin air?

When Neil Armstrong descended from his spacecraft and became the first human to set foot on the moon in 1969, he uttered the famous words, "One small step for man. One giant leap for mankind."

One of the qualities required by every scientist, pilgrim and artist that dares to walk the spiritual path is the courage of astronauts to leave this world behind and travel beyond the boundaries of human experience. The one small step is, in fact, a giant leap in faith:

> *To be still and know that you are not born separate from the Infinite Eternal All.*

To be still and know that your Natural State of Being already has everything you are looking for.

POINTS OF REMEMBRANCE #5

- Your connection to your Source exists through your spiritual center, your heart, your sixth organ of perception.

- Go to where the money is: stillness is your gateway to blissful communion with your Source.

- Separation and isolation—resistance to what is—are essential for your ego's survival.

- To end suffering you must overcome the ego's power.

- To be the stillness is to be a speck of attentiveness flowing with the tide of Consciousness.

- Know, trust and love your Source.

- The three major Attitudes of Abundant Living—Giving, Forgiving and Thanksgiving—reveal your Natural State of Being and empower your experience of it.

- You cannot give what you do not have, and you cannot have what you do not give.

- Forgiveness is your greatest gift to humanity.

- Thanksgiving is the attitude of gratitude

PART II

SUFFERING

"This union [with Spirit] is within us of our naked nature and were this nature to be separated from [Spirit] it would fall into nothingness."

The Blessed John Ruysbroeck

5 THE FALL INTO NOTHINGNESS

THE CYCLE OF SUFFERING

IF, FOR SOME reason, a magic wand was waved and every trace of ink vanished from the face of the earth, all the letters in this book would instantly disappear and there would be nothing but blank pages. There would be no more libraries, no more magazines, no more newspapers, no more photographs.

Likewise, if our Source were to vanish from the universe, all life as we know it would instantly disappear: we, like the letters separated from the ink, would "fall into nothingness", as articulated by the Blessed John Ruysbroeck in the quote heading this section. Swallowed by the Immensity, we would simply cease to exist as we know it. (Author's note: It is important to be aware of the apparent paradox of words here. The word "nothingness", as used in the above context, means the nothingness of non-being, as opposed to the "No-thingness" that we have been using to describe the Source from which everyone and everything in the universe is created.)

Although our Source would never remove itself from creation (if it was going to happen, it already would have), this very situation can be, and is continually, duplicated in the minds of every human being: we can literally feel as if our life has fallen into non-existent nothingness. This fall, in fact, is the visible and tangible consequence of forgetfulness, the initial mistaken belief that we are born unconnected to Spirit, that we have been banished from Paradise and have arrived in this world with nothing. Our belief in separation from Spirit is the magic wand that removes every trace of our Source from our life.

The resultant fall into nothingness is felt as an uneasy slide into despair and isolation. We become hollow, haunted by the sensation that something is missing in our life and always will be. Emptiness and incompleteness become constant companions, which we know already as those feelings associated with the perceived absence of our Natural State of Being—the feelings of sadness, insecurity, rejection, turmoil and limitation.

Worse, over time, the seed of isolation embeds within the womb of forgetfulness, then duplicates and grows into an embryo of fear. As discussed in Chapter 1, we feel the presence of this unwanted pregnancy in three main ways, as the fear of darkness (vulnerability), the fear of death (loss/annihilation), or the fear of desertion (abandonment). It more often than not registers as a subliminal feeling of perpetual dread, a gnawing in our belly that something is not quite right, but sometimes more alarmingly as an overwhelming sense of terror, panic and insanity.

Left unchecked, fear continues to grow and mature until it eventually spawns its own child, the feeling of need, in particular the self-perpetuating need to do something about our anxiety-riddled state of being. This need to do something is an irrepressible urge known as the "fight or flight" response.

Gripped by this urge, we either feel the need to fight the fear that has emerged from the dark pit of isolation (sadness, insecurity, rejection, turmoil and limitation), or we begin to feel the opposite, the need to flee toward an antidote to annul those feelings of fear and emptiness, to seek a relieving injection of joy, safety, importance, peace or freedom. Because of fear, we feel the need to fight the pain or flee toward a more pleasurable outcome (which we have previously discussed as the pleasure principle).

But the need to fight or flee only strengthens the grip of our ego and reinforces forgetfulness, the illusion of isolation, thereby deepening our fall into the void of non-existent nothingness. Our lives become nothing short of a cycle of suffering, a frightening

THE FALL INTO NOTHINGNESS

whirlpool in which we spiral out of control and feel we cannot escape.

This destructive cycle is visually represented in *Figure 4: The Cycle of Suffering* below. Take a moment to reflect on it, taking particular note on how Forgetfulness, Emptiness, Fear, and Need have played a role in any suffering you may have experienced in your own lifetime.

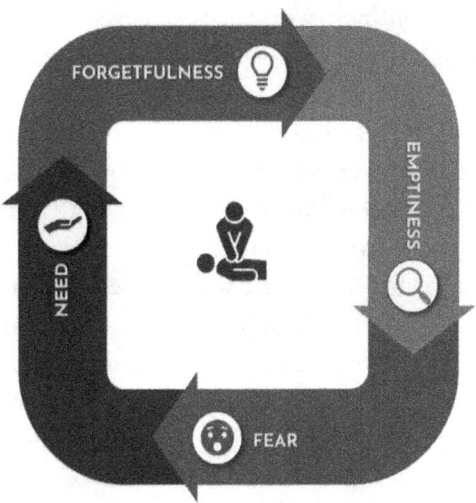

FIGURE 4: The Cycle of Suffering

Suffering, therefore, is not just a result of hunger, thirst, injury, or destitution, nor is it confined to any particular race, sex, continent, or era. It is more than just a physical problem. Suffering is a psychological (consciousness) issue with its roots in spirituality, a self-perpetuating cycle of pain with four distinctive but overlapping and recurring phases:

-> Forgetfulness (the belief in an isolated self or ego).
-> Emptiness (the fall into nothingness).
-> Fear (of darkness, death and desertion).
-> Need (the fight or flight response).

FORGETFULNESS: GRASPING AT SELF

Michael B., a friend and ex-colleague, spent the time of his mid-to-late twenties as a junior doctor working in the UK. It was the decade of the 1990s, and it was a decade in which he was having a great deal of difficulty. He lived a privileged life, compared to the physical suffering of the Third World, and yet it felt as if his existence had slowly become a nightmare, in particular his job situation. He routinely worked six or seven days a week of up to seventy to eight-five hours, which left a meager eighty to ninety hours for the remainder of the week to sleep and rest, study for further exams, travel to work, partake in a relationship and if there was any time left over, relax and have a social life. He complained that there never seemed to be any time to do the simple things like eat and sleep, let alone do the things he wanted to do. His job was dominating his life and it felt wrong. He constantly struggled to get up in the morning. He took a lot of sick leave, and he was more and more unlikeable as a person, especially to himself. He knew that something had to change, and quickly, or he would soon have a nervous breakdown.

The imbalance in Michael B.'s life was a commonality he shared with many other doctors. In 2000, a survey of GPs in Great Britain revealed that seventy-five percent wished that they could leave the workforce before the normal retirement age of sixty-five. The ill feelings that Michael and other doctors harbored about their working life, however, were not only confined to the medical profession. Another survey around the same time gave people traveling on the London Underground a hypothetical choice: Would they rather go to work or be dead? Unbelievably, fifty-five percent responded that they would rather be dead than face their work.

Although these were small surveys performed nearly a decade ago and in only one city in the world, they still give pertinent and intriguing insights into the psychological and spiritual erosion that has been chipping away at Western society for some time now. Something is wrong in a lot of people's lives, as Fritjof Capra, author of *The Tao of Physics*,[11] laments:

> *Most people are aware of themselves as isolated egos . . . engaged in endless conflicts generating continuous metaphysical confusion and frustration.*

Like a surgeon's scalpel in the hands of an amateur, Michael B. and many others like him have used the dual edges of ignorance and self-importance to slice their ego from Spirit's Personality. In doing so, they have inadvertently created a detached, isolated identity with which they no longer know what to do. Instead of recognizing the mistake and suturing the split personality back onto the Real Personality, instead of re-grafting their little self onto their Higher Self, they continue to nurture the confused creation into adulthood, where it remains lost and frightened in the darkness of separation, an isolated ego "engaged in endless conflicts".

To further assist our understanding of suffering and its causes, forgetfulness, it will help to briefly reconsider the nature of reality in the terminology we have been employing to date, specifically the concept of duality and its relation to life and the universe. To recap, reality can be considered to be True (Absolute) or conventional (relative). Absolute Reality is the purest, most truthful order of the universe—peaceful, perfect, enlightened—in essence, our Natural State of Being.

Diametrically opposed to Absolute Reality is the conventional reality of duality, the relative world of opposites in which delusion, suffering and disharmony run riot. This universe can

---

[11] *The Tao of Physics: An Exploration of the Parallels Between Modern Physics and Eastern Mysticism*, Fritjof Capra, Flamingo: 3rd Revised Edition, 1992

be considered an imperfect form of Perfect Formlessness, a disturbance or ripple of Silent Stillness, and from this concept we can understand the origins of the previously quoted Buddhist aphorism, "Form is emptiness, and emptiness is form."

From our perspective, what separates our felt sense of the Absolute (and thereby the stimulus of pain and suffering through the blockage of the day-to-day experience of our Natural State of Being), are corruptions of our own making. They are misplaced practices of the mind and harmful emotional burdens that have arisen from one basic misconception, forgetfulness: we believe ourselves to be isolated and separated from everyone else, nature, the world, and our Source.

As discussed previously, Buddhists regard this forgetfulness or misconception as ignorance of the Nature of Reality, or "grasping at self". Christians, Muslims and Jews regard this as sin, which is none other than turning our back on Spirit and ignoring our Source. Once "grasped" or "born in sin," our ego convinces us from an early age that it and its will alone is more important and beneficial than our Natural State of Being.

As a consequence, we become unconscious of Reality as it Truly Is (can the psychological state of lower consciousness be called anything else than "unconscious"?), seeing not the underlying Absolute Universe supporting every moment but only its shadow, the universe of duality. Ricocheting between polar opposites, the ego's pleasures and needs take precedence over Spirit's Will, our Highest Wisdom and Knowledge and Power. We end up spending most of our lives chasing after the ego's desires, trying to fulfill its every whim and fancy, and avoiding the things that cause it displeasure and discomfort. The resultant experience is akin to a lifetime of running after a three-year-old toddler, forever trying to please its whimsical desires.

The constant ebb and flow of isolation and despair, fear and need, pain and pleasure, day after day, week after week, month after month, year after year, is the inevitable consequence of grasping at self. In other words, the cycle of individual and collective suffering (see *Figure 4*) is the direct and natural experience that arises from the constant and deliberate misidentification with the ego.

Shantideva, here quoted from *The Healing Power of Mind*,[12] relates his strength of feeling on the matter:

> *All the violence, fear and suffering*
> *That exists in the world*
> *Comes from grasping at self.*
> *What use is this great evil monster to you?*
> *If you do not let go of the self,*
> *There will never be an end to your suffering.*
> *Just as, if you do not release a flame from your hand,*
> *You cannot stop it from burning your hand.*

Grasping at self, the dismemberment of our small egoic self from our Higher Self, is the single most definitive factor in the causation of psychological unease and inner suffering in humanity, and it can happen in any number of ways. The most common manner is the creation of an identity or self-image using the dualistic parameters of mind and body only, thereby limiting the sense of who we are to certain forms (shapes) and conditions, both physical and psychological. The creation of an isolated ego, therefore, stands in direct contrast to our Natural State of Being, which is Formless and Unconditional.

Our ego's defiant stance splinters it from our Source, the painful consequence of which is an interminable fall into nothingness.

---

[12] *The Healing Power of Mind*, Tulku Thondup, Shambhala Publications Inc., 1996

EMPTINESS: THE FALL INTO NOTHINGNESS

Globally, humanity's recent history and current behavior reflects an underlying pain that has never been dealt with, only covered up or swept under the carpet. More than ever, as a race, humans are suffering under the interminable weight of spiritual grief. A dark cloud hangs over our heads blocking out the light of the sun. Whether we accept the fact or not, we seem to be in a constant state of mourning over the loss of connection with our Source. We constantly yearn for the end of our suffering.

Anjam Khursheed says this in *The Universe Within*:[13]

> *The unity of mind and body depends on our experience of [Spirit], yet the vitality of this spiritual experience has been progressively lost over the past few centuries.*

This loss of spiritual experience on a worldwide scale manifests as collective grief. As a collective whole, we seem to be mourning not only our inescapable individual deaths but also our very existence. We have lost our "vitality" and we are sad to be alive.

Most notably, this sense of grief heightens around the age of fifty, the age at which we experience what is commonly known as the mid-life crisis. Needless to say, one doesn't have to be fifty or sixty to feel this crisis. It can happen at any time but it does seem to be felt most profoundly around middle age. What, though, is it we are grieving?

Isolation.

We grieve our loneliness in the universe and the loss of connection to the Whole.

The unavoidable consequence of denying our Higher Self, the inescapable result of blinkering our eyes to the truth that we are not alone, that we are part of a Greater Picture, is grief.

---

[13] *The Universe Within: An Exploration of the Human Spirit*, Anjam Khursheed, Oneworld Publications, 1995

THE FALL INTO NOTHINGNESS

To forget or ignore our innate connection with our Source is to forget or ignore the omnipotent presence and help of our Higher Intelligence. As we have seen, forgetfulness leads to a state of unconsciousness, which is just another way of describing each person's "fall into nothingness" and the inevitable consequence of living each day with "metaphysical confusion and frustration". Or, as we have come to understand it, living with the dark void of sadness, insecurity, rejection, turmoil and limitation. That is, fear.

Unfortunately, unconscious spiritual isolation has existed in the hearts of men and women for millennia, both individually and collectively, but it is no more acutely felt than now. A kind of separation anxiety runs deep through our sense of being as an uneasy feeling that something is missing. The unhappy reality is that our individual and cultural unease has been neglected for so long it has developed into a disease that threatens the wellbeing of the planet and every species living on it. Worse, it has become a pandemic illness which we seem unable to vaccinate.

As already discussed, we take more drugs than any other time in our history. We divorce more. We change jobs and partners more frequently. We gamble to the point of bankruptcy. We all do this in the hope of relieving our sense of isolation. But it is all to no avail:

We still feel lonely because our spiritual problems cannot be resolved by material means.

This feeling of isolation is a child of our own making, born out of the perceived severance with Spirit, our Universal Self. But isolation, no matter how real and overwhelming it is, is false; it is an illusion, it is forgetfulness. We are not alone. Spirit is always with us and is continually communicating its Presence as Consciousness, Life and Love—the deep and abiding felt sense of Goodness, Truth and Beauty—only we don't seem to be receiving the message.

The reason seems to be threefold:

1. Either we are unaware that the message is being sent, or
2. We choose to selectively block it out and listen only to what we want to hear, or
3. We don't know (or have forgotten) how to tune in and listen to it.

Or all of the above. Deepak Chopra hits the nail on the head in *Ageless Body, Timeless Mind*:[14]

> *Any appearance of separation [from Spirit] is only the product of the limitation of your senses, which are not attuned to these energies [of an underlying Source].*

Isolation, therefore, is an "appearance of separation" from our Source, and that is exactly what it is, an appearance, an illusion, that our Higher Self is no longer an essential part of our lives. The illusion of isolation is what we are feeling individually and collectively, albeit subconsciously, and this heartache presents itself as a kind of spiritual angst, a disjointed unity with the wholeness of everything.

Some might say we have become dysfunctional.

The In-Out World

Whilst cogitating one day on the problems that were confronting me more regularly than I wished, I realized that I had fallen into the trap of persistently separating the outside/ external/ material world from the inner/ internal/ spiritual world. It was as if I had drawn a line between what is physical and what is spiritual, as if there were no connection uniting the two.

I asked myself this: "How do I see myself? Am I really living in the limited confines of time and space, or is my true abode the eternal and infinite Source?"

---

[14] *Ageless Body, Timeless Mind*, Deepak Chopra, Rider, 1998

THE FALL INTO NOTHINGNESS

The answer I received was immediate and profound. Not as a voice or vision, but as a simple knowing of what is, a clarification of Truth:

> *There is no separateness between me and the Infinite, between me and the Eternal. There is no separateness between me and Love, between me and Being. There is no separateness between me and the Light, between me and Consciousness. There is no separateness between me and my Source.*

The realization struck me that there are no in and out worlds, no duality driven subjective and objective reality, rather a united, singular "In-Out" world of Absolute Reality; there is no separation, no dividing line between the two, only the illusion of separateness.

The In-Out world, I had now come to understand, cannot be divided except through the illusion of appearances—*forgetfulness*—which stemmed from an egoic identity that needed to separate itself from everything else to maintain that sense of individual identity. I also understood, finally, the essential message that spiritual masters had been trying to convey for thousands of years:

> *The illusion of separateness creates the sense of isolation, and isolation leads to suffering.*

Suddenly, that great depressing millstone that had been hanging around my neck for so many years began to feel so much lighter.

Illusion or not, however, and no matter who we are, the pressing sense of isolation is very real. It is often all we know. Once we feel isolated and lonely, whether we believe in a Higher Being or not, the cycle of suffering turns another notch, fear and need arise, and pain strikes at our sense of self. Different people may experience differing degrees or depths of isolation, but no matter how little or how much is experienced, it is still intimately related to the strength of attention, or inattention, to our Source.

This is because of one simple fact of existence:

The focus of our attention determines our experience of life.

What we surrender our attention to, in other words, we become. Indeed, that upon which we apply our attention creates our identity and becomes us. In essence, you reap what thoughts you sow. If we use our ego as a lens to continually focus attention upon our individual isolation, to identify with it, to proclaim it as the truth of who we are, then that is what we will experience and become, a life that is continually empty, un-whole and devoid of meaning:

If we remain focused on nothing, we feel as though we have nothing, which leads to the feeling that we are nothing. We fall into non-existent nothingness.

On the other hand, the opposite is also true. If we use our Natural State of Being as a beacon to draw attention to our inner Oneness with our Source, then that is what we will experience and become, a life that feels complete and whole. One that is joyous, secure, worthy, peaceful and free. The Buddha said:

We are shaped by our thoughts, What we think, we become. When the mind is pure, joy follows like a shadow that never leaves.

Yet, this is not the reality most of us know or experience. To our detriment, we tend to forget and overlook that our thoughts have immense power in determining our experience of life. We have become unaware of the medium through which we experience reality—our belief system—and we live each day in a hazy cloud of unconsciousness, which, drip-by-drip, irrigates the roots of our suffering and pain.

The Identity Trap

The end of suffering and pain begins with our beliefs.

Beliefs direct the focus of our attention. Hence, because all life-experience occurs within the Spectrum of Consciousness, beliefs direct the actual experience of who we are. The belief and assumption that we are born separated from everything—*forgetfulness*—that we are born with nothing and must start from scratch, diverts our attention away from our inner state of connectedness and redirects it onto the empty void of isolation, a dark abyss from which the feelings of emptiness and meaninglessness bubble continuously to the surface. In this dark, empty abyss, there is no frame of reference upon which we can form a conscious identity, nothing with which we can say, "This is who I am." It is devastating to the ego.

Consequently, our ego snatches and grasps at anything it can to gain a foothold of selfhood. The ultimate outcome is the misidentification with the physical and mental sides of existence and the unconscious creation of a false or limited image of our self. We see our body and feel its emotions and say, "My being is confined to this physical form." This spawns lesser idioms and viewpoints, such as, "I am what I eat," and, "Might is right," that reinforce the original belief of the individuated and isolated self.

We listen to the never-ending stream of thoughts running through our mind and come to the conclusion that mirrors the philosopher Descartes' famous remark, "I think therefore I am." We become impressed with our ability to reason with logic and common sense. We start to believe our own hype, worshipping humanity as the highest form of consciousness in the universe. We then wield our self-proclaimed superiority like a sword to justify our destructive actions against the environment, the animal kingdom and other human beings.

Like an elastic band that has been stretched until it snaps, the habit of using the mind and body to define who we are (grasping at self), results in the eventual loss of touch with our Natural State of Being, our true abode. Focusing our attention onto the image of a separated self actually severs (or covers beneath a thick, impenetrable layer) the connection with our eternal Goodness, Truth and Beauty, and, consequently, restricts the belief and definition of who we are to the mind and body only. Inevitably, we become an ego-dominated "mind-body" being, one that is limited, confined, reactive, unconscious, and time pressured, all the things that our Natural State of Being is not.

The void of isolation, emptiness and hollowness that ensues is not surprising, nor is its domination of our sense of who we are. We think that this is what it is like to be human and that there's nothing more to it than that. We think that this is life, that this is being.

We have made ourselves in our own image and have fallen into non-existent nothingness.

Mind-Body Personalities

At their very core, mind-body personalities believe only in the end-point, or product, of life. The creative process of life itself is dismissed, or, at worst, completely neglected. Take the analogy of a river, for example. If mind-body personalities were to consider their life as a flowing river, they would probably see themselves as the river mouth (or some other point along the river's course that they have now arrived at) and not the pure source from which the river began its journey. They would see their abode as the marshy delta, not the river's original spring.

By grasping at self, mind-body personalities remove themselves so far from their source that, for all intents and purposes, it becomes lost and forgotten in the jungle of their mind. Worse, it becomes irrelevant. For when the delta, wittingly or unwittingly, removes itself from its origins, or dams itself against the flowing waters, the very thing from which it is continually rejuvenated and refreshed, the quagmire of stagnation, salinity and lifelessness becomes a very real possibility.

The river's original source, however, is not just the physical spring from which its waters first emerge trickling from the ground. The original source, in fact, is the infinitely refreshing Fountain of Youth that continually bubbles forth with life. The Source is simultaneously the whole river and its individually defining stages—beginning, middle and end. It is who we really are, our Natural State of Being, our true abode. The river mouth or delta is only one point along the river's meandering course, which is defined by the four-dimensional conditions of space and time. It is only a frame of reference, a context, with which we can use to express our Natural State of Being. It is not the entirety of the river's being.

Yet, paradoxically, if we were to look closely at the delta, we would catch a glimpse of the essence of the Source immanent within it. We would see the Water of Life.

> *Look well at each letter: thou seest it hath already perished but for the face of the ink, that is, for the Face of His Essence.*

To reclaim the lost spring, the Fountain of Youth, to therefore end suffering and find salvation, a shift in perspective is required. This entails a small, but significant, redirection of focus upon the Spectrum of Consciousness from its end-point (mind-body) to its beginnings (Source). Like a boat on a river, our awareness must set sail upstream from the delta to its silent origins. For if we are ever to release the grasp we have on our egoic self and stake a serious claim to our own essential Origin, our Natural State of Being, we must release the grip on our mind-body and return our conscious identity to our Source—we must repatriate the image of our essentially dead self to our Homeland.

Alas, mind-body people dominate the planet so much that the

state of grasping at self is considered a normal function of the human condition. It is as if disease has become the normal state of affairs and healthiness the abnormal state. The ego has usurped the soul; three-year-old toddlers are running the house.

Thankfully, it is rather easy to spot an unconscious mind-body personality. It is not too hard to identify someone who has fallen into non-existent nothingness and who lives with the continual companionship of emptiness and hollowness, one who has forgotten to live with the abundance of their Natural State of Being. Certain characteristics make them recognizable:

- They see themselves as separate from others and are fiercely proud of their independence.
- Survival is paramount; they believe "It's me against the world," that life is a dog-eat-dog existence.
- The end justifies the means.
- They harbor feelings of superiority, or the reverse, worthlessness; if they have succeeded in "beating the world", they feel superior, and if they do not see themselves as having material success they feel worthless or angry.
- They strive to impress or to be impressed.
- They hold onto grievances for inordinate periods of time, even a whole lifetime.
- They believe the biggest rat wins the rat race, are likely to despise those who are successful, and take glee from another's fall from grace; they may say, "Things never go my way. I never have any luck," or, "She deserved every piece of misfortune she got. I hope she suffers for her actions."

- They never give to beggars or donate to charity, or if they do, only with an obvious tax deduction in mind; they may say things like, "All women are the same," or, "I never had any help when I needed it, why should I help other people."

Typical behavior patterns exhibited from this restricted and conditional way of thinking include:

- Always wanting to win.
- Dissatisfaction with themselves or others; an "intolerance of fools."
- Forever chasing the elusive "perfect" partner, job or home.
- Constant despair, resentment or cynicism.
- Continual manipulation of other people and situations to suit their own ends.
- Refusal to take responsibility for their actions, quickness to blame others or God for any pain or misfortune, and the first to demand compensation for any accident, no matter how minor.

Mind-body people sound pretty horrible when written down on paper in this manner, but we can all recognize in our own personal thoughts and behaviors, now or in the past, some or all of the character traits just mentioned. Mind-body personalities align themselves against the world (as opposed to their Natural State of Being, which is aligned with the world). The world must be conquered and made accountable to the will of the personality.

If mind-body people could be defined by one word, it would be resistance. Mind-body people resist everything and anything, and resistance in its extreme is violence. Characteristically, they try to use force to resolve their issues, whether it be mental—belittling, bullying, verbal abuse, emotional abuse, blackmail, sexual manipulation, and so forth—or physical force, in all its manifestations from pushing and shoving to domestic abuse and even murder. Fired up with anger, hatred, frustration, indignation, or even jealousy, they try to bulldoze through any barrier that stands in their way. Non-violence, non-resistance, is simply not an option if it doesn't resolve the situation immediately. They reject the notion that the only way to completely destroy an enemy once and for all is to make him your friend. They also cannot see that coming from a position of peace (the peace that is not of this world, the peace of our Natural State of Being) is eminently more powerful in instigating change in the world and resolving disputes than anger or hatred can ever be, despite any short term gains these emotions might provide.

What frightens the mind-body personality most, in all of us, is change. The ego will always resist change, because to change is to die. The immediate retort of the ego to any threat to its comfortable way of being is, "Why should I change? I'm all right, aren't I?" The next question is invariably, "What if I like who I am? What if I don't want to change?"

What the ego is really afraid of is that if it changes into someone or something else, what will become of the someone or something that it thinks it is now?

But change is the natural order of the universe. As Heraclites, the ancient Greek philosopher, famously said,

Change is the only constant. Change alone is unchanging.

Change is evolution and the universe is constantly evolving, developing and bettering itself. Change is growth and the universe is constantly growing, emerging and expanding. Change is renewal and the universe is constantly renewing, refreshing and rejuvenating itself. To try and remain as one is to resist change, is to resist the natural state of life itself. So why would anyone in their right mind resist life? Forgetfulness, of course. Unfortunately, little do we realize the extent of our forgetfulness and the degree to which we misidentify as a mind-body being, until it's too late. Little do we realize the extent of our fall into non-existent nothingness, nor the depth to which we have become immersed in the cycle of suffering (*Figure 4*), the cycle of pain and pleasure that inevitably results from grasping at self and almost always leads to a life of fear and addiction.

THE SYMPTOMS OF FEAR

When we fall into non-existent nothingness and are immersed in the void of emptiness and isolation, we see and feel the abyss of oblivion. Fear arises. We feel helpless and vulnerable. We feel the threat of extermination and annihilation. We feel the backstabbing betrayal of abandonment and the utter despondency of forsakenness.

Fear is like a heavy cloak of doom and gloom weighing down on our state of being morning, noon and night. It affects everything we see, think, say, feel, and do. We feel vulnerable, seeing danger around every corner and under every rock. The threat of dismissal from friends, family and colleagues gnaws at our stomach. Disaster shadows our every footstep and, detained within a mental prison of self-limitation, the world appears to actively conspire against us, a cold, impersonal force that inhibits and crushes our every move.

The symptoms of fear can thus be summarized as:

-> Despair
-> Danger
-> Dismissal
-> Disaster
-> Detainment

These symptoms—the effects of fear on our state of being—are none other than the subtle yet destructive manifestations of what we have come to understand, respectively, as sadness, insecurity, rejection, turmoil and limitation.

What is felt and experienced during our fall into non-existent nothingness is, in actuality, the absence of our Source. In our unconscious state, we see no more Light, only darkness. We sense no more Life, only death. We feel no more Love, only desertion. The Presence of Spirit has been snuffed out. It is no less than hell on earth.

Yet, although fear arises from the illusion of isolation, from forgetfulness, the experience of it is anything but unreal. Fear, as some authors have insisted, may be False Emotions Appearing Real, but its destructive impact on our life is certainly real and genuine. It is very real to a mother whose daughter has just been diagnosed with leukemia. It is very real to a wife whose husband has just been sent to a foreign war. It is very real to a father who has just lost his job and has little prospects of finding another.

Allowed to grow into its extreme, fear is petrifying. It seizes control of all aspects of our body and prevents any rational thought. We freeze in terror. We cannot think without panic. The world as we have known it is tossed upside down. This alone is very real.

If we are fortunate enough, we may never experience fear in its extreme. Alas, for many in this day and age, life is still a continual, daily struggle with fear. Humans may no longer dwell in caves or struggle for survival against the threat of prehistoric beasts, yet regardless of our age, sex, race, or socio-economic status, fear is still the main motivating force for doing what we do, the fuel driving our wants and desires. Its presence is so prevalent and pervasive it is considered a normal part of life.

Nevertheless, fear takes more from us than what it gives. As President Franklin Roosevelt warned in his inaugural address in 1933, the only thing we have to fear is fear itself. Like a vampire, fear sucks our lifeblood until we are nothing but an empty, lifeless shell.

The fear of loss slams the door on our dreams and locks us into a lifetime of scrounging in the dark for safety and survival.

The fear of rejection bars us from loving and makes hermits of our hearts.

The fear of failure hampers our risk taking and leads us along the congested highway of predictability and humdrum.

With fear as our master, we become the walking dead.

But, to our detriment, as previously stated, it is an unfortunate but common fact that we are our own worst enemy, our own nemesis. Just as we create problems through the judgement and labelling of situations and circumstances surrounding our life (see Chapter 1), fear too is a creation of our own consciousness—its presence is our responsibility.

At its heart, fear is just a problem taken to the nth degree:

- -> Fear of darkness is nothing more than a heightened problem with our own *vulnerability*.
- -> fear of death is nothing more than a heightened problem with our own *mortality*.
- -> fear of desertion is nothing more than a heightened problem with our own sense of *isolation*.

There is not one fear that didn't begin its existence as a problem.

Fear, accordingly, does not happen to us. Rather, it comes through us. Like any problem, fear is attributable to the entity that is our very self and, hence, it is something from which we cannot run. Says Kahlil Gibran in *The Prophet*,[3] again at his poetic best:

And if it is fear you would dispel, the seat of that fear is in your heart and not in the hand of the feared.

The Only Way Out

For many, our safety in the world is in doubt. The world is a dangerous and unfriendly place to live, where everyone and every thing is an imminent threat to our survival. Our eternal nature is not something that is practical or relevant to our current situation; we feel vulnerable and at imminent risk of injury, death and abandonment.

As the months and years pass, however, after surviving most threats to our early existence, we may arrive at the conclusion that we are actually more resilient than we initially thought. In fact, we start to think that we are resilient enough to tackle almost anything that comes our way. We convince ourselves that we have the strength, the guile, and the will to overcome anything that jeopardizes our life. As long as we have the financial resources, the ego starts to believe, we have the ultimate power of all, the power to defeat death, at least for the time being.

But if the underlying belief of separation is still intact, if we still believe that we are independent from our Source, we have achieved nothing more than a momentary reprieve. The fear, still feeding upon the incendiary flames of isolation, is soon rekindled, this time as a fear of old age. To our horror, our money, intellect and network of influential contacts have done nothing to smother the fire. The fear is still with us, only now we have projected it into the future in our attempts to avoid it.

We begin to doubt that we will be able to cope in our retirement. Old age becomes a dreaded curse, a time where only death, disease and decrepitude are our companions. We then react by throwing our elderly into institutions so that they cannot remind us of our hopeless fate, or by trying to buy our way out of it through pension schemes and superannuation plans, or by endlessly searching for the magical fountain of youth. Insurance companies, plastic surgeons, and cosmetic companies make a fortune out of our fear of old age.

THE FALL INTO NOTHINGNESS

Doubt for our continuing existence and wellbeing now and in the future is just one of the many manifestations of fear, just one of a multitude of fear's disguises. Doubting our survival puts into question the validity of our Source but doubt itself is not the problem. It is a symptom of a much more insidious disease, a reaction of the ego to its felt isolation.

Another example of fear, in fact one of humanity's greatest fears, is the loss of a loved one, especially the loss of a parent, partner or child. It can cause untold worry and suffering and it can even dictate the manner in which we behave toward that person we fear will be lost.

A parent can live in terror at the thought of his son or daughter becoming the victim of pedophilia or cancer, his fear so great that he virtually imprisons his children in their own house. A child can have nightmares at the possibility of her parents' divorce and potential abandonment, so much so that her fear literally causes her to wither and stop growing. A wife can be consumed with paranoia over her husband's closeness with his secretary and, in her fear, becomes obsessively watchful of his movements and phone calls, even to the point of stalking him.

Fear of this kind, conscious or unconscious, can usurp our sense of who we are and thus affect our attitudes and actions. But the truth is, hard as it is to acknowledge, we will experience loss of some kind at some point in our life.

For example, either we will die first and lose those who are closest to us, or they will die first, and we will still lose them. In essence, our mind, or more to the point, our ego, fears what is inevitable. In its desire for things to remain as they are, and for itself and loved ones to last forever, the ego continually resists the natural cycle of death and decay. It tries to control death. It tries to force its will upon life, so that everything it comes into contact with conforms to its idea of what should or should not be.

Our ego has a major problem with impermanence and immortality and its inability to deal with these issues manifests as a fear of loss, and the greatest loss of all is death.

In effect, our individual and collective behavior is and has been for thousands of years, controlled and manipulated by fear, not by love. Yet we can break through the shell of fear and crush its influence over us if we see it for what it really is, a warning signal alerting us to the degree to which our ego is subjugating our Natural State of Being, a red flag signaling the ego's hegemony over our sense of self. We can, in fact, turn it to our advantage by using the strength of its emotion to warn us of danger ahead. Not the danger of darkness, death or desertion, but the danger of further extrication from our Source.

Using our own consciousness as a mirror, fear can be shown for what it truly is, a vampire with no reflective image, a beast with no life-source other than what we feed it. Consciousness slays unconsciousness. Awareness shines a light on the darkness, and simply being aware that fear is a product of the belief in an isolated ego—*forgetfulness*—of grasping at self, can bring us back into Spirit's Presence, Spirit's Light, and light is something no vampire can bear.

Those who experience a deep connection with the Presence of Spirit, those who know and are intimate with their Natural State of Being, know that they cannot not be. They know that they exist forever in the Eternal Memory of Spirit like a drop of water in the Vast Ocean of Life.

Living with Spirit's Presence, however, does not mean that fear will instantly vanish from your life. As long as you are alive in human form you will have an ego, and as long as you have an ego you will have fear. Rather, what you will come to experience is a drastic reduction of its impact, a slackening of its tether, a dampening of its control, as Love begins to take over the reins and becomes your predominant experience and motivation for life. Death of the ego, as some seekers have interpreted it, is not a literal death of the personality but merely a death of the ego's influence, which is fear. But as Helen Keller once cautioned:

Fear: the only way out is through.

Living with the Presence of Spirit's Love means that despite the fear you feel, you will still move forward. You will no longer remain paralyzed. You will have clarity of thought and peace of mind. You will have the courage and security of your Natural State of Being.

Living with Spirit's Presence means that though you walk through the Valley of Death, you shall not fear anything but fear itself.

POINTS OF REMEMBRANCE #6

- Suffering is a self-perpetuating cycle of pain with four distinctive but overlapping phases: Forgetfulness, Emptiness, Fear, and Need

- Humanity grieves its loneliness in the universe and the loss of connection to the Whole.

- The focus of your attention determines your experience.

- A mind-body being is limited, confined, reactive, unconscious, and time pressured, everything that your Natural State of Being is not.

- The symptoms of fear are despair, danger, dismissal, disaster, and detainment.

- Fear does not happen to you, it comes through you.

6 THE CYCLE OF ADDICTION

NEED

IF NOT STOPPED when fear arises, the cycle of suffering (review *Figure 4*) rotates to the next phase, the feeling of need. More often than not, our need falls into two reactive responses, fight or flight: the need to fight or resist our pain, or the need to flee toward or pursue something pleasurable.

Diagram 1: The Weed of Need, is a visual representation of how our emptiness, fears and needs grow from the seed of forgetfulness. The diagram shows how the roots of fear—vulnerability, loss/annihilation and abandonment—which are deeply embedded in the fertile soil of emptiness, grow from forgetfulness into despair, danger, dismissal, disaster and detainment, then sprout as the need to fight or flee: pain avoidance or pleasure seeking.

Although the reactive need to counteract our fear is real and painful on a mental and physical level, it is in fact, on the level of our Natural State of Being, of Absolute Reality, an illusion. It is forgetfulness and there is a direct correlation between ignoring Spirit and the need to flee or fight our fear, to seek pleasure or avoid pain.

As we have seen, misidentification with the ego, grasping at self, leads to an unhealthy mental state of psychological isolation and fall into unconscious nothingness. If ignored and left unchecked over time, this unhealthy mental state can even manifest as physical illness or morbidity: tiredness, insomnia, high blood pressure, hair loss, and many other symptoms of stress, including, in the most severe forms, heart attack and stroke.

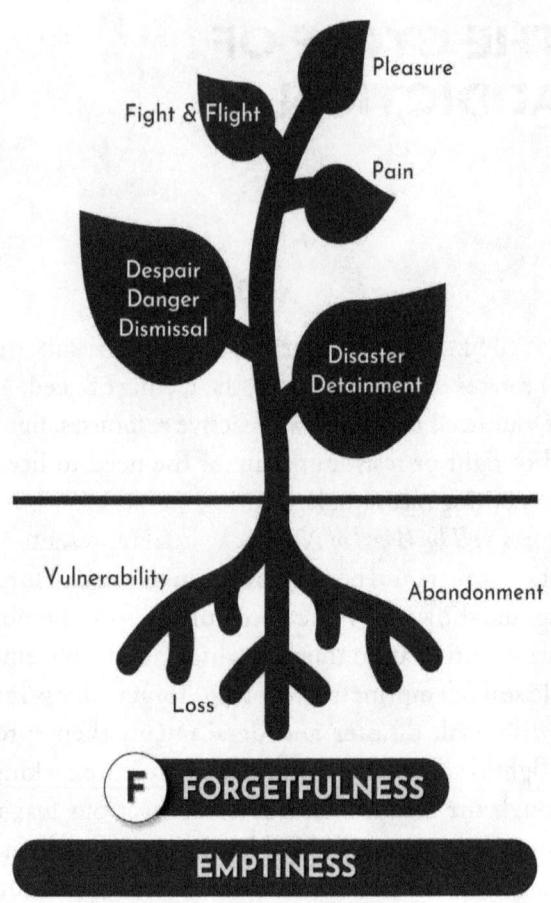

DIAGRAM 1: The Weed of Need

Although the consequent desire for an end or cure to the pain we feel is an inevitable and normal reaction to seek wholeness and wellbeing, to simply feel better, our efforts to escape our suffering and feel whole again are usually in vain. Forgetfulness can only be healed through remembrance, and the only permanent way to heal the emptiness of isolation is through the reconnection with our Natural State of Being, by communing with our Source. But failure to recognize this leads to the interpretation of spiritual suffering as having mental or physical causes, which then triggers the irrepressible urge for outside cures instead of inside ones.

In other words, in the vain hope that we can fill the empty void inside, we reach out and grasp onto material cures for our unhappiness, insecurity, rejection, turmoil and limitation. We snatch at any worldly promise to end our pain and suffering. What better way to feel happy and safe and important and peaceful and free than to buy a diamond ring, or a new sports car, or a new house? What better way to numb the fear of vulnerability, loss or abandonment than to spend or drink our feelings away?

The world as we know it is being crushed under the stockpile of material wealth that has been accumulated in fear of what we think we are presently lacking, or in fear of what we will lack at some point in the future.

The advertising and marketing people know all about our sense of fear and un-wholeness, and they are relentless in their determination to hide the error in misidentifying with our ego. Those inside the advertising and marketing industry know all too well that if we no longer needed material goods to make us feel complete, then they would be out of a job. We, especially our children, are easy prey for the glitzy and glamorous messages they deliver second after second, minute after minute, hour after hour, day after day.

The marketing machine is relentless, seductive and powerful. It tells us that we all have needs, that it's simply human to have desires, that our fantasies are important and deserve to be fulfilled.

"Desires and emotions are what make us uniquely human," the marketers say, ignoring the fact that even the pet dog and other animals also have emotions, that they too can feel love, happiness, depression, greed, and anger like us, even to the point of having likes and dislikes. To our detriment, we believe them. But, even though emotions and desires contribute to our humanness, they do not make or define us. Our Natural State of Being does.

Once hooked, however, the marketing machine then tells us that the only way to meet our basic human needs and desires is to purchase one of their products, if not two or three. Preferably right away, now, before stock runs out. The advertising industry pretends to look after our interests, but it only exists to fulfill and serve its own requirements and this it does by perpetuating the fallacy of need for as long as possible.

If advertisers truly wanted to limit our pain and suffering and make us feel whole once again, if they truly wanted the world to feel happy and healthy, they would advertise the benefits of reconnecting with our Infinite Source rather than the benefits of reconnecting with our credit card or bank manager. But they don't. They want us to remain in a state of needful suffering, in a state of duality, disconnected from our true self.

What the advertising industry won't tell you is this:

> *Permanent and abiding joy, security, acceptance, peace and freedom arise from the abundance of our Natural State of Being.*

They are free of cost. We don't need to purchase them and we don't need to purchase anything else to obtain their benefits. The need for these things is therefore a need for our self, which is futile, if not insane, like a snake eating its own tail to satisfy its hunger.

Is it really a healthy state of being to need what we already have, to thirst when the well is full? Is it really a healthy state of being to continually ignore who we are, to forever ride on an ox looking for an ox?

The Six Thieves

The main issue facing humanity, in the context of ending suffering and finding salvation, is that grasping at self is often a process that is sub-conscious and habitual. We don't realize that we're doing it.

THE CYCLE OF ADDICTION

But there are certain emotions specific to the character of need and wanting that we can identify, if we maintain sufficient and continual awareness of our underlying feelings, and thus put the machinations of the ego under the microscope of our consciousness. These emotions are:

-> Anger
-> Hatred
-> Greed
-> Pride
-> Idolatry

More will be said on these issues in *Part III, Love*. Suffice it to say, at heart these five emotions of need are non-other than the children of fear. Fear, in all its manifestations of darkness, death and desertion, is a productive breeding ground for the emotions of anger, hatred, greed, pride and idolatry.

On a lighter note, fans of Star Wars will be familiar with Yoda's often-quoted axiom on fear and anger:

Fear is the path to the dark side. Fear leads to anger. Anger leads to hate. Hate leads to suffering.

Together, fear and its children are a family of thieves that I call "The Six Thieves", stealing from you what is rightfully yours, your Natural State of Being.

The modus operandi of The Six Thieves is to support and strengthen the illusory image of the ego—*forgetfulness*—thereby supporting and strengthening the illusion of separation from our Source. Their actions can be subtle or obvious, invisible or visible.

Here are some examples of how the awareness of your Natural State of Being can be stolen by anger, hatred, greed, pride and idolatry:

-> Anger can arise when your need to avoid pain or to gain pleasure is not met within a satisfactory timeframe. Anger can distract your attention from your Natural State of Being and mesmerize you by igniting the effigy of the ego and keeping the false image alight with its self-destructive flames.

-> Hatred can arise when someone else, or some other community, has what you think you need to avoid pain or to gain pleasure and they do not share it with you. Hatred can numb or anaesthetize the sense of connection with your Natural State of Being by intoxicating the ego's individual and cultural identity, which then staggers and stumbles forward like a drunkard hankering for a fight.

-> Greed can arise when your need to avoid pain, or to gain pleasure, is ravenous and insatiable. Greed can overpower and negate the felt presence of your Natural State of Being by fueling the ego's desire, which then hungers for immediate gratification.

-> Pride can arise when your efforts to avoid pain and fulfill your pleasures have been successful. Pride can dismiss and ignore the Goodness, Truth and Beauty of your Natural State of Being by continually pampering and praising the ego's self-importance and needy requirements.

-> Idolatry can arise when the cure for your pain, or the object of your pleasure, is set over and above everything else. Idolatry can usurp your Natural State of Being by placing external, material things upon a pedestal, which the ego then carves as a magnificent idol to worship in its own image.

THE CYCLE OF ADDICTION

Although these emotions can affect your state of being in a detrimental way, they can, like fear, be turned to your advantage, if you remain conscious enough, that is, and don't surrender your attention (identity) to them.

As long as you remember to look beneath their mask, anger, hatred, greed, pride and idolatry will reveal their underlying need (fight or flight, pleasure and pain). A thief can only steal from you when you are in the dark as to who and what it is, when you are unconscious of its true intentions. Identifying the underlying need catches the thief in the act of stealing and pulls the mask off its face, as it were. Once its real identity has been recognized, the thief drops its booty, your Natural State of Being, and flees out of sight.

But, as the police well know, catching the little guys of the criminal ring will only achieve a momentary respite unless the mastermind, the ringleader giving the orders, is also caught. Thankfully, once the need to fight or flee has been revealed beneath the masks of emotion, then the ringleader, Mother Fear, is not too far behind.

The trap has now been sprung and the whole criminal infrastructure begins to unravel. For once the ringleader (fear) is in the crossfire of your consciousness, it too reveals its source, the abyss of isolation, which itself is brought on by the initial grasping at self and misidentification as a mind-body being. Once this is acknowledged, coupled with the will to stop your unconscious forgetfulness, the end of suffering is not too far away.

More often than not, however, these thieves are given free rein to run riot in our house. Anarchy is the norm, not the exception. Our needs to fight our pain or flee toward material sources of pleasure are, more or less, left unchecked and the cycle of suffering becomes a closed loop (*Figure 4*).

It in fact becomes a negatively reinforcing cycle. Our repetitive patterns of behavior reinforce the belief systems that created them, thus fortifying the very thing that caused the problem in the first place, our egoic grasping at self, forgetfulness. Caught in the cycle of suffering, we become mentally and physically unhealthier with each rotation until, if we continue failing to recognize that our own beliefs instigate the downward spiral of suffering, our patterns of helplessness and despair become our grave clothes.

We run the very real risk of creating the most unhealthy state of need possible, a cycle of addiction.

Need & Gratificaion

The cycle of addiction is recognized within the medical profession as one which follows a need-gratification-need cycle. Too much need, whatever its cause, and whether it is felt physically or psychologically, invariably leads the individual down a tired and familiar path: the temptation to seek out the means of fulfilling that need in a cycle of never-ending desire.

Addictions are very seductive. They appeal to our basic, childlike desire to never have to pay the cost of succumbing to it, and they fool us into believing we don't have to take responsibility for the consequences of our actions. They tell us it's okay to have everything we want now, that it's stupid to delay the gratification of our desires.

But the allure of addictions is a lie:

> *There is always a cost of seeking pleasure for pleasure's sake, there is always responsibility to be accounted for in avoiding pain, and there is always a price of having it now instead of waiting.*

Nonetheless, it is very rare for a person to completely avoid the cycle of addiction throughout their lifetime. Due to its subtle nature, addiction can afflict each and every one of us at some stage in our time here on earth.

THE CYCLE OF ADDICTION

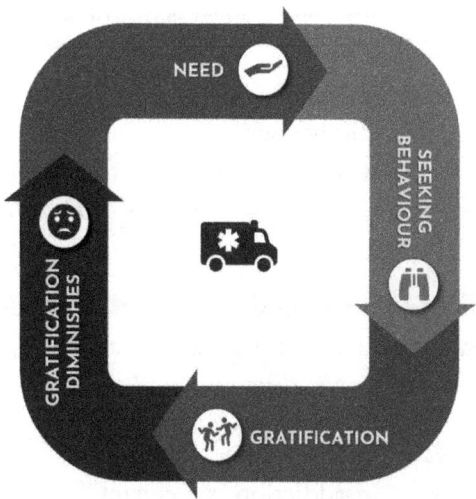

FIGURE 5:   The Cycle of Addiction

Addictions to gambling and to drugs, such as alcohol, coffee, nicotine, sleeping pills, heroin, to name a few, are, of all the addictions that exist, probably the better known. There are numerous TV, radio and magazine commercials advertising a thousand ways or more to kick our cigarette habit. Most people have heard of Alcoholics Anonymous and its Twelve Steps. There is also a heightened social awareness to the dangers of heroin, cocaine, methamphetamine, and other drugs of dependence.

However, there are plenty of other addictions that are not so easily recognized. Addictions to food, sex, money, entertainment, and even adrenaline, are just as prevalent in society but less well understood and recognized because we don't see them as a problem. In fact, they are generally considered a normal part of life.

If we go so far as to acknowledge that our psychological and physical health is a reflection of our state of spiritual health (that is, a reflection of our connection to our Natural State of Being), and if we recognize that addictions are a symptom of some underlying need, we can then begin to accept that addictions are actually physical and psychological symptoms of an underlying spiritual problem.

Christina and Stanislav Grof, transpersonal psychologists and specialists in addictive behavior in the USA, argue that the craving for alcohol or drugs is, in actual fact, a craving for spiritual transcendence or wholeness. In a chapter of *Paths Beyond Ego*,[15] they write:

> *For many people, behind the craving for drugs, alcohol, or other addictions is the craving for Universal Self [Source] ... For many people, drug and alcohol dependency and other addictions are forms of spiritual emergency.*

In other words, an addiction is a craving for what we already have. It is an extreme case of forgetfulness and, although each person is unique and individual, there are two common addictive cycles in which we can find ourselves trapped: money and relationships.

THE MONEY CYCLE

When I met Sandra D. she was spiraling into the kind of "spiritual emergency" that Christina and Stanislav Grof would readily recognize. Her emergency, or crisis, took the form of an addiction to money.

Although she seemed completely unaware of it, her addiction followed the characteristic addiction cycle (*Figure 5*): the need for more money (desire), the search for money (her job), the initial gratification upon receiving the substance of her desire (her paycheck), the rapid decline in gratification soon after, and finally the re-emergence of the need for more money. It was a monthly cycle of twenty-nine to thirty days of desire and need

---

[15] *Paths Beyond Ego: The Transpersonal Vision*, R. Walsh, F. Vaughan, Penguin/Putnam Inc., 1993

and only one day of gratification. Her life had become a misery because she was stuck in a job she didn't like and yet couldn't leave it because she felt she needed the money that it paid.

To make things worse, she borrowed money to buy a car that she didn't need, which only served to get her deeper into debt and make it increasingly more difficult to leave a job she resented. Her life was spiraling into chaos.

Like Sandra D., many people live in a cycle of debt repayments that seem will never be paid off, yet we don't call their debt cycle an addiction cycle even though it is essentially the same. Debts don't get labeled as addictions because they are seen as a normal part of life. Addictions are viewed as something abnormal, something that involves alcoholics and drug addicts, but not so-called "normal" people. But if we look closely at the money cycle we see it for what it really is, a cycle of addiction.

But people need money to live, don't they? How is anyone supposed to buy food, pay the rent or mortgage and be entertained without money?

When we identify ourselves only as physical and mental beings, mind-bodies, and continue to deny our spiritual core through ignoring Spirit, our Higher Self, only physical or material remedies will make sense. But, as with any addictive problem, the answer lies beyond the ego.

Reconnecting with our Natural State of Being is the ultimate cure we are all seeking for our needs, because that is where we made the first underlying mistake—*forgetfulness*—the severance of our umbilical lifeline from our Source. Without getting to the root of a disease, any cure is only temporary, a bandage on top of the wound. Our superficial attempts at a cure for our needs even make the situation worse.

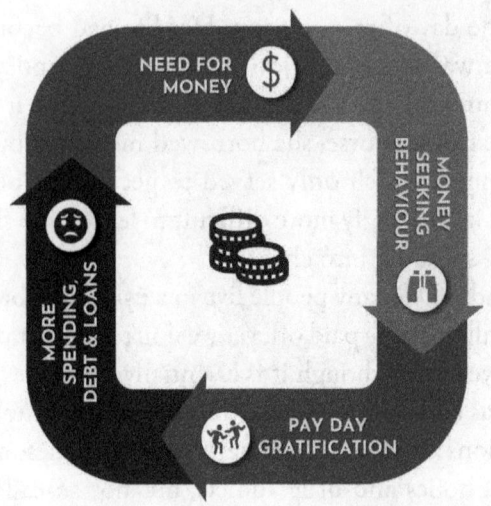

FIGURE 6:   The Money Cycle

The problem of need is perpetuated because the original cause has not been dealt with, which is still free to continue manifesting unease and suffering beneath the surface. To use a builder's phrase, a coat of paint only masks the rotting wood beneath it.

Serving Mammon

I know through firsthand experience the pain that accompanies the addictive cycle of money. Midway through my studies as a junior pediatric trainee at the Royal London Hospital, I decided to resign from my post and begin a career of fulltime writing. I had spent my whole childhood fascinated with books and wanting nothing more than to tell my own stories and write my own novels. But instead of writing, I had chosen the safe option of going to medical school and getting a "proper job" after matriculating from high school. Writing was a hobby, I had been taught to think, not real work, something to do in my spare time or when I retired.

University only reinforced this belief. I was well aware that only five percent of writers, like actors, painters, musicians, and dancers,

THE CYCLE OF ADDICTION

actually made enough money to earn a livelihood from their endeavors. It was foolish to contemplate it as a fulltime occupation.

Nevertheless, I eventually did just that. I quit, albeit fifteen years later. I took off my stethoscope and took up the pen. I did what I believed I had been called to do since high school, tell stories. I thought I was finally following my Life Purpose.

How silly. I was broke and humiliated within six months. No magazine editor wanted to print my articles. No publisher wanted to publish my manuscript. No competition judges wanted to shortlist my stories. I felt sure I was following my Higher Will and Purpose, but I wasn't progressing as far or as fast as I believed I should have been. I wasn't achieving anything more than I thought I could have achieved had I stayed in my job and earned more money. I wasn't happy. I felt let down. I felt abandoned and forsaken. Worse, my friends and family were calling me mad behind my back and sniggering at my failure.

"How can I pay the rent?" I cried out to the heavens. "How can I afford to pay for food? I NEED MONEY!"

I cried myself hoarse a dozen times or more. I was certainly no grateful Job, appreciative and reverent of God despite my privations. Sure, I wanted to follow my calling, but I didn't want to lose money or my lifestyle in doing it. I didn't want to be forced out of my home and humiliated in front of my friends and colleagues.

"I NEED MONEY!" I shouted again and again.

My ranting and raving, however, didn't do anything to stem the bleeding. The more I yelled at God, the quicker the money disappeared from my savings account. I was obviously missing some vital point. Then, after who knows how many times, something in the dark shell of my ego cracked and through it a beam of light shone upon my consciousness:

I need money, yes, but I need God more.

I need God more than money? Really? For what?

For eternal life. For being. For love.

As if an earthquake had shaken my fragile psychological terrain, the idol I had made to Mammon was sent crumbling to the ground. From the cloud of dust, Jesus' words echoed in my ears: "No one can serve two masters . . . both God and money."[2]

My need for cash had unwittingly grown into an unhealthy dependence and misguided love of Mammon, which had caused me to lose sight of the bigger picture, to lose focus on my Essential Nature. Sure, money could buy me the nicer things in life—holidays in the sun, fancy cars, city apartments, champagne breakfasts—but there is one thing that money cannot buy, the one thing that only God can provide, the permanent Light, Life and Love of my Natural State of Being.

How small everything suddenly looked. Money, I realized, could only provide me with material things, things that rust and get eaten by moths, things that by their very nature are temporary and cannot last. Losing focus on my Natural State of Being had caused me to place an unhealthy importance on impermanent things, the small things that come and go, things that need to be constantly replaced, which had invariably led to an unhealthy reliance upon the provider of these things, money. This reliance had been the cause of my suffering. Money was an addiction, my idol, and my needy desire for it had widened the rift between me and my Source. All my pain I had created myself.

Needless to say, despite this moment of insight, the landlord still wanted his rent-check every month, the utility bills still needed paying and the local supermarket didn't deal me any handouts. God, it hurt to realize, wasn't a fairy godmother or a genie in a lamp. He didn't wave a magic wand or cast a spell to make my problems go away.

But this I now knew: through Grace I had been given the abiding joy, security, acceptance, peace and freedom of my Natural State of Being to help resolve my problems and fears, to help pierce the heart of any need I might have had, any addiction, something no amount of money in the world could ever do.

If only for that, I need God more.

THE RELATIONSHIP CYCLE

Sandra D. came to work one day looking very pleased with herself. On her finger I noticed a sparkling diamond ring that had not been there the day before and I understood the cause of her sudden happiness.

Previously, Sandra had been in a loveless relationship for eighteen months. In fact, it was one of the reasons she had found herself in debt. Continuous phone calls to her foreign boyfriend and dashes overseas had taken a toll on her bank balance but, ultimately, it ended in misery, frustration and unhappiness. Many one-night stands and fleeting romances following her break-up had led her to the conclusion that she was never going to find a husband, and finding a husband was just the cure she needed to solve all her problems. To Sandra's delight, her newest fiancé had proposed just six weeks into their relationship.

Many of us know or have heard of someone like Sandra D., someone that hops from one relationship to another, one bed to another, never happy with the partner they are with and are continually on the lookout for another potential partner, even when they are in the middle of a relationship. Many people take this attitude into their marriage, so it is not surprising divorce rates in the First World are now around fifty percent. Soon more than one in two weddings will end in separation.

The problem, of course, is rooted in the duality of mind-body consciousness. Love and hate, like pain and pleasure, are two sides of the same coin called need, separated from one another only by the passing of time. Like pleasure, we can't flip the coin to always land on the side of love. Sooner or later, any time from six hours to six months, we start to fall "out" of love with our new partner. The little idiosyncrasies we found so amusing and were so incredibly tolerant of (much to our surprise) at the beginning of the relationship when we were "in" love, now become irritating annoyances that chip away at our patience until we can no longer stand them anymore.

Thus the mind-body relationship of two egos fluctuates between love and hate, like and dislike, sometimes with the same partner for life, often with many different partners. But ego relationships are always the same. They have to be. When our Natural State of Being is forgotten or ignored, there is no other way of existing than in the world of duality.

As we will be discussing in Part III, there is much confusion surrounding the topic of love. Ask one hundred people what they think love is and you will probably get one hundred different answers. Often it is spoken of or thought of in the context of something or someone we like excessively ("Ooh, I love that!), not as the Love of Spirit, which is pure and has no opposite. In other words, love is commonly used to describe the pleasure that arises when our needs for happiness, safety, belonging, peace and freedom are fulfilled.

But need fulfillment is not love: it is simply the sensation of gratification. And gratification, as with contentment, satisfaction and every other pleasurable emotion of need fulfillment, is an integral player on the roulette wheel of addiction.

When one or both partners in a relationship focus purely on the fulfillment of their ego's needs or desires, when they focus on what they can get out of the relationship over and above what they can bring to it (that is, their Natural State of Being), a cycle of addiction is established. With each rotation of need-gratification-need, an addictive pattern of pleasure seeking and pain avoidance, of love and hate, attraction and repulsion, is created within the relationship. We literally become addicted to our partner.

THE CYCLE OF ADDICTION

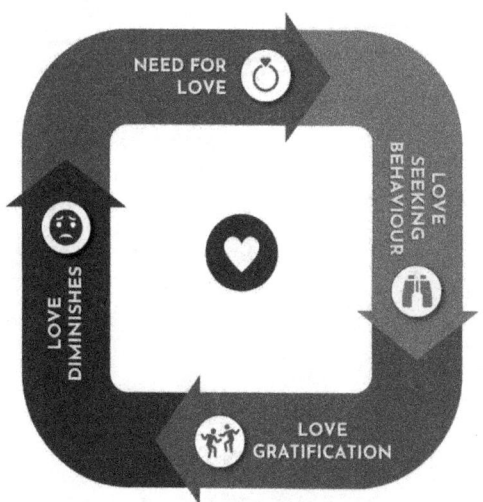

FIGURE 7: The Love Cycle

When they provide us with what we need, we interpret the pleasurable feelings of gratification as the feeling of love; and when they fail to provide us with what we need, we hate them for the pain and hurt we continue to feel. We can't live with them, and we can't live without them.

The problem, as with every addiction, can be traced back to the initial need. Needs and wants are insatiable. They are bottomless pits which no amount of gratification will fill—a need will always need more of what it needs. This is true for all addictions, whether they stem from the need for heroin, alcohol, gambling, or the need for a partner to gratify our sense of happiness (pleasure), safety, belonging, peace and freedom. As long as our partner can meet our escalating needs, we tend to stick with them. If not, if we don't feel love (or what we mistake as the continuing pleasure of need fulfillment) in our relationship, we blame our partner and look for it elsewhere. Like Sandra D., we jump from bed to bed, relationship to relationship, never satisfied for long, always on the hunt for someone better.

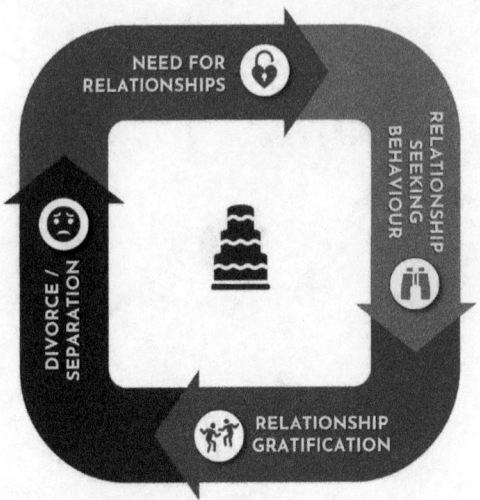

FIGURE 8:   The Relationship Cycle

Besides Sandra, I have known many other men and women, young and old, who have also been addicted to love for a great proportion of their life, or what they think of as love, the gratification of pleasure, safety and belonging. They are constantly in search of the perfect partner to fill their emptiness and make them feel complete. They aren't aware of their addiction to others because being with a partner makes them feel so whole.

In fact, so intoxicating is this feeling of wholeness that when they are no longer in the company of somebody else, they feel utterly inadequate and incomplete, which ultimately leads to the harrowing feeling of loneliness. Some, men and women alike, are so caught up in the addictive cycle of relationships that the instant they are alone they immediately go on the hunt for another partner, sometimes succeeding in capturing one within hours of breaking-up with another. The addictions can become so rampant that they end up dating multiple partners at once, often juggling dates on the same night. I have known of one particular young man whose physical and mental health suffered continually with the anxiety of getting caught out by one of his girlfriends, which eventually, and not surprisingly, regularly happened.

In its extreme, the addiction to pleasure, safety or belonging can manifest as an addiction to sex. Sex, although initially satisfying, becomes unfulfilling when it is performed only as a physical act, when one's heart is not in it. The gratification of a sexual conquest soon diminishes, often as soon as the sexual act is completed, and the feeling of need rears its ugly head once again. Men and women can bed hop for years, little knowing that they are caught in an addiction cycle, little knowing that they are a slave to their ego's desires and needs.

Multiple partners are therefore a symptom, not a cause, of relationship addictions. However, it is appropriate to give a word of caution: abusive and aggressive partners should not be tolerated, and if that means separation or divorce, then so be it. Although there exists a strong religious doctrine surrounding this topic in a number of faiths, a violent relationship is infertile ground for spiritual growth and is completely incapable of sustaining a healthy state of being. It is even worse when children are involved. Violence begets violence. Those who are abused often become the abuser. The cycle of violence must be stopped, even if that means separation or divorce from the violent partner.

Violence, though, is not the commonest grounds for divorce in Western society. "Irreconcilable differences" are, and irreconcilable differences arise in relationships when needs are felt wanting and the cycle of suffering continues unabated.

THE END OF SUFFERING

It took a decade or so of relentless soul searching to finally realize that my own addictions, whether they were addictions to money, relationship, sex, food, drugs, or work, had a common root, a similar cause of origin—*forgetfulness*—grasping at self. It took a long time of surgery in the operating room of my mind, of excising the tumors both large and small, to realize that I, myself, was the cause of my own problems. It was humbling, if not initially devastating, to confront the reality that my own belief in a separated self was actually oxygenating the cycle of suffering and turning my mind into an unlivable malignancy of isolation, fear and need. I had spent years searching outside myself for the bandages to dress my spiritual wounds, but it was my very behavior in seeking out what I believed was lacking in my life that nurtured, not healed, my addictions.

Many people I know, through personal and professional experience, are suffering as I did, and for identical reasons, forgetfulness. In fact, it can be argued that any illness from anxiety to hysteria, obesity to anorexia, depression to mania, can be caused by grasping at self. Whatever the illness, though, the consequences are the same:

> *Like Frankenstein and his hideous creation, we are gripped in a life of disease and disaster from the very thing that we created.*

For instance, when the cycle of suffering (*Figure 4*) and the cycle of addiction (*Figure 5*) are combined, it can be seen how the two cycles feed off each other in a never-ending frenzy of self-destruction (*Figure 9: The Cycle of Illness and Decay*).

Need is the common link. It has its roots in fear, emptiness and forgetfulness, but it grows out of control in the cycle of addiction. Each cycle reinforces the other; suffering reinforces addiction, and addiction reinforces suffering. Our need becomes so insatiable that we demand instant gratification in just about every aspect of life—food, entertainment, sex, promotions, sport, travel, to name a few. We want things fast and we want things now. The gluttony of need is an illness not too unlike a malignant cancer that is consuming the planet at an unprecedented rate.

THE CYCLE OF ADDICTION

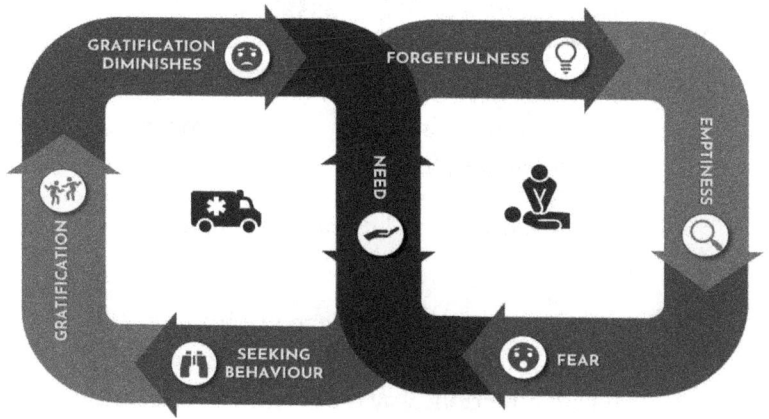

FIGURE 9: The Cycle of Illness & Decay

This is nothing new, however. In the second chapter of the Bhagavad-Gita, like a prophecy from the ancient past, we are warned that desire or need is inevitable when the rambling senses are allowed to take control, when we focus upon and become attached to external, material objects. From desire comes anger, the Gita counsels, and from anger comes a cascade of unrelenting, destructive emotions, which, in the end, become our ultimate ruin. We are like a boat on the sea driven from its course by stormy weather. Our judgment is lost, and there can be no salvation, no tranquility, until all our power is focused upon freeing the senses from attachment and egoism.

This, in fact, is the promise of all religions. For those that want it and seek it out, there is a cure for our individual and collective suffering. The end of fear, need and addiction happens when we first acknowledge that the cause of suffering and pain is deeply seated in our grasping at self, in forgetfulness, and then we develop the will to do something about it.

Our suffering begins to end when we start grasping at our Higher Self, when we actively start grasping at Source.

POINTS OF REMEMBRANCE #7

- Your need falls into two reactive responses: the need to fight or resist pain, or the need to flee toward or pursue pleasure.

- Forgetfulness can only be healed through remembrance.

- Certain emotions are specific to need: anger, hatred, greed, pride, and idolatry—thieves that steal your attention away from your Natural State of Being by supporting and strengthening the mind-body image.

- A thief can only steal from you when you are in the dark as to who and what it is.

- Addiction follows a need-gratification-need cycle.

- A need will always need more of what it needs.

- The cycle of suffering and the cycle of addiction feed off each other in a downward spiral of self-destruction.

7 GRASPING AT SOURCE

IDENTIFICATION & REMEMBRANCE OF SOURCE

For complete mental, physical and emotional healing, resolving the disease of need and addiction must occur at its root cause, which is achieved by re-establishing the connection with our Source. It cannot be resolved with superficial bandages. To fix a severed artery, a doctor must first recognize that the artery is severed. This may seem obvious, but the symptoms of internal bleeding are often difficult to detect and many patients suffer significant morbidity or die because of an initial misdiagnosis when they present at hospital. But when a doctor does recognize that a patient has internal bleeding, the patient is rushed to the operating room and the hemorrhage fixed from within.

Likewise, to heal a spiritual severance with our Source, we need to first acknowledge the severance. Many people, however, fail to recognize the symptoms of internal spiritual hemorrhage and hence fail to act constructively to fix the leak.

The problem, in fact, is not even acknowledged; it is misdiagnosed.

Too often we apply bandages to our internal spiritual bleeding—multiple relationships, career changes, lifestyle choices—and are surprised when the loss of spiritual energy isn't halted, when our lives continue to feel sad, insecure, insignificant, chaotic and stagnant. But when we try to solve a spiritual problem by means other than spiritual, the result is simply more problems and more despair. The root of the problem has not been addressed—we are using outer bandages when internal surgery is required—and we continue the endless search for an end to our deep-felt suffering.

If we therefore want to do anything about breaking the cycles of suffering and addiction and once again feel the abundance of The Five Pillars of Love in our life, we must stop grasping at our mind and body, stop identifying with the little self, the small mind of ego, and begin grasping at Source as readily as a child would grasp her father's hand to cross the street.

Grasping at Source, not the selfish ego, is the practice and philosophy that will resolve many of the problems that afflict the world. Once achieved, we can begin to focus on the certitude that we are not born separate from the Source of Consciousness, Life, and Love, that we are not born with nothing and have to start from scratch, but that each and every one of us has been given as much Goodness, Truth and Beauty we could ever want or need.

Grasping at Source is not difficult. It simply involves a two-fold process of:

1. Identification with our Source.
2. Remembrance of our Source.

To begin with, to grasp at Source is to identify with something bigger than we believe we are. Too many times we fall into the trap of identifying only with the five senses of the body—sight, sound, touch, taste, and smell—our unconscious mind-body image.

Identification with our Source involves not seeing our self as something lesser, not seeing our self as separate from our Essence, but identifying with our Big Mind, our Universal Consciousness. It also involves identifying with our Greater Being, our Higher Self, and identifying with our Eternal Beloved, our True Love.

Previously, I made the point that identifying with something other than what we already are runs the risk of polarization, of splitting the Formless Self into forms, an ego "me" and a "something other than me". Separation, though, is ultimately futile, like trying to break the speed of light or force a square peg into a round hole. But the word identity we are using here is meant to be used in the context of attentiveness and awareness—being aware that you are already that which you find yourself attracted to, which is Love.

The second step in grasping at Source is a voluntary but necessary reconnection with the Spirit of Life. It is remembering that our Source is always present as the underlying, deeper sense of our own being, remembering that our Source is the sensed presence of our own consciousness.

It is the disbandment of disbelief, the remembrance and the acceptance of our connection with a Higher Intelligence.

GOODBYE TO FEAR

The two-fold process of grasping at Source, identification and remembrance, is essential if it is your will to confront the suffering in your daily life, for without including your Source in your healing process you are in fact disconnecting yourself from the major essence of your total makeup. To only participate in fifty percent of a football game, to leave the field at halftime and never return to complete the match, would be suicide to any football team. So why would you only participate in fifty percent of life?

There was a time when I was only participating in fifty percent of everyday existence. As mentioned previously, I too suffered through various society-condoned addictions, one of which was an addiction to money, the unconscious worship of Mammon. The worship of money probably extended over thirty years of my life (I was a devout follower), but it seemed to peak during my intern year at age twenty-four. Such was the depth of my poor mental and spiritual state at that time, not only was I living on the fragile backbone of personal loans and credit card debt, but my physical health also suffered.

To my horror, the threat of early baldness was extremely real. Many mornings I would despair at the sight of dark hair covering my pillow. Worse, every shampoo and brush revealed more and more of my naked scalp, which my hairdresser even advised I start protecting with sunscreen!

I only began to recover my debts, and my hair, years later when I realized that the cause of my problems was self-created. Namely, the underlying notion of separation from my Source. It was as though I had foolishly handcuffed my hands together and then swallowed the key—the very thing that I needed to release myself from my suffering was inside me. Slowly but surely, with the realization that my belief in isolation—*forgetfulness*—was the cause of the mess I was in, I became aware of every dark fear and false need I was harboring. When I realized that I had all the joy, security, acceptance, peace and freedom I could want, I realized that I actually didn't need to fear anything, nor was there any condition or any thing that I needed outside myself to experience and express these things.

And with the end of fear and need comes the end of suffering and addiction. Of course, I still had the responsibility to pay off the debts and loans I had accumulated over decades of worshipping Mammon, but I didn't need money to know the Light, Life and Love of my Natural State of Being. In fact, I know now that the opposite is true. The experience of relative poverty and privation, in my case, was a journey of negation that I needed to make in order to remember that the Source of Consciousness, Being and Love was accompanying me every second of the day. I needed to know what is not in order to know what is. For this is what is revealed:

Discard the unreal and that which persists is real.

Extrapolating the lesson that can be taken from our addictions:

Gasping at Source, or reconnection with our Higher Self, is a movement of consciousness upstream to Higher Consciousness, a movement from a place of separation to a place of wholeness and Oneness.

GRASPING AT SOURCE

It is a movement from forgetfulness to remembrance.

Which, in fact, neatly defines the spiritual journey—the stripping away, layer by layer, like an onion, of our unconscious mind-body ego to the full Consciousness of Self. This stripping away of unconsciousness feels like a movement toward Higher Awareness. That is why it is called a journey, or pilgrimage, even though we don't physically go anywhere.

> *It is the hero's journey, going deeper into yourself, fighting the demons and monsters of your own unconsciousness and confronting deserts and mountains of your own making.*

Even so, it is the journey spiritual masters say we must make if we wish to overcome suffering and pain. For once we have moved or detached the focus of our attention from lower-self consciousness to a position of Higher-Self Consciousness, we can, like an army general positioned on high ground above the battlefield, look down upon our false beliefs and plan an assault on our unhealthy state of affairs. We can see the patterns of our addictive behaviors and thus head them off before they can trap us in an endless cycle of suffering.

If anything, the main difference between grasping the mind-body-self and grasping at Source, between living in the stagnant delta and living in the Infinite Spring, between being fifty percent human and one hundred percent human, is identification with our Natural State of Being. This simple act gives us the controlling edge over our ego and our fears by arming us with the awareness that we already have everything we could possibly want.

Probably for the first time, identifying and remembering that we have all the Goodness, Truth and Beauty the universe can provide, we say goodbye to a life of need and say hello to a life of abundance and plenitude.

Probably for the first time we really start to live. We say goodbye to a life of fear and say hello to a life of love.

POINTS OF REMEMBRANCE #8

- Grasping at Source is a two-fold process of identification and remembrance of your Source.

- Without including your Source in your healing process you disconnect yourself from the major essence of your total makeup.

- The very thing that you need to release yourself from suffering is inside you.

- Sometimes you need to make a journey of negation—to know what is not in order to know what is.

- Grasping at Source is a movement of consciousness upstream to your Higher Consciousness, a journey from forgetfulness to remembrance.

- Your spiritual journey involves stripping away your unconsciousness to reach your Higher Consciousness.

PART III

LOVE

"You want to know your lord's meaning in what I have done? Know it well, love was his meaning. Who reveals it to you? Love. What did he reveal to you? Love. Why does he reveal it to you? For love."

Dame Julian of Norwich
(14th Century)

8 THE POWER OF LOVE

ATTENTIVENESS

Throughout history, men and women alike have searched for the meaning of life. Pilgrims have searched far and wide for it. Scientists have split the atom and scanned the universe for it. Artists have tried to copy and mimic it. Some have stumbled upon it in places they never thought possible, finding it in every single moment of existence. Some have searched for it their whole life and departed this world disappointed, having never found what they were looking for. Some have never bothered at all, citing the futility of searching for meaning when no meaning exists (and, as such, have inadvertently given meaning to life through the negation of it: the meaning of life is that it has no meaning!).

The meaning of life, it may or may not be of surprise to learn, is none other than love. Meaning is therefore both personal and general. It is both unique and significant to each particular individual as well as having an overarching importance that embraces the entire spectrum of life throughout the universe, including the human race. The meaning of life—love—has a local meaning and it has a broader meaning.

But what is love? Can it actually be defined?

Awakening Love

Throughout the chapters so far, love has been briefly mentioned and described with many different metaphors. I have said that love is the Source that fills us with joy, security, acceptance, peace and freedom. I have quoted the Bible and said that God is love.

I have even said that love is the unifying force of the universe, the Personality, or Soul, of Spirit. I have said that love is that face we recognize as clarity of mind, the face of Perfect Beauty whose radiance captures and pulls us unceasingly closer with its inescapable gravity. As such, love is palpable, love is real and, yet, perhaps something so common we barely notice it. Or, if we do, we take it for granted.

I have also said that love is often misused in the context of something or someone we like excessively. For many, it is simply another addiction, commonly confused as the pleasure or gratification arising from the fulfillment of our needy desires (as opposed to the felt sense of Oneness with our Source). I have said that for the majority, those of us caught in the mind-conditioned duality of this world, love is nothing more than the antithesis of that other extreme emotion, hate.

Love awakens and heals us, and in that sense it is an active, not passive, process. In *The Road Less Traveled*,[16] M. Scott Peck writes that love is not a feeling; it is a verb. That is, love is an action, not an emotion, and he expands his definition of love as being:

> *The desire or intent for another's, or your own, spiritual growth.*

Attention is probably the best word to describe love in the sense of being a verb, an action. Attention is paramount to loving others and our self. Children, especially, thrive on attention. When we give children our utmost attention, they feel joyous, secure and worthy. They feel at peace with themselves and free to be who they are. On the contrary, a child will wither when ignored, especially if they are ignored over a sustained period of time. In essence, paying attention to others is an act of loving them.

---

[16] *The Road Less Traveled: A New Psychology of Love, Traditional Values and Spiritual Growth*, M. Scott Peck, Touchstone, 1998

This is because when you give attention to somebody (or our self), you are actually giving them a gift of recognition and belonging, which is non-other than a gift of remembrance and Oneness. The attention you give, in fact, is more akin to a key that opens a door than a present or a physical package that can be received and unwrapped.

Loving attention arouses in others their own sense of love, the love that is already there inside them as their Natural State of Being, but which has hitherto been lying inactive and dormant. Acts of love—attention—toward another person energizes and arouses in them their dormant sense of Goodness, Truth and Beauty. That is, attention energizes and arouses in others their innate sense of Being.

Attention is also being centered, and this is especially true when giving attention to our self. When we are centered, we are balanced. A spinning top can be tipped from side to side without tipping completely over because the centrifugal forces keep it centered and balanced. Love, as attention directed toward our inner self, is like a centrifugal force keeping us from tipping over. When we give attention to our Natural State of Being, we are centered and balanced:

> *A major crisis may occur, tipping us from side to side, shaking our senses, but because of the centrifugal force of attentive love we remain upright.*

This leads to yet one more meaning of attention, which is being aware. Attentiveness of something is awareness of it, of awakening to its presence. Conversely, inattention to someone or something is being unaware or unconscious of that person or thing, and because attention is a loving act then it follows that inattention, or unconsciousness, is an unloving act.

Just as a drowning man will pull you beneath the waves if you are not careful or attentive, consciousness will always be dragged down by unconsciousness. Likewise, if you are not being aware of your Natural State of Being, you are not paying it any attention, resulting in a slipping of awareness into unconsciousness. Which, in the end, is an act of un-lovingness.

Attention, therefore, is the loving act that prevents us from drowning in unconsciousness.

Healing Love

The definition of love as a verb is as good as any definition of love I have found. It embraces both the personalized and generalized meaning of life. If every man, woman and child were to etch this philosophical template into their hearts, it follows that all our attention—our thoughts, words and behaviors—would be designed to benefit the spiritual journey of everyone we encountered, including ourselves. We would cultivate compassion and loving kindness in our minds; we would speak with kindness and gentleness to our neighbors; we would be proactive, not reactive, in our day-to-day activities.

Yet, as good as the benefits would be to the global community should everybody on the planet embrace it en-mass, the definition of love as a verb does seem slightly unbalanced and tipped toward the intellectual experience of what love is and thereby somewhat biased against the delicate, heartfelt experience of it, which simply has to include our emotions and passions. The definition of love therefore needs expanding to include, though by no means become the exclusive domain of, the personal feeling of love.

This is necessary because the absence of love is disastrous for our state of being and sense of who and what we are:

> *The feeling of being unloved can be fatal and we can literally die of a broken heart.*

There exists a vast body of scientific research that has explored the absence of love and its consequences on the human body. Studies conducted since the 1990s examining the survival rates of people suffering an acute myocardial infarction, or heart attack, have shown that those people, especially men, who are married or in a long-term relationship tend to live through their crisis, whereas those, again especially men, who have never married or are divorced tend to fare much worse.

Interestingly, a figure has even been established to quantify love's effect on the heart. Heart attack survivors who have the love of a close friend or family member have an approximately fifty percent less likelihood of suffering another heart attack within the subsequent year, as compared to those who do not have the love of a close confidant. Although it could be argued that those lacking close friends and family are more likely to abuse alcohol, smoke more cigarettes and use illicit drugs, some studies have shown that when these and all other factors of heart disease are taken into consideration, they alone do not significantly increase the survivor's future heart attack risk. Indeed, even though the love of a confidant may express itself in a practical sense, such as helping survivors adhere to treatment regimens and attend hospital follow-up appointments, the effect of love is consistently shown in various independent studies to exert a mysterious and unknown factor on our physical state of being.

What's more, feeling loved is not only good for the heart, it is also beneficial for the rest of the body, such as our immune system. The immune systems of people in love, it has been shown, consistently out-perform the immune systems of those men and women not in love. Certain white blood cells, the cells involved in fighting infections, are higher in people who are in love, or at least claim to be, compared to those who are not. On average, they catch fewer viruses and are afflicted less by illnesses. Not only that, love also affects our hormonal systems. It appears to reduce our cholesterol levels and this has obvious impact on our general state of health, especially our cardiovascular health.

Some researchers, however, in the attempt to demystify love, have reduced it to a purely chemical experience. One particular hormone, oxytocin, has been labeled the "love hormone", or "cuddle hormone", due to its presence in the bloodstream during sex, childbirth and subsequent mother-child bonding. Love, these researchers claim, is just an illusion of chemical tricks and mirrors: when the oxytocin wand is waved, we feel loved. Nothing more. Nothing less. All in all, they conclude, love is something we really don't have any control over. It's just a question of luck and genetics.

A few researchers even go so far as to suggest that every emotional experience—anger, jealousy, happiness, greed, excitement, sadness and so forth—is the result of balances and imbalances of chemicals in the brain, chemicals such as dopamine, serotonin, endorphin, oxytocin, and vasopressin. This, of course, poses an interesting question, the classical chicken and egg paradox: is love an effect or an affect? Is love the result of our chemical makeup or is it the cause of it?

Notwithstanding the differing research data on love, however, it has been my professional experience that any clinical statistic, whether they support or detract from our own personal beliefs and philosophies, must be thoroughly scrutinized before becoming an accepted fact. All data can be manipulated to suit the needs of the researching scientist or sponsoring company. Money and prestige, I have found, can have a greater effect on the outcomes of research than mere observer influence.

Despite this, the just mentioned studies on love and its physical effects are still noteworthy. Whether or not we take them as fact or not, they still highlight the benefits of the felt presence of love in our lives, especially its extraordinary healing qualities. They show that love is a cathartic force:

> *We humans are healthier and feel better when love is a constant presence.*

Love has the capacity to mend our broken hearts. This is its power, but people actually know this innately without all the research. Interestingly, the more we believe in love, the greater its impact in our lives. When we don't believe we are loved, we don't feel it and when we don't feel loved we are more depressed, more prone to getting angry, more frustrated with others and ourselves, and we generally behave like a stick-in-the-mud.

When we do believe we are loved, however, we feel loved, and when we feel loved we feel joyous, safe, worthy, peaceful and free. We are mentally and physically the better for it. Love transforms us. It washes away our pain and suffering.

It could be argued, in fact, that love is our salvation.

LOVE CONSCIOUSNESS

Earlier in the discussion on Light, Life and Love, I made mention of the Zen saying, "Grasping the essence of life in the living of it." We are now at the point where we can gain a better understanding of why Zen Buddhists place so much emphasis on it. However, if we wish to delve even further into its deepest meanings, it will be of some benefit to first translate the sentence into the words and concepts we have become comfortable with, in particular the words and concepts of Consciousness, Being and Love. To do so, we will break the sentence into three parts, "Grasping", "the essence of life", and "in the living of it."

To begin the translation process, the first word in the sentence, "Grasping", can be interpreted and reworded as something along the lines of "becoming conscious of". To think of it another way, the intellectual act of grasping something, in the context of mental comprehension, means figuring it out, to understand the concept of it, to get its gist, to take it on board—to become aware of.

Next, the middle part of the sentence, "the essence of life" can be interpreted and restructured into something that means "the emotion of love." That is, of course, we accept that Spirit is Life and that its Essence is Love, and we also accept that its gravitational force has the power to attract and move us—that Love is an emotive power.

Lastly, the final words of the sentence, "in the living of it", can be interpreted and reworded as meaning something like "in its being". Likewise, we could also reword it as meaning "in its heart" or "in the existence of it". It simply means to fully experience the beingness of life.

Fully translated then, using the words and concepts familiar to this book, the Zen adage reveals its secrets. "Grasping the essence of life in the living of it" now reads like this:

Becoming conscious of the emotion of love in its being.

True to its Zen nature, the act of becoming conscious of the emotion of love in its being actually goes some way to solving the which-comes-first conundrum of the chicken and the egg. It does so by revealing the answer to the question we posed earlier: Is love an effect or an affect? Is love the result of our chemical makeup or is it the cause of it?

Consider the analogy of reading a book. Becoming conscious of the emotion of love in its being is, in a way, not too unlike reading a novel and examining its theme: it's knowing the how and the why of the story. In any good book (or poem, or song), the theme is the invisible thread weaving together all the characters, places, action, dialogue, tempo, and plot. (For example, religious scholars have acknowledged that love is the central theme uniting every word in the Bible.) Flick through the pages and dissect your favorite book into its constituent parts, there will be nothing physical—no words, no sentences, no paragraphs, no chapters—that can be pinpointed and mounted upon the shelf as the actual theme, except, of course, if the entire book is considered as a whole.

Yet the theme, although intangible, is greater than the sum of the whole book:

The theme is the spirit of the story, the invisible, organizing force holding it all together.

Without its spirit, its theme, the plot becomes nonsensical, the words become jumbled, the sentences garbled, and the characters have no intrinsic personality or grounding. Without the spirit of the story, without its theme, the whole story becomes chaotic and useless.

Yet books and stories do flow from beginning to middle to end in an orderly sequence (at least the good ones do)—the characters are real, the dialogue tight, the plot believable, the tempo appropriate—which is only possible because every word is held accountable to a central meaning by the underlying theme. The theme, therefore, is that force (will) of the writer which slots every letter, word and sentence together in a structured and meaningful sense but which, although invisible to the reader, has become known to the reader through its story. In actuality, the theme is the original source or inspiration from which the story is created, the primary template from which all its characters and places are written. (For instance, the theme of this book, the invisible spirit from which each page has sprouted forth, is the belief that you already have what you are looking for.)

The theme of a book or story, therefore, is first cause.

Love is like the theme of a good book. If the universe is the greatest story ever told (or the greatest ode ever recited, or the greatest song ever sung), then Love is the invisible thread weaving together all its characters, places, action, dialogue, tempo, and plot. Flick through the pages of history and dissect the universe into its constituent parts, there will be nothing physical—no atoms, no chemicals, no materials, no buildings—that can be pinpointed and identified as the actual essence of Love, except, of course, if the entire universe from its birth to its death is considered as a whole.

Yet Love, like the intangible theme of a book, is greater than the sum of the universe's constituent parts:

Love is the Spirit of Life, the invisible, organizing force holding it all together.

Without Love, without Spirit, the universe becomes nonsensical, the building blocks of matter become jumbled, the laws of physics garbled, its life forms no intrinsic basis or grounding:

Without Love, without the gravitational will of Spirit, chaos rules the universe.

But it doesn't, does it? Stars embrace one another to form galaxies; planets orbit the stars with elliptical precision; laws of physics command order in the entire universe. But this is only possible because everything is held accountable to a central meaning by an underlying theme, which is Love.

Love is that Force (Will) of Spirit which fits every star, planet and person together in a structured and meaningful sense but which, although invisible to humanity, has become known to humanity through the story of life.

Although invisible and intangible—and initially experienced by most people as a vast, empty nothingness, or an immeasurable "dark cloud of unknowing"—the Loving Will of Spirit, is very real. Like the thread weaving together the stories of the Bible, Love is the Original Theme (dare I say Commandment?) of the universe. It is God's Grand Plan that Christians speak of, the Fundamental Template from which everything is created and maintained.

Just as passion excites within us feelings and emotions, Love is the Primary Inspiration from which this universe and its creations—its *effections*—are aroused. From Affectionate Love stems the how and the why—the *effectiveness*—of life.

Love is first cause, and its affection becomes its effection.

THE LANGUAGE OF LOVE

The concept of Love as first cause is a difficult concept to grasp. To look at it from a different angle, I invite you to now take a step through the foyer of your mind and go behind the scenes of your local theatre company, to where a choreographer is rehearsing with her cast.

Ask yourself this: what message is she trying to convey with this particular dance routine you are now privy to? What concept is she hoping her audience on opening night understands with the vernacular of dance? In fact, what is any creative artist trying to accomplish in their chosen field?

The answer: pure, untainted emotion.

In essence, dancers, painters, poets, sculptors, actors, singers, musicians, and every other artist, are attempting to do nothing less than capture the precise moment of an emotion and present it to us in the language or dialect of their art. Like a statue sculpted from marble, art in its purest form is an emotion carved in time, in the sense that the chosen art form is the delivery vehicle for that emotion. Just as tears are the physical manifestation or evocation of non-physical emotions, such as sadness or joy, art forms are physical manifestations of the emotional essence or source from which that art form has arisen. Without emotion, tears would never arise. Without an emotional source, art forms would never be created.

Consequently, when we cut through to the emotional source of art we get to the very heart of its life, and when we do we actually feel its beat, its power, its energy, in our very own heart. Anyone that has been moved by a poem or ode, or been so engrossed with a story that they can't put the book down, has actually connected with the creative essence behind the words of that poem or story. Anyone that has felt a stirring of the heart upon hearing a sonata or symphony, or felt it squeeze tight at the vision of a dance recital, has experienced unity with the emotional essence behind the performance.

When the artist's emotion is identified in the moment of witnessing their art, the emotion transforms and becomes us: we are infused with the power of the emotion, its life, its being; we are its possession. In fact, the extent to which an artist is able to capture an emotion and have it arise in our self, have it impregnated within our own sense of being, is the extent of power contained within their art, which itself is a reflection of the artist's mastery of their craft.

Put another way, the degree to which we are possessed by the artist's emotion and become as one with it—the degree to which we become conscious of the artist's emotion in the art—is both the degree of power from which that art has been created and the degree of genius to which that artist has grown to be. Is not an accomplished actor someone that is so involved in the role that we no longer see them but the actual character they are playing, someone who in fact takes on board the personality of the character so much so that they become that person on stage or on film? Is not a masterful musician, a virtuoso, someone who feels and becomes one with the emotion of the music they are playing and thereby infuse it within us, the listener?

Our Higher Self, Big Mind, is such a powerful genius, such a masterful artist. Like the portrait of a great painter, we become conscious of its emotion (Love) in its art (Creation).

> *When we see through created life to its emotional essence, we in fact see and become One with the Source from which life has arisen—Love—the very thing that without which life would never have been created.*

Once drawn in and possessed by the Beauty of Love, we have clarity of mind, pureness of being. and we now see Love as first cause. We see, and come to know through direct experience, Love as the Primary Inspiration that aroused this whole universe through its passion for Goodness, Truth and Beauty. We now know the how and the why of life, we begin to sing in salutation and praise of it, and we understand the deeper meaning of St. Theresa's words quoted at the beginning of this section:

> *You want to know your lord's meaning in what I have done? Know it well, love was his meaning. Who reveals it to you? Love. What did he reveal to you? Love. Why does he reveal it to you? For love.*

This may seem a little daunting to anyone still harboring an innate fear of God's Power, but we are invited to revere, not fear. We are invited to let go of our worries and become conscious of Love and its healing presence, which in the human condition is essentially the sensation of being drawn toward Goodness, Truth and Beauty.

Love is nothing to be afraid of, just as our own reflection in the mirror is nothing to be afraid of. Once we are truly conscious of the Essence of Love as the basis of creation, once we are fully aware of our Source as the motivating power behind the design of the universe, we are swept along in the tide of its unifying force and thus come to "live in union with God, and God in [us]."[2]

Once we are conscious of Love as it is in the process of its unique manifestation in our individual lives, once we grasp the essence of life in the living of it, we begin to access the greatest power in the universe and reap the benefits of its manifestation in all aspects of our life and the lives of others we touch, physically, mentally and spiritually.

We come to feel truly blessed.

POINTS OF REMEMBRANCE #9

- You are healthier when love is a constant presence.
- Attention is a loving act to others and to yourself—it is giving recognition, being centered, and being aware.
- Love has the capacity to mend your broken heart.
- The more you believe in love, the greater its impact in your life.
- Grasping the essence of life in the living of it is becoming conscious of the emotion of love in its being.
- Is love an effect or an affect?
- Like the theme of a good book, Love is the invisible thread weaving together all characters, places, action, dialogue, tempo, and plot.
- Love is the invisible Force (Will) of Spirit that can be known through the story of life.
- Love is first cause.
- You are invited to revere, not fear.

9 THE MANIFESTATION OF LOVE

THE THREE FACES OF LOVE

JUST AS BEING exists as the trinity of Light, Life and Love, just as our Source flows with Goodness, Truth and Beauty, just as Spirit is the three-fold Intelligence, Power and Personality, so too Love, being the Willful Theme of the Universe, expresses itself as a triune. It too has three faces, three manifestations:

1. Love which is all-embracing.
2. Love which is unifying.
3. Love which is self-sacrificing.

The first people to recognize these three categories of love were the ancient Greeks. Five hundred years before the birth of Christ, with the relative peace and freedom that democratic union brought to the Athenian mainland and its islands, the Greek philosophers found that they had significantly more time to observe, rather than fight, the inhabitants of the country as they went about their daily activities.

In the cities and villages, these philosophers began to notice and document consistent patterns of human relationship-behavior that we would well recognize today—young lovers passionately embracing in the parks, mothers nurturing their babies in the home, siblings banding together in the streets, friends and colleagues showing camaraderie in the workplace, even neighbors acting compassionately toward strangers—and they came to the conclusion that love expressed itself in three distinctive, and sometimes overlapping, ways:

1. *Unconditionally*, such as the love of a parent for their child.
2. *Desirously*, such as the craving of one lover for another (an emotion which the Greeks believed was the direct result of Cupid's arrow striking our hearts, an emotion which they also believed we had no control over, being the direct will of Eros).
3. *Friendly*, or welcomingly, such as the bond of belonging struck between friends or siblings and even the long-term companionship between husbands and wives, the bond that can grow so strong we might even be compelled to lay down our life for the person we so love.

As a testament to the Greeks' fascination with the subject, over three hundred words in the modern Greek and Latin dictionaries define or contain the word "love", words such as aphrodisios, kupris, anerastos, eramai, philippia, lussa, but of their multitude we shall employ only three: Agape, Eros and Philos. From herein, Agape shall be used in reference to unconditional, all-embracing love; Eros shall be used in reference to love that is desirous and coveting; and Philos (the Greek word that is both a possessive term for beloved, or dear, and a verb to act in a friendly, kindly spirit) shall be used in reference to the love of companionship and friendship, the love that takes us under its wing and makes us feel as though we belong to an individual person or a wider family or community of people. (It is interesting to note here that the Modern Greek word for friend is *filos*.)

Ultimately, though, each Face of Love—unconditional (Agape), desirous (Eros) and friendship (Philos)—are simply the individual viewpoints or perspectives of the Eternal Fount as it is able to be understood by any specific personality. It is a personal relationship of sorts, the subjective interaction with that Infinite Sea which is without opposite, the private intercourse with that Uncreated Spring which exists even before space and time has been created. This individual relationship we have with Love is therefore the individual relationship we have with our Source.

If you wish to have a more intimate relationship with Love, if you wish, in particular, to expand your knowledge of the process of loving, you need only follow this simple rule:

Love yourself as Love would.

At heart, this rule is nothing more than an invitation to love yourself unconditionally, to love yourself with desire and to love yourself as a friend.

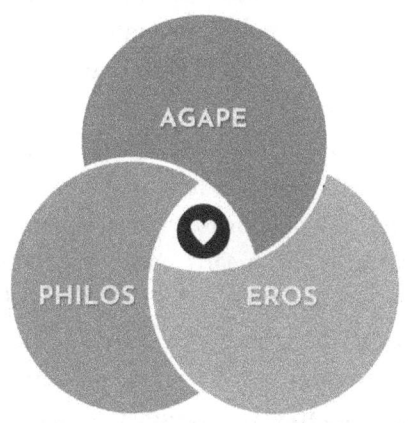

FIGURE 10:   The Three Faces of Love

AGAPE

To expand your understanding of the process of your Beloved's Unconditional Love for you, to visualize the Face of Absolute Love, first love yourself as you would love your child or future children.

Remember that there is perfection in the process; you are not a finished product.

> *You are forever a work in progress, always learning, always growing, a perpetual apprentice of life.*

Forgive yourself easily and often. Don't be too hard on yourself for making mistakes. Be kind to yourself for not always doing things right, for not being perfect or not playing in tune and take joy in yourself as you grow in Spirit. In this way, you will come in time to understand your Source as the gentle emanating presence of Unconditional Love; you will come to know in your own experience how the darkness of isolation magically vanishes in the presence of light.

If there is a concept to describe the Face of Unconditional Love, it is that force or presence which is all-embracing. Love's All-Embracing Presence means that wherever we are, so is Spirit, now and evermore. It means that "wheresoe'er be the letter, there with it is always its ink." Spirit's Unconditional Love is all-inclusive of everything and everyone. Nobody and no-thing is excluded. It is irrelevant who or what a person or thing is, they are always accepted in the sweeping embrace of the Absolute.

For who or what would Spirit reject if all things are of its essence? Would your Source reject itself? Would the ink reject the letter for being what it is?

Unconditional Love is therefore that Higher Awareness which recognizes and expresses its innate Oneness with All That Is. It is the love that breaks down and transcends all barriers of age, gender, race, wealth, class, sexual attraction, physical appearance, occupation, and all human-imposed requirements for approval. Human beings express this unconditional love, consciously or unconsciously, through the total acceptance of other people, things and events as they are without the need for anyone or anything to be other than who or what they are. In other words:

Humans can express unconditional love by allowing what is to be what is.

Unconditional love is the love we all know we are capable of, but are unable to explain where it comes from or how it came to be. Unconsciously, it usually happens without thought, as an instinct, a love that is spontaneous in its expression and which comes without the need for reciprocation or recompense. Consciously, it is an action centered in our Natural State of Being, an acceptance that is abundant and without need, and which, more importantly, comes without cost. When we love unconditionally, we know that nothing is taken away from our Natural State of Being or its essential qualities.

For when we love in this way we are actually loving our self.

EROS

Second, to expand your understanding of the process of your Beloved's Desire for you, the burning love of Eros, love yourself as you would love a partner you have just met, full of yearning. Want to be with yourself as much as you can. Make yourself the focus of your affections. Even be jealous of other people's attention and the threat they pose of diverting your focus away from yourself. Draw closer to your inner core and feel the abundance of your Natural State of Being. Do this and in time you will come to understand the unifying love of Spirit, you will understand how your Source is constantly drawing you closer to its core.

If there is a concept to describe the Face of Desirous Love, the

Face of Eros, it is that force of attraction which unifies all created life. If we are characters in the greatest story ever told, if we are protagonists in the Great Book of the Universe, then Desirous Love is that theme which pulls us back into alignment with its central core and holds us accountable to a central meaning (Oneness).

> *It is the invisible thread weaving together all the people, places, action, dialogue, tempo and plot throughout our lives, which, as living characters, we feel as the irresistible attraction to Goodness, Truth and Beauty.*

We know, feel and understand Love's infatuation, its yearning, its gravitational pull, as our own passion for charity, science and art. The zealous commitment of the scientist to seek the Truth is non-other than the heartfelt sense of Love's unifying force drawing her closer to itself, to Big Mind.

The enthusiasm of the pilgrim for Goodness or to do what's right (incidentally, the word enthuse stems from ancient Greek and means to be infused with the energy of the gods) is non-other than the heartfelt sense of Love's unifying force pulling him closer to itself, to Higher Being.

The infatuation of the artist for Beauty and purity is none other than the heartfelt sense of Love's unifying force attracting her nearer to itself, to Universal Soul.

We know, feel and understand the Love of our Source as the heavy feeling of weight in our heart for all things Good, True and Beautiful. As such, Desirous Love, Eros, is the most emotional of the three Faces of Love. It is the Face of Love most of us recognize, the one most written about in books and acted out on stage or on screen. It is also the emotion that is most commonly misinterpreted as the gratification of need fulfillment, which, as discussed previously, has the dangerous potential for untold suffering and the insuperable addictiveness of lust and jealousy. Moreover, it is also the emotion many of us have come to fear.

Why? Because it is unreasonable. We fear its lack of logic and reason. We fear its spontaneous and untamed nature. We fear it because, once swept up in it, we cannot control it. We fear it because we believe this kind of love can only lead to one inevitable conclusion: pain.

But there is no need to fear Eros. In the words of the Bible,[2]

There is no fear in love. But perfect love drives out fear.

The essence of love, as stated before, is as a purifying force: it clarifies the mind and cleanses our sense of being. Like iron in a blacksmith's forge, our impurities are incinerated, making us clean, making us stronger and yet, paradoxically, more malleable to the will of his hammer blows.

Likewise, the sizzling arrow of Cupid burns away our fear when it strikes our heart, and what remains is the untainted essence of our Natural State of Being. For this is what the Love of Eros does and its very intention: it brings us back to our self.

PHILOS

Third, to expand your understanding of the process of your Beloved's Friendship for you, love yourself as you would love a brother or sister, or even a close colleague. Support yourself when you need help. Lend a hand to yourself when you're in a spot of bother. Welcome yourself with open arms. Listen without judgment to your problems and give yourself a shoulder to cry on. Make yourself feel as though you belong to the family of the whole world, even the entire universe. Act this way, and in time you will come to appreciate the utter benevolence of your Source.

If there is a concept to describe the Face of Friendship Love, it is self-sacrifice. One of the characteristics of true friendship that sets it aside from all other feelings is altruism—it grieves us to see our fellow human beings suffering from pain, from despair, from anguish, and we want to unburden them of their pain. We want to take their suffering on board. We feel a need to carry their cross.

As the Face of Friendship, Philos is probably the closest of Love's three manifestations to the definition of love as a verb, of acting toward the spiritual growth of another or one's self.

When my daughter was only nine or ten months of age, I came to understand firsthand the Love of Philos and its daily impact on my life. At the time, my daughter was suffering from a minor surgical condition that needed hospitalization and treatment, which, although non-life-threatening, was on occasion extremely painful. On the day of surgery, before my wife and I had taken her to the hospital, my daughter began squealing in agony. She couldn't as yet talk, only look at us with questioning, tear-soaked eyes.

While my wife hugged and tended to her, I began wishing that I could do something to ease her pain and suffering.

"Jeez, she's only a kid," I said quietly, directing myself to God. "She doesn't need to go through this. Just let her be. Give me her pain. I can handle it. Let me take her pain on board and set her free."

It was then, at that moment of asking for her pain to be transferred to me, I was struck with the sudden immensity of what Jesus had done on the cross at Calvary. Such was his love for us that he took on board all of humanity's suffering and pain in order that we would no longer have to endure it.

I had wanted to unburden one instance of one person's pain, my daughter's. Jesus had been whipped and nailed to the cross to end the suffering of the entire world, to ease every single instance of pain that had been, and will be, endured by every man, woman and child in the history of humanity. The very thought of it was mind-boggling. But imagine actually doing it! I came to understand for the first time, because of what Jesus went through, because of his love for humanity, this incredible truth:

I no longer needed to suffer the despair and anguish of separation from Source.

He had taken on board all our pain and set us free. But whether or not we believe in the deification of Jesus or the purpose of his life, we can still believe in his intention and hope for his fellow man. It is not a prerequisite to believe that he is the Word made flesh to believe and understand his personal feelings for us as individuals. Nor is it necessary to be a Christian to understand and believe in his passion for others.

At the very least, Jesus was a man who loved humanity, one who meant every word when he said: "Greater love has no one than this, that he lay down his life for his friends."[2]

Other than the self-sacrificial act of the crucifixion itself, Jesus no more succinctly related the strength and power of his love for humanity than with those words. Like a loving parent, like a good friend, like a beautiful spouse, he wanted nothing more than to take on board humanity's grief and sorrow in order that we would no longer have to live with it. He wanted to give us an outlet. He wanted to mend the broken bridge with our Source, by laying down his own body across the gap so that we could cross over it. His deepest desire was to fulfill his destiny upon the cross so that we could unburden our pain and suffering, and therein live with peace and harmony—our birthright—in this lifetime.

Jesus' hope, it can be argued, was that his presence in our hearts should open the door to the felt sense of our Natural State of Being. His hope was that we should be filled with the joy of eternal life, the strength and courage of unity and companionship, the sense of belonging and worthiness, the peace that is not of this world, and the freedom to be who we are. His hope was that with his presence we should be, and feel, loved. For eternity.

Philos is therefore the ultimate act of benevolence, the act of giving one's self to another for the benefit of that other. It is selfless. It is altruistic. It is self-sacrificial.

There is no greater love in the heart of any man, woman or child than the desire to surrender one's self for the benefit of another.

THE GREAT AFFAIR

In the months preceding my thirtieth birthday, after much introspection and questioning of my life's meaning and the meaning of life overall, I came to the decision that before I died I wanted to have a great love affair. I wasn't exactly sure what I was asking for, but I knew that I wanted to be the best that I could be in my short time here on earth. I also knew that I wanted to live my life to the fullest and experience the utter majesty, awe and wonder this universe had to offer, and the best way I thought I could achieve this was through love.

I guess I was somewhat of a closet romantic. My head was swimming with great expectations of adventure and fantasy, swashbuckling heroes (me), swooning heroines and damsels in distress, but I had no idea how to put these notions of love together in any real or practical manner. I didn't know or understand yet the three Faces of Love. Love was still, in my mind, very much Eros based—desire, desire, desire—but something inside me knew that there was more to know about love and about life.

I was also under no illusion that a lifetime of learning was set before me. As far as I was concerned, love was always going to be difficult. But I also knew that the greatest people in history—Jesus, Rumi, Ghandi, Mother Theresa, Martin Luther King, to name a few—shared one commonality: they all had a great relationship with humanity.

All these great men and women had a great love affair with the people of the world, and they expressed this love in one form or another through service and contribution to other human beings. So, for me, the path was obvious: to love greatly.

THE MANIFESTATION OF LOVE

At first, my great love affair was focused solely on my partner, now wife. I wanted to start my adventure with love by taking small steps. If I could love one person fully and properly, it would benefit my goal of developing compassion and loving-kindness for everyone (I had discovered Buddhism about this time).

But then, some while later, it became clear that what I had really asked for was a great love affair with God. I realized that the journey of life is about learning to love not just your partner, your children, and your extended family, but that life is learning to love God through humanity and through self. The great men and women I so admired and had set up as role models, the people I deemed the greatest of all and who I respected over and above everyone else, had a deep and passionate love for God, and this love manifested as a love for their fellow human beings.

As the months and years passed, I then came to understand, through various readings and personal experiences, God as the Intelligent Spirit of Love and not as a preternatural being made in the image of man (the image classically portrayed in Michelangelo's centerpiece of the Sistine Chapel, where Adam is reaching up to touch the outstretched finger of God, a white-bearded old man in the sky). In gradually weaning myself off the image of God as human, in gradually realizing the Intelligent Spirit of Love as the Source of all things, it became clear that my intent for a great love affair was in actuality a wish for a great affair with Love itself.

Finally, during a meditation session, Love was revealed to me as a vision of a constantly blooming rose, which simply meant that once the seed of Love was planted in my heart, its flower would never die. I also like to think of it another way:

Love is always in the process of being what it is becoming.

It is also interesting to note the dual definitions of the word 'becoming' in this context, of meaning something that is never complete but always bettering itself and, second, that which is flattering and appropriate. The phrase, "Love becomes you," now takes on multiple meanings.

This vision of the rose helped to clarify the intention I'd had to have a great love affair.

In other words:

> *To be better today than yesterday, to be better tomorrow than today. To constantly blossom.*

My Great Affair, I at last knew, was a never-ending journey, a constant pilgrimage, from Eros to Philos to Agape, and then back to Eros again. I had come to learn that life is a closed circle, and that, although all earthly affairs must eventually come to an end, the Great Affair is eternal.

THE LENS OF LOVE

If it is our intent for a Great Affair to manifest and become a reality in our daily existence—a love of Life, a love of Spirit, a love of Love, a love of humanity—the concepts of Love as that which is Unconditional (Agape), that which is Desirous (Eros), and that which is Friendship (Philos), must, through necessity, be acknowledged and willfully embraced.

Even though Love, as the Source of all things, is beyond the duality of time and space, even though Love simply is and cannot be held or limited to a single definition, it is read or understood through its three differing facial expressions, Agape, Eros and Philos, which in turn represent both the how and the why of Love's manifestation.

> *Love is both the action and the thing doing the action. It is the verb and the noun. The complete sentence, in other words.*

THE MANIFESTATION OF LOVE

First of all, Agape, Eros and Philos are how we, as duality-bound human beings, experience and identify Spirit's Love in the day-to-day events of our life, the magnifying glass through which we read the Words of Love written throughout the story of the universe. Second, Agape, Eros and Philos are Spirit's Theme, the Why, the Grand Plan, the reason for which everything exists.

Just as the Uncreated Light is both the visual light of the observed object and the means of perceiving that light—sight—so too Love—Agape, Eros and Philos—is the lens through which Love visualizes itself—unconditionally, desirously and friendly.

Through the 'how' we understand the 'why', and through the 'why' we understand the 'how'. This is just another way of saying:

In the deepest Being of Love the observer and the observed are One.

A sure sign that we have come to live with the Oneness of Love, that we have come to live in union with Spirit, is the amount of creativity and play that we employ in our everyday activities. It is the amount of freedom with which we live. This is because freedom is an essential quality of Agape, Eros and Philos. Love is, in a word, free.

True to the tripartite nature of Love, the meaning of freedom can be interpreted and experienced in three distinct ways. First, Love is free from conditions. It is unconditional. We do not need to do anything to have it. We do not need to pay a price for it. It is a gift. It is free.

Second, Love is free from limitations. It is boundless. It is infinite and eternal. It has no shackles or fetters. It is free from the chains of space and time.

Third, Love sets us free. Our past is forgiven. Our present is given a purpose. Our future is secure.

With these three facets of Love, we can honestly expect to live our life with the freedom that is our birthright and inheritance.

Stolen Love

Unfortunately, the experience of Love is far removed from most of our daily reality. Sadness, insecurity, rejection, turmoil and limitation—disharmony from the felt sense of our Natural State of Being—is generally the norm. Negative, self-destructive emotions tend to subordinate positive, inspirational emotions. The feelings of fear, anger, hatred, greed, pride, and idolatry—'The Six Thieves'—habitually steal the experience of who we really are, which is love. Through our unconscious identification with them, The Six Thieves pilfer or extinguish any spark that might otherwise shine forth from the center of our being.

No matter how strong or powerful they may feel, however, emotions are only messengers. The Six Thieves and their progeny—bitterness, frustration, resentment, gluttony, sloth, arrogance, righteousness, lust, and so forth—merely indicate the lens or filter we are using to view the universe. Emotions are only informing us which lens or filter we are using to sift and analyze the data we are receiving from the world in and around us.

An important point is that these emotions are not the lens or filter itself, although they are often confused for it and frequently blamed as the cause of suffering. When this happens, a negatively reinforcing downward spiral is established, one that threatens to keep us in darkness for an entire lifetime. It is not uncommon for our mind to turn in on itself, to become constantly negative and self-destructive.

How often have we feared our own fear? How many times have we been angry at being angry? How easy is it to become frustrated at being frustrated?

Through blaming the emotions for how we feel, the mind can hide within many dark places, places where the flame of love has little or no chance of survival.

THE MANIFESTATION OF LOVE

But there is no point in shooting the messenger. In truth, we should be blessing and showering praise upon these harbingers for the information they present to us. Blaming the emotions themselves for how we feel will do nothing to abate our suffering.

Instead, we must get to the heart of the matter and find out what is causing our fear, anger, hatred, greed, pride, and idolatry to arise in the first place. If these emotions predominate our sense of being, we must find the lens or filter through which they are being visualized and experienced before we make the mistake of totally surrendering our self to, and identifying with, them and thus inadvertently become them.

The lens or filter, of course, is forgetfulness, the belief that we are born isolated from our Source and must accumulate material possessions and wealth to make up for the shortfall.

Fear, anger, hatred, greed, pride, and idolatry are simply the result of viewing the world through the lens of forgetfulness.

They are the messages that are sifted through the filter of isolation. But changing the filter of forgetfulness to the greatest, most open lens or filter available—Oneness—swapping it with the belief that we are born connected to our Source, has the effect of freeing our Natural State of Being. Through the lens of Love everything is renewed, made fresh, reborn. Even though we are still in the same place, we literally see another world.

It stands to reason, therefore, that because the awareness of Oneness is integral to the definition or makeup of Love, the greatest, most open lens or filter available to humanity is Love itself.

When we experience the world through the filter of loving eyes—Oneness—we see the sacredness of everything.

We see the Presence of Spirit, the Essence of Light, Life and Love in everything.

We see, as Paulo Coelho writes in *The Witch of Portobello*,[17] a world that is

> *... full of love, regardless of how that love is manifested, a love that forgives our mistakes and redeems our sins.*

When we gaze lovingly at humanity, we see people in their totality, their wholeness, and no longer stare and reduce them to numbers or individual body parts.

When Jesus advised us to love God with our whole heart and to love our neighbor as we would love our self, he did so because he knew love works both ways:

Love is the process and *the destination.*

Love is that which we use to experience the very thing that we use. When we find that we aren't experiencing the abundance of our Natural State of Being has to offer, our emotions are telling us that Love cannot express itself through us, which is the very reason we are here, to shine with Spirit's Light. Something is blocking our awareness of the Theme of Life.

Contrary to what might initially be thought, anger is not the block, only the sign that we are blocking the expression of Love. Greed is not the block, only the signal that a blockage is occurring from our Natural State of Being.

When water is flooding from the kitchen sink onto the floor, the problem is not the water but a blockage in the pipes. Fear, anger, hatred, greed, pride, and idolatry are the mess upon the kitchen floor. They are not the blockage of Love, only the result of it. If the blockage is not attended to, the mess stagnates, and what was once a pure, flowing Force from the Source becomes an unpalatable, angry, frustrated experience of life.

The point is this:

---

[17] Paulo Coelho. *The Witch of Portobello.* Harper Collins Publishers, 2007

Blockages are the telltale signs that the lens we have chosen to see the world through is too narrow, that our filter is too small.

The repercussions of our blockages, emotions, and The Six Thieves especially, are therefore a choice, often an unconscious choice, of which spectacles we wish to don. They are a choice of which lens we wish to identify with and view the world and our existence in it.

Human beings are the only life forms on the planet that have the ability of self-determination—how to react, how to respond and how to behave. You have the power, the free will, to make a choice of what lens to see through in every moment of your life. You have the power, in every moment, to choose how and what to be—who you are is a choice.

How you see the world and your place in it is your responsibility.

But if we choose to react, respond and behave with emotion, we can literally become carried away by that emotion. So the question remains, what do you choose?

Do you choose to wear the spectacles of forgetfulness and see the world and yourself unconsciously with anger, hate, greed, pride, and idolatry?

Or do you choose the spectacles of remembrance—Oneness—and see the world and yourself consciously with joy, security, acceptability, peace and freedom?

Do you choose to see the cup half empty, or half full?

Do you choose to SEE the Source of all that is Love?

POINTS OF REMEMBRANCE #10

- Love expresses itself in three main ways: unconditionally, desirously, and friendly.

- Unconditional Love, Agape, is your Higher Awareness which recognizes and expresses your innate Oneness with All That Is.

- Desirous Love, Eros, holds you accountable to a central meaning, Oneness, which you feel as the irresistible attraction to Goodness, Truth and Beauty.

- Friendship Love, Philos, is the self-sacrificial act of giving yourself to another for the benefit of that other.

- The Great Affair is a constant pilgrimage from Eros to Philos to Agape and then back to Eros again.

- Love is both the action and the thing doing the action, the verb and the noun, the complete sentence.

- Love is free.

- Emotions are only messengers.

- The most open lens available to you is Love.

- How you perceive the world is your responsibility—who you are is a choice.

PART IV

PERCEPTION

"It is the nature of an hypothesis, when once a man has conceived it, that it assimilates every thing to itself, as proper nourishment; and, from the first moment of your begetting it, it generally grows the stronger by every thing you see, hear, read, or understand."

Laurence Sterne; Tristram Shandy
(18th Century)

10 BIG MIND, SMALL MIND

1 + 1 = 3

To feel the constant Presence of Spirit, to see the Goodness, Truth and Beauty that is not of this world—to live with The Five Pillars of Love on a permanent basis—it is important to understand the mechanism of perception itself.

If the goal of salvation, and thereby the end of suffering, is to perceive the Uncreated Light, the Infinite Life, and the Eternal Love, to SEE our Source and live in the Heart of Spirit, it is to our benefit to become familiar with the process by which we make that observation. Just as a TV repairman must know how to assemble and disassemble every electrical and physical component of a TV set, we must also get to grips with the components of the pathway of perception and dismantle the body, brain and mind in order to fully appreciate the process of knowing Reality.

The human condition, in fact, has a very interesting way of seeing the universe both within and without. In essence, perception follows a set pathway beginning with the five sense organs of the "flesh" and finishing with the construction of a mental image of what we think is "out there" or "inside our self". The process is both physiological and psychological, both scientific and creative.

Ultimately, though, perception comes down to one thing, *choice*, and it is either a process that occurs consciously or unconsciously.

The Brain is Not the Mind

Before discussing the anatomical pathway of perception, however, an important distinction must first be drawn between the mind and the brain. It is worth noting that contemporary science and medicine makes no such distinction; the brain and mind to most doctors and neurological scientists are one and the same.

Without question, the brain is an important organ of the body, like the liver or the heart. It is not, however, in my experience, the entity we understand as the mind, as much as London is not the cultural entity we know as the United Kingdom, although it is its thriving nerve center.

For several decades now, a body of scientific thought has grown to accept the distinct possibility that the mind is a non-localized entity. The premise is that the mind is more like a field of energy, like a magnetic or gravitational field, than a quantifiable physical organ that can be weighed, measured and dissected.

As such, the "mind-field" cannot be seen, only detected through the force it generates and the effect it exerts on its surroundings. Just as the first person to break the shackles of gravity and orbit the earth, cosmonaut Yuri Gagarin, professed upon his return to the Soviet Union that he hadn't seen God while he was floating above the planet, there is no physical evidence of the mind to be found in the brain. Slice open the grey matter and we won't encounter a single thought. Blend it to a pulp and we will only find a soupy slop of water, proteins and carbohydrates, without so much as a single dream, idea or flash of insight. The mind-field is non-physical.

As an aside, it is also notable that the philosophical basis of ancient Chinese medicine centers on such an invisible field of energy, one which has many similarities to the non-localized mind-field we are proposing. This invisible energy flows through and around the human body. Blockages of this flow of energy, if not attended to, are eventually expressed as physical pain and disease.

Acupuncture and other techniques aim to resolve these blockages and restore the natural flow of energy and, thus, bodily health.

Whether or not, however, we consider this invisible energy field as the mind itself, the surprising conclusion that any scientist, pilgrim or artist in the habit of seeking Truth, Goodness and Beauty must eventually accommodate is that, in keeping with the nature of an energy field or force, the mind is not enclosed within the confines of the skull.

The mind permeates the body and the world around it.

The Mind-Continuum

Having believed for so many years that my own mind was imprisoned within the thick cage of bone sitting atop my spine, the first time the revelation that it was actually boundless and not limited to the confines of my body came, not surprisingly, as a sudden shock.

It happened on a trip to South Africa. I was contemplating the nature and relationship of the mind to the outside world in a seaside café, when suddenly, like the waves crashing onto the nearby beach, I was inundated with the conviction that my mind was not separated from the rest of the world, and in fact the universe, because it is intimately one with the Mind of God, Big Mind.

The sensation was that of receiving an infinite amount of knowledge in a split second, an instant spiritual "download" from the Universal Super Computer, as it were.

Paradoxically, there was no longer any "me" consciousness, just Awareness. I felt as if I was at the same time infinitely vast and infinitesimally minute, bigger beyond contemplation and smaller than could be imagined. I understood with utter certainty that God's Consciousness and my consciousness were united as one within a Spectrum of Awareness: my mind was a continuum with Big Mind.

Then the moment ebbed away and I was back in the flow of my limited "small mind" consciousness again, but the feeling that I had been soaked with the Fullness of Spirit lingered with me for a long while afterward.

I knew with complete surety that no consciousness exists other than God's—there is no consciousness but Consciousness—and that any awareness I happen to use in my day-to-day existence is none other than Source Awareness. Much like a PC with intranet capabilities, I was linked to the Universal Super Computer via an internal connection that could not be switched off, only ignored or put to sleep. I also knew that I could no longer hang onto the belief that my mind and my consciousness were limited to the space between my ears. My brain and my mind were not the same thing.

Although far from offering this episode as valid scientific proof of a Higher Intelligence or Big Mind, this account of Source Awareness does highlight the fundamental error we can make of mistaking our brain for our mind. If we wish to perceive and experience our Natural State of Being on a permanent basis, it is imperative that we become comfortable in distinguishing between the brain and the mind.

As previously touched upon in the first chapter:

We must become comfortable with the fact that we are bigger than we think we are.

The brain is not the source of our consciousness, our mind, just its receptacle. Scientists and most doctors claim otherwise. As with any analytical interpretation of the world, they have a top-down approach to the brain and mind as opposed to a bottom-up approach. The top-down approach says that consciousness arises from biology. Biology is primary, consciousness secondary—in essence, first the brain then the mind. Look at evolution, the scientists and doctors say. See how consciousness grows and advances with every leap in evolution, from amoebas and bacteria to fungi, plants and trees to insects, fish and reptiles to birds, primates and humans.

Consciousness progresses and evolves with each stage of biological development, especially neurological development. We are the highest form of intelligence on the planet only because our brain has evolved the most in comparison to other species. Granted, they say, the chemicals and proteins of the brain's interconnecting neural network does not fully explain the phenomenon of consciousness, but neither does it refute the notion that consciousness is founded in biology. Consciousness, they counter, is just a case of the sum being greater than its parts.

In essence, whether you want to believe it or not, the evidence points irrefutably to the fact that $1 + 1 = 3$.

The bottom-up approach, in contrast, says biology is a product of consciousness. Consciousness is primary, biology secondary—in essence, mind first, brain second.

The bottom-up approach does not ask you to believe in nonsensical equations like $1 + 1 = 3$, nor does it ask you to refute the scientific fact of evolution, just to believe that Consciousness is the foundation upon which everything is built, the Formless Source of all form.

Since the Big Bang, all Consciousness has done is to keep asking biology to meet it halfway. Consciousness has been, and always will be, the impetus for evolution. From it biology derives the evolutionary drive to progress from amoeba and bacteria all the way through the insect, plant and animal kingdoms to humanity, and even beyond. (The evolutionary drive, of course, manifests on many different levels of awareness: geographical, environmental and natural selection; chromosomal aberrations and genetic mutation; the instinct to protect and survive; sexual drive; pleasure seeking and pain avoidance; fear and love; transcendence and Oneness, and so forth.)

Looking at it from the bottom-up perspective, life on this planet really is greater than the sum of its parts, but not because of its biological nature—because its nature lies beyond biology.

In respect to the differentiation between the brain and the mind, Buddhists have a simple analogy that helps to understand the bottom-up approach. The human condition, they say, is like a cup dipped into a river. In other words, we are part of a greater whole:

> *We are a part of the Whole that is not apart from the Whole.*

Although this cup and river analogy is open to many kinds of interpretation (which is its true intent, to stimulate understanding of the true nature of life), one way of considering it, in the context of our brain and mind, is that our mind is the river into which our brain, the cup or receptacle, can continually dip and replenish itself with ideas, thoughts, wishes, will, and enthusiasm.

The cup does not create the water, the conscious mind. The water is primary. The cup is just the receptacle for the water.

What we must now ask is this: Am I the cup, or am I the river?

TIME-BOUND MIND

As we will discuss shortly, the process of perception in a healthy person occurs stupendously fast. From the moment our eyes catch sight of a bird swooping from a branch, or our ears catch orchestral music floating across a concert hall, the time it takes our mind to register these events is a matter of microseconds.

But the fact that it takes any time at all means that we always perceive events in the past, never in "real time." This time lag between what is happening and the perception of it, albeit extremely small, gives an intriguing insight into the workings of the mind.

Our mind, like our body, is time bound. Big Mind, our Source from which everything is created, lies beyond the physical universe as we experience it and thus beyond space and time. That is why Yuri Gagarin couldn't see God while he was orbiting the earth.

Yet God is still immanent in creation and the universe, in time and space. This may or may not be of any comfort to know, but it is the way it has to be for humans to exist and continue to experience this particular moment in four-dimensional reality. As the only consciousness that exists is Spirit's, the fact that we are able to be aware of our body and the outside world is because we use Spirit's Awareness. Big Mind is intimate and personal with our small mind, just as the ocean is intimate and personal with all the fish that swim in its waters.

The Spectrum of Awareness is intimate and personal with every created thing in space and time.

In its transcendent position outside the four-dimensional universe, Big Mind is aware of everything that has ever happened, is happening, and will happen. But this does not mean we know everything. Human beings could not function in this state. We would be overwhelmed with sensory input and, like a computer suddenly overloaded with data, we would simply freeze and cease to work.

All at once, we would see dinosaurs roaming the prehistoric earth. We would hear the screams of millions of babies being born. We would taste exotic fruits from the distant planets of future humans. From the abyss of time we would hear everyone's thoughts, feel everyone's desires, see everyone's dreams. The chaos would be catastrophic for any one individual.

Because it could not function knowing everything at once, our small mind is deliberately limited to the temporal experiences of one particular person. It has been created or projected from Big Mind with the sole purpose of maintaining our distinct and unique position in time and space.

Some people, however, have the unexplained ability to garner awareness or knowledge beyond the accepted physical reaches of their brain and body. They have the gift of reading somebody else's mind (ESP), or they can see into the future (prophesy), or even manipulate objects distant from themselves (telekinesis).

In fact, most people have had an extrasensory experience at some point in their life, even if it is something as simple as hearing the telephone ring and knowing without a shadow of doubt who is calling before they pick up the handset. Documented medical examples also exist of clairvoyance. For example, twins having the uncanny ability to feel each other's sudden pain, or a mother knowing the exact moment her child has been injured, even when they were separated and incommunicado at the time.

In the general population, though, these experiences are weak and unreliable. Yet, on the other hand, extrasensory experiences do lend circumstantial evidence to the fact that the mind's behavior is not confined to the spatial or temporal frameworks of the brain. The mind, it appears, operates more like a field or force of intelligence extending from the body and capable of "touching" and interacting with other minds or mind-like fields.

THE MIND-FIELD

Most high school physics or science students are aware that the flow of electrical energy through a metallic wire generates a magnetic field around that wire. There is a direct correlation between the strength of the electrical current and the strength of the magnetic field generated: increase the current of electricity and the power of the magnetic field increases; turn the electricity off, and the magnetic field disappears.

In addition, a wire with high resistance or opposition to the flow of electrical current through it will produce a comparatively weaker magnetic field than a wire with less electrical resistance (or its converse, more electrical conductivity).

Placing a compass in the vicinity of an electrical wire and watching the effect upon the needle when the electricity is turned on and off is the easiest way to replicate these findings.

FIGURE 11:   The Electromagnetic Fiel

The flow of electricity, however, does not create the magnetic field. Using imagery provided by quantum physics, the electrical current serves only to direct the force or power of magnetism that already exists as a waiting potential in the greater body of the electromagnetic spectrum. The magnetic field is therefore a relative field, one that comes into being through its relationship to the flow of electrons. The electrical current through the wire simply brings out, or coaxes from hiding, what is already waiting as an uncreated formless entity in the uncertain realm of quantum dynamics.

The manifestation of a magnetic field by an electrical current is, in fact, similar to the events at the creation of the universe, a small-scale version of the Big Bang—it calls forth into four-dimensional reality of space and time what had hitherto existed un-manifest in the non-dimensional, infinite and eternal "nothingness" from which everything was created. If anything, the generation of a magnetic field is an act of re-creation.

Likewise, if we consider a living entity to be sustained from birth to death by a life-force or life-energy, then the flow of life-energy through a living entity has a similar effect of generating a field in and around that entity, from an organism as small and simple as a bacterium to something the size and complexity of a human being. Living entities or cells, in this sense, are conduits of life-energy, although the field that is generated is not a magnetic field but a field of awareness—a mind-field.

This mind-field is a field of intelligence permeating the living organism as a direct result of the flow of life-energy through the organism's cells, a kind of containment field of consciousness that localizes a focus of awareness to that unique and specific individual organism.

Comparatively speaking, the power or force of intelligence of a bacterium is billions and billions of times weaker than the power or force generated around the human body, but it still has consciousness, a mind-field, albeit one that is working on a subliminal or sub-conscious level not much different from vegetation. This level, in fact, prevents us from participating in any kind of meaningful communication or exchange of information, similar to the way in which the evolutionary advances of software and hardware prevents modern computers from directly communicating or sharing information with their ancestral computers of the 1960s.

Furthermore, the power or force of the mind-field generated in and around a neuronal cell, for example, is significantly greater than that generated in and around a blood cell or muscle cell, even though the flow of life-energy is equal throughout every cell of the body.

The cells of the brain have evolved a remarkable ability to amplify the current of life-energy flowing from our Source, or at least reduce resistance to it, and thereby generate a stronger, more powerful field of consciousness than the cells in the rest of the body, almost as if they have the ability to generate a field within a field (see *Figure 12* below).

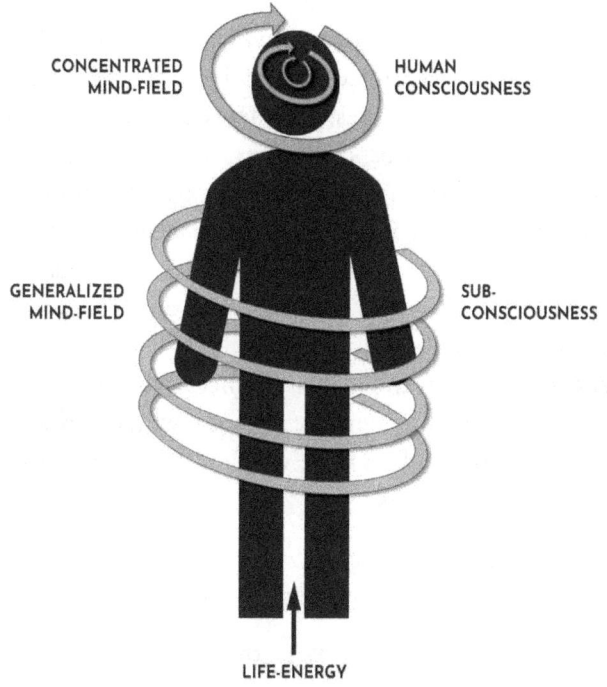

FIGURE 12: The Mind-Field

In essence, the brain has evolved to become the dominant powerhouse of mind-field generation, which serves to focus and thereby give the impression that consciousness originates there. But it doesn't, the only awareness that exists is the Uncreated Light. No consciousness exists other than Spirit's.

Confusion as to the origins of consciousness therefore arises in humans because consciousness is highly concentrated in and around the neuronal cells, but the brain is by no means its exclusive domain. This dominant awareness of the mind-field generated by the brain, however, is what we have come to know, rightly or wrongly, as the human consciousness, and the general awareness of the mind-field generated by the rest of the body is what we have come to know as the sub-consciousness.

The origin or fountain from which life-energy flows is the Formless Realm of our Source—Light, Life and Love—the Infinite, Eternal All. For our purposes, life-energy can be thought of as the highest form of consciousness that exists, or supra-consciousness, and when it flows from our Source through the human body it generates, in an analogous manner to the electromagnetic field, a localized relative field of awareness in and around that individual body—a mind-field—with a strong bias and focus around the neurons of the brain.

Please note, however, for convenience of the analogy, the body is taken to be a separate conduit through which supra-conscious life-energy can flow, like a wire, whereas in reality nothing exists other than Consciousness.

Everything we see, every form, is a manifestation of Consciousness at some relative level of awareness.

As such, Consciousness may be thought of as flowing through itself, a self-perpetuating flow of energy that generates the illusion of variable levels or qualities of awareness—sub-consciousness, consciousness, and supra-consciousness—much as the temperature of the ocean is layered with currents of coldness and warmth but is still one single body of water. Ascending through the levels of sub-consciousness, consciousness and supra-consciousness, is therefore like rising through the thermal layers of Big Mind.

Putting it another way, the flow of life-energy through the body, as with our high school experiment with electricity and magnetism, is only indirectly responsible for the creation of the human mind-field. Just as the electrical current through the wire directs the force or power of magnetism that already exists as a waiting potential in the greater body of the electromagnetic spectrum, the flow of life-energy through the cells of the body brings out or conjures what is already waiting as an uncreated entity in the Formless Spectrum of Awareness, what already exists without form in Consciousness.

> *Like the magnetic field around an electrical wire, the mind-field is a relative field, in that it only exists in relation to the flow of supra-conscious life-energy through the body, and in particular the cells of the brain.*

This unique mind-field permeating in and around the body is a focus of awareness within the greater Spectrum of Awareness, Big Mind, a localization of consciousness that we have come to recognize as the awareness of the self. With it we are aware of our position in time and space as an individual living and breathing and thinking in our own particular manner. We are aware of our bodies and what is around us. We are aware that I am "me" and you are "you."

This localized field of awareness of the individual self is known as the ego.

EGO CONSCIOUSNESS

The oldest tale of awakening to ego consciousness is in Genesis, the fall of Adam and Eve from Grace. Having lived in communion with God in the Garden of Eden, shame and guilt descended upon them once they had taken a bite from the forbidden fruit.

"Who told you that you were naked?" God asked of them.

Adam and Eve trembled in their hiding place because they were suddenly aware of their individual nakedness, awareness that was a direct consequence of eating fruit from the Tree of Knowledge. And with the knowledge of themselves as individuals came the inevitable separation from paradise and separation from God.

There is something of that moment in Eden in all of us. The creation of an isolated ego (eating the forbidden fruit), from our Source (Eden) has the inevitable consequence of banishment from paradise. In a sense, it isn't technically banishment but a logical result of cause and effect, like telling a child that if they put their hand on a hot stove they're going to get burned.

In other words, if we insist on wanting to know about the duality of good and evil, then we have to leave paradise—the Land of Absolute that has no opposite, only Goodness, Truth and Beauty—to find out what it really means. We have to become conscious of our individuality and thus separation from God.

Through the process of negation, we have to know what is not to know what is. We have to know sin.

Before Adam and Eve descended from Eden, they communed as one with All That Is. They lived in infinite and eternal bliss. They had abiding joy, security, acceptance, peace and freedom. They had the Love of God.

Once they took a bite from the apple, however, they were confronted with the dawning of themselves as isolated egos, unique individuals separated from paradise. That which was infinite and eternal in Eden was now experienced as finite and temporal, a frightening world bound by space and time. The relative world of good and evil, duality, was suddenly made known to them. They now experienced the opposite of Eden in all its horror—sadness, insecurity, rejection, chaos and imperfection. Most of all, they felt utterly abandoned and forsaken by God.

The important point here is not the banishment from Eden, but the fact that it is an illusion—a failure to remember our true self. Eating the fruit from the Tree of Knowledge is like Snow White eating the poisoned apple handed to her by the queen, her evil step-mother: it sends us to sleep.

The poison seeps into our being and clouds our consciousness in a fog of forgetfulness. Like Adam and Eve, we forget that we are still connected to our Source, to the paradise from which we are created and still belong. We forget that our mind is just a localized field of awareness that has been generated from the flow of life-energy through the conduit of our bodies, that our human intellect is an intimate product of the Light of Intelligence shining upon it.

In our forgetful sleepiness we live in sin, the belief that we are isolated and separated from God, abandoned and forsaken. We forget that we have been born with everything we need. We forget that the connection to Big Mind is an essential part of who we are and that we don't have to accumulate material wealth in order to fill the dark void of isolation.

In our foggy slumber we forget our Natural State of Being and live a life of illusion and suffering. Like Snow White, we await the handsome prince to save us from our fate.

But has the savior not already come to kiss our lips and awake us from our slumber, to live happily ever after in His Kingdom?

POINTS OF REMEMBRANCE #11

- Your brain is not your mind.

- The bottom-up approach to the nature of reality states that consciousness is primary, biology secondary.

- Your mind permeates the body and the world around it.

- No consciousness exists other than Spirit's.

- You always perceive events in the past.

- The mind-field is a relative field.

- Your brain has evolved to become the dominant powerhouse of mind-field generation.

- Like Adam and Eve, it is easy to forget that you are still connected to your Source, to the paradise from which you have been created and still belong.

11 THE PATHWAY OF PERCEPTION

SENSORY PERCEPTION

HAVING DRAWN THE distinction between the brain (the organic conduit of life-energy) and the mind (the localized field of awareness), we can now turn our attention to the physiological and psychological aspects of perception.

In humans, the pathway of perception goes something like this: small nerve endings or receptors of the five senses of sight, hearing, smell, taste, and touch react to an inner or outer stimulus, which then pass on this information through the nervous system into our brains, which is then interpreted by the mind and made conscious as a mental image, with more often than not the added attachment of a label or judgement—good, bad, like, dislike, hate, pleasurable, and so forth.

The continuous reproduction of labeled conscious images flick from one to the other like the still frames of a movie reel. It is, in fact, like watching a never-ending documentary across the cinema screen of our mind with the added commentary of our own narrative voice.

As such, there are six basic steps in the pathway of perception.

-> Step 1: Stimulation of sense receptors.
-> Step 2: Relay of sensory information to the cerebrum via the nervous system.
-> Step 3: Packaging of sensory information as neurochemicals in the cerebrum.

-> Step 4: Sensory analysis and image construction by the mind.

-> Step 5: Image labeling and naming.

-> Step 6: Relay of image response from mind to body.

Step 1: Stimulation of Sense Receptors

Step 1 in the pathway of perception involves the activation of our body's sense receptors by an external or internal stimulus.

For instance, the receptors located in our retina detect photons of light, either as color or as black and white, entering our eyes through the pupil. The ear also has two main types of receptors. The outer eardrum, or tympanic membrane, detects the vibrational movements of sound, whereas the inner ear, or cochlea, monitors our movements and position in three-dimensional space so that we know whether we are up or down, left or right, forward or backward in relation to the outside world.

Skin receptors also detect many things in the strange and varied world of our environment, including pain, temperature (hot and cold) and touch (pressure). Inside our mouth, our tongue's taste buds tell us what food is sweet or sour or bitter, and its pain receptors can tell us what meals are spicy. The olfactory bulb positioned high in the back of our nostrils, the most prehistoric sense receptor we have, can alert us to the danger of smoke or the delight of oven-baked bread.

Beauty and ugliness, pleasure and pain, good and bad, all the experiences of the physical world, are first communicated by sight, sound, smell, taste, and touch.

The five sense receptors, however, are only the embarkation point in this line of communication.

THE PATHWAY OF PERCEPTION

Step 2: Relay of Sensory Information to the Cerebrum via the Nervoucs System

Step 2 in the pathway of perception involves, like a simple telegram, the body's receptors sending the information they have detected to the brain via the myriad of connections in the nervous system, the body's equivalent of telegraph lines. If the nerves are intact and in healthy condition, the message sent from the receptor(s) arrives in a split second at the brain, the body's sorting room or telegram interchange.

Although all messages arrive in the part of the brain called the cerebrum, they don't all arrive at the same place. Messages from our eyes get sent via the optic nerve to the back of the brain in an area called the occipital lobe. Surprisingly, all images from the retina are sent upside down due to the optical inversion of the eye's lens and cornea, which must be then turned or flipped the right side up by the mind!

Messages from the eardrum get sent to the lateral side of the brain called the temporal lobe. Pain, touch and temperature messages from our skin arrive at different locations in the parietal lobe, located toward the rear-central part of the brain (and then in separate locations dependent upon what part of the hand, arm, foot, leg, abdomen, back, chest, neck, and face they have originated).

Taste, too, arrives in its own department of the parietal lobe, whereas messages from the olfactory bulb arrive at an area in the olfactory lobe called the piriform cortex (which is concerned with odor identification) and other areas such as the medial amygdala (believed to be associated with social functions, such as mating) and the entorhinal cortex (believed to be associated with memory).

Figure 13 below is a diagram that will help to visualize the parts of the brain we are discussing:

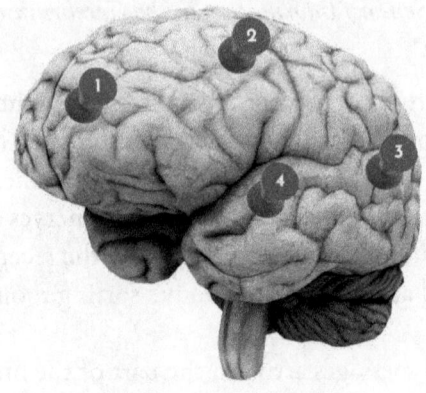

FIGURE 13: Brain Lobes (1) Frontal (2) Parietal (3) Occipital (4) Temporal

Step 3: Packaging of Sensory Information as Neurochemicals in the Cerebrum

In Step 3 of the pathway of perception, the information arriving at the brain is then stored and packaged in the cerebrum as chemicals known as neurotransmitters, such as acetylcholine, serotonin and dopamine.

Like a computer that cannot discriminate between the 1's and 0's of its binary data, where a potentially devastating recipe on making a nuclear bomb is treated no differently than an inspirational piece of classical music, the brain doesn't discriminate between the various assortment of chemical data arriving from the five senses. To the brain, the chemicals of a rose's scent and that of a decaying carcass are the same; serotonin is just serotonin, dopamine is just dopamine.

Being a non-discriminatory organ, the brain will harbor both criminals and saints. It is the mind (the conscious mind as opposed to the subconscious mind), not the brain, which analyzes the sensory data packaged within the cerebrum, seeing and hearing a world of wonder. Serotonin and adrenaline, acetylcholine and

THE PATHWAY OF PERCEPTION

dopamine, just another day at the office for the brain, are but for the conscious mind the continuing images of sight and the endless sounds of life.

The brain, as it turns out, is just a highly developed relay center, an organic, biological interface between the rest of the body and the mind-field.

THE BRAIN

To better understand the functioning of the brain, consider the circumstances of a person that has suffered a tragic accident and is now considered brain-dead.

Although his brain is in decay, life-energy still flows from his Source through his body generating a localized field of awareness—a generalized mind-field—thus enabling his other organs to function, such as his heart to continue beating in regular rhythm and his kidneys to continue filtering the blood of its poisons.

The system of government in the UK is analogous to the human body in this sense. For instance, if the Houses of Parliament were to suddenly sink into the River Thames, if the government were to lose its head, as it were, the system of law throughout the local councils and boroughs would continue to function and support the country at some basic level and thus prevent the UK collapsing into ruinous anarchy.

Similarly, a person's body can still operate on some fundamental level when the brain has died. Although the main executor of the mind's will is no longer functioning—the now deceased brain— the surviving cells of the rest of the body still detect and respond to the invisible power of intelligence, or life-energy, flowing through them from his Source.

The brain-dead person is not dead. He simply can't interact on a human level anymore; the communication center between his mind-field and the outside world is no longer operational. Yet the continuing flow of life-energy through the remainder of the body ensures that the mind still exists in some manner or form, albeit as a field of awareness lacking the amplification of the neuronal cells (see *Figure 12*).

The brain-dead consciousness is therefore a consciousness that is functioning below normal, everyday human awareness or "awake-ness", a sub-conscious mind-field that has lost its means of translation, its ability to share and experience any kind of meaningful human relationship. That is why doctors advocate euthanasia in these circumstances, why they advise relatives to switch off life-support: dead to the world around them, the brain-dead person is "as good as dead".

Consequently, in our scientifically developed society, for better or for worse, the organ of the brain has come to symbolize our essential humanity. Its death represents our own death. The unconscious vegetative existence, however, in which the brain-dead person is totally dependent on intensive medical intervention to prevent starvation or thirst, doesn't detract from the underlying point that, although an extremely vital organ, the brain is nothing more than a highly developed interface between the body and the mind. The brain is just a communications center that relays information of the environment to our consciousness (and relaying the mind's will or intentions back to the body, the creative process of thought which we will discuss in Step 6). In its initial role, the brain's foremost concern is focused upon sorting and storing the chemical data it has received from the rest of the body, somewhat like a biological recording device, and to then present this data to the mind for analytical interpretation.

To further complicate matters, the neurons of the brain are not the only cells that can act as an interface and transmit sensory information to the conscious mind. Just as every cell in the body acts as a conduit for the flow of life-energy and generation of a mind-field (albeit weaker than that generated by the flow of life-energy through the neuronal cells), every cell in the body also acts as an interface for transmission of information to our awareness—liver, kidneys, pancreas, stomach, spleen, marrow, heart, and so forth. The two processes are so interlinked and interdependent that they can, for our purposes, be considered one and the same thing.

> *The process that generates the mind-field in and around the body is the same process that transmits information from the body to the mind and its field of awareness, and vice versa.*

Accordingly, the transmissions of information from the cells of the body are relatively weak (sub-conscious) compared with the transmissions of information from the neurons of the brain (conscious). They occur beneath the normal level of mind-field awareness or awake-ness that has been established by the dominant neuronal interface of the brain, sub-conscious transmissions that would in fact overwhelm us in their sheer volume if we were to be constantly aware of them.

Take, for instance, the bone marrow. Total body production of red blood cells is approximately one million per second. That's sixty million cells per minute, three hundred and sixty million per hour, and over eight and a half billion per day (which sounds astounding, but this figure doesn't even include the production of white blood cells, the cells that fight off infection). We do not need to be aware of each and every blood cell absorbed into the vascular system, we would get bogged down in the detail. We only need to know when something goes wrong with the production, when there is an over or under supply of blood products, as in diseases like leukemia, lymphoma, pancytopenia, and thrombocytosis.

Even then our awareness of the body's imbalance is usually superficial and vague, more akin to a "gut feeling", a feeling that something is wrong but exactly what remains unknown. These vague feelings are the subconscious background transmissions from the cellular level creeping into our general awareness.

For the purposes of general perception, however, it is the function of the brain cells that is of main interest. In keeping with their dual purpose, not only have the neurons evolved to amplify the flow of life-energy into a concentrated field of awareness, they have also become highly adapted and specialized in transmitting sensory information of the world to the mind, so much so that their transmission "noise" all but drowns out the background transmission "noise" of all the rest of the body's cells combined.

This dominant or relative intensity of neuronal transmission noise from our neuronal cells is a key factor in determining for the majority of our life, what gets filtered through to our awareness and made conscious. Our level of perception, in other words. The glut of information is so great it is easy to become bedazzled and preoccupied with the five senses. Cellular transmission from the rest of the body, as in the case of bone marrow, simply gets relegated to the domain of sub-conscious; we barely notice it. Like a smitten child, the mind then picks and chooses what sensory information it wants from the neurons.

We see what we want to see and hear what we want to hear.

But that is of no concern to the brain. The brain is a constantly replenishing smorgasbord of neurochemicals and the mind is welcome to help itself to whatever it wants.

The brain is a happy servant.

RENUNCIATION OF THE SENSES

Understanding the brain's role in the pathway of perception sheds light on Evelyn Underhill's earlier advice that, to find a permanent end to our pain and suffering, the self or egoic mind "must turn from the sense-world to some other with which it is in tune."

We can even begin to fathom the reason why all legitimate spiritual paths advocate some kind of purification or cleansing of the self, or chastity, at least for a while. The discipline of chastity isn't confined to the practice of sexual abstinence, which most of us living outside a convent or monastery not uncommonly find a little bizarre and abnormal, even counter-evolutionary. There is much more to it than that.

Chastity is the deliberate poverty or renunciation of the senses in order to obtain spiritual purification. The theory behind its practice involves the difficult task of disabling our mind's preoccupation with the sensory input of our brain so as to disable our identification with the five senses and, hence, identification with the limited self (mind-body ego image) that is created by those senses. Once we have disabled our identification with our limited self, we can then begin to identify with our Unlimited Self, our Source.

It is a difficult art to perfect. Many seekers are unable to deny themselves short-term pleasure for long-term spiritual gain, and in failing to do so they fall short of the mark. Just as many overshoot it, turning the body into a thing to be hated and despised instead of loved and nurtured, punishing themselves unnecessarily for normal human desires and demonizing their sexual feelings as wanton and lustful, thereby unwittingly reinforcing the very thing they were supposed to renounce in the very beginning, their five senses.

Renunciation of the senses—the turning of the self "from the sense-world to some other"—does not mean that we should deny what we see, hear, touch, taste and smell as a delusion. This is not the aim of chastity. Rather, it is more concerned with the continuing practice of refuting the delusory belief that the senses can describe the totality of all there is in the world. The senses tell us of pleasure and pain, of form and duality, but nothing of the Source from which those sense experiences arise.

For those who do manage the delicate balance of chastity and contemporary living (and we don't have to live in a convent or monastery to achieve it), turning from the sense-world to some other is akin to switching off a noisy radio. It means becoming in tune with the purity of the Silent Stillness. It means tuning into the life-energy flowing through us from our Eternal Fount.

Moreover, it means becoming receptive to the Sight beneath the sight, becoming receptive to the Sound beneath the sound, becoming receptive to the Taste beneath the taste. It is grasping the essence of life in the living of it.

> *Look well at each letter: thou seest it hath already perished but for the face of the ink, that is, for the Face of His Essence.*

Turning from the sense-world to some other means becoming receptive to the Mind beneath the mind.

IMAGINARY PERCEPTION

With this understanding of the overlapping but differing roles of the mind and the brain in the pathway of perception, we can now turn to our attention to Step 4. As a reminder, a summary of the first three steps we have covered so far is thus:

- -> Step 1: Receptors in our eyes, ears, nose, mouth, and skin detect light, sound, aromas, tastes, and pain/temperature/pressure information, respectively, on the world outside and inside our bodies.
- -> Step 2: The receptors relay this information via the myriad of nerves to different areas of the cortex, such as the occipital, temporal and parietal lobes, depending on what type of information is being sent and where it has come from (see *Figure 13*).

THE PATHWAY OF PERCEPTION

-> Step 3: The brain stores and packages the information it has received from the receptors in the form of neurotransmitters and neurochemicals for the mind to access and interpret.

Step 4: Sensory Analysis and Image Construction by the Mind

In Step 4, having arrived at the appropriate lobes of the brain, the various sensory messages must then be analyzed and interpreted by the mind into an appropriate image. What started out as a photon of light impinging itself upon a receptor in the retina of the eye, or a sound wave vibrating against the tympanic membrane of the ear, is now a packet of chemicals sitting in the cerebrum of the brain. Exactly how a molecule of dopamine or serotonin gets interpreted as the color red, or the aroma of coffee, or the toot of a trumpet, remains a mystery. This is because perception is as much a creative process as it is a scientific one, a process that is beyond the physical limitations of the brain.

The detection of one thing (object) by another (subject) occurs at a level of awareness above that of our sub-conscious bodily reflexes, a level of awareness called cognition. (Interestingly, memory is a case of re-cognition; when we recall something or someone, we re-cognize them.)

Cognition is a process confined to the workings of the conscious mind—everything we see, hear, feel, eat, and smell is a replication or reconstruction "inside" the mind-field of an object that is "external" to it. This reconstruction is an imaginary creation, a virtual replica, made of nothing but the fluctuations of mental energy. Every image we perceive is in fact a psychological construction.

Consider a movie at the cinema. We do not actually see the real actors or scenery being shown on the big screen, only a moving image of them. Similarly, we do not see the reality of people and places around us, only images constructed from the pattern of sensory neurochemicals projected upon the organic "big screen" of the brain. It is not the neurochemicals per se that are analyzed or observed by the conscious mind but something deeper at the very core of their essence, their energy patterns.

The basic building blocks of life are not atoms and electrons but energy, as demonstrated by Einstein's equation $E=MC^2$, which states that mass, the very thing that constitutes our physical body, is pure energy. Every atom, ion, chemical compound, DNA molecule, and organ in our body first originates as a spark of energy in the quantum domain, including the brain's neurochemicals, and it is the unique combinations of energy patterns or fingerprints of acetylcholine, dopamine and serotonin that the mind recognizes and learns from birth to adapt and manipulate into specific images that best match the object being observed.

Some neurological illnesses like schizophrenia, or drugs (for example, LSD), can alter the levels or distribution of our neurochemicals and project a distorted energy pattern to the conscious mind, which then interprets the distorted pattern into a distorted image. In other instances, our mind doesn't learn how to interpret the energy patterns correctly, even though the brain is functioning normally. (This kind of mental disorder is more often than not the result of some trauma, neglect or abuse suffered in childhood.)

In either situation, cognition is impaired. We can begin to see things that are not present in physical reality, hear voices that haven't been spoken, hallucinations in other words. It is the role of psychiatrists and psychologists to recognize in a patient which underlying defect is at fault and to treat the affected individual by either readjusting the chemical imbalance with antipsychotic drugs, or by re-educating the maladjusted mind with psychotherapy. Usually, treatment consists of a blend of both modalities dictated by the needs of the patient at the time.

Other illnesses, such as pathological memory loss, are also a cognitive problem of Step 4. In Alzheimer's Disease, for example, amyloid plaques deposit in the brain leading to atrophy or shrinkage of the grey matter and gradually affecting the way a patient interacts with the world; he forgets where he put the car keys; he forgets whether or not he ate breakfast this morning; he starts accusing his closest relatives of stealing his reading glasses and his wallet.

It is his short-term memory that is mostly affected, the things that happened just a moment ago, and learning new skills is therefore an extremely difficult proposition for him. His long-term memory remains comparatively intact, however, the memory of past persons and places that was established before any significant deposit of amyloid plaques had occurred. He can still read and write and hold a logical conversation, even recall events experienced decades ago with sharp and vivid detail. But it is his newer memories that are prevented from becoming embedded in the mind.

Once established, the deposits of amyloid plaques begin to interfere with the transmission of sensory information from the patient's neuronal cells to his mind. They distort or "tangle" the neurochemical energy patterns in such a way that his mind-field can no longer interpret the data it is receiving except within the context of old behavioral patterns. Pain is still pain, pleasure is still pleasure, but the only way his mind can make sense of anything that is happening is through the eyes of the past.

Consequently, over a period of gradual decline, the patient with Alzheimer's Disease loses the ability to interact with his environment within the context of the present moment. His mind loses its sense of time and place, its current orientation with the rest of the world. Confusion sets in. He wanders away from home. He gets angry and aggressive.

Unable to make new memories, he becomes trapped in the pages of history. His perception of who he thinks he is, his identity, his frame of reference, can only be made in comparison with the things he can remember, mental images of previous events, people and places. He is a virtual time-traveler, lost and confused like a child separated from his mother in a crowded market.

But what do the pathological processes of psychotic events and memory loss actually reveal of the imaginary nature of perception? In particular, what are the implications for the perception of Spirit?

If our Source is not an object external to us like a person or a place, is what we SEE of Goodness, Truth and Beauty simply a figment of our imagination? Is the abiding presence of joy, security, acceptance, peace and freedom an illusion too far?

SPATIAL PERCEPTION

For good or for bad, it is the nature of an image to represent an approximation of the object it is trying to portray. A photograph is not the real thing. A photograph can only detail certain aspects of reality due to inbuilt constraints (there's only so much that can be done with paper and ink), and although a good likeness it may be, it can only ever be a two-dimensional image of a three-dimensional object.

Likewise the mental images or psychological photographs we use to navigate through life. By their nature, they can only ever represent an approximation of reality. A perceived image is not the real thing. Our mental perceptions can only detail certain aspects of our environment due to inbuilt constraints; they can only give us a four-dimensional picture or map of a multi-dimensional universe and this mind-made picture or map is what determines our relative position in four-dimensional space and time. Step 4 in the pathway of perception is therefore where we gain our sense of where and when. It gives us our relativity, our frame of reference, our orientation.

That space is relative is self-evident. Things look smaller

the further away they are and bigger the closer they are—their appearance is determined by our relative position to them in three-dimensional space. The word appearance is vital in our understanding of perception. Things appear smaller the further apart we are from them, but this appearance is not objective fact but subjective distortion. The object itself doesn't change size when we observe it. It only appears to enlarge or shrink depending on its distance from us, an optical illusion rooted in relativity.

Artists, in fact, use this optical illusion by painting far away objects smaller than nearby objects, thus creating an illusory three-dimensional picture on a two-dimensional sheet of canvas. The appearance or perception of a spatial object in our mind is a similarly relative and creative act.

> *Using the sensory information provided by the brain, our mind paints an optical illusion of the world according to its relative position to that world.*

This has repercussions for our perception of Spirit. If we hold to the belief that we are separate from Spirit, if we consider our self an isolated entity somehow independent of it, then its appearance will necessarily be determined by our relative position to the image we have created of it.

Is Spirit far? Is Spirit close? Is Spirit big? Is Spirit small? Is Spirit absent?

Of course, Spirit is none of those things. Spirit is as it is. Spirit is not an object with self-defining limitations such as big, small, far, close, or absent. These are the defining criteria of a limited mental perspective deeply embedded in the mistaken belief of disconnection from our Source—*forgetfulness*. The subsequent positioning and relativity to Spirit is a direct corollary of such a belief. But Spirit is not relative to anything. There is nothing that is not Spirit—our Source is One and All—so there is nothing to be relative to except itself.

This is why Zen Buddhists say, "Kill the Buddha!" and why the Bible commands us not to worship false idols. It is also why the Koran strictly forbids any images to be made in God's likeness. Our psychological images of the deity we believe in (for example, an old man in the sky) only reinforce forgetfulness, the false belief that we are somehow separate and relative to him, which makes God an object.

Any image of God we hold is therefore an idol and necessarily false. It is a lesser God.

TEMPORAL PERCEPTION

Like the relative nature of space, the nature of time is also relative. Most people are familiar with the effect age has upon our experience of the days and the years; most know how a woman experiences temporal reality differently in her seventies than she did when she was six. As an older woman, time flashes by. She blinks once and a week has passed. She blinks twice and half the year is over. As a child, however, time passes relatively slower. A day for her is long and drawn out, a week like a month. A year until the next Christmas takes an eternity. Age ages us.

The issue of time's relativity is more complex than the mere date of our birth, however. One hundred years ago, Einstein revealed to the world just how bizarre and quirky time really is with his famous equations on relativity (as briefly mentioned throughout the book). Well before the construction of particle accelerators, he was able to demonstrate through "thought experiments" that for any person able to break through the impossibility barrier and travel at the speed of light, time amazingly comes to a halt. Not for anyone else, only for them. Hurtling through space on a lightship, the galactic traveler doesn't age, whilst hundreds, if not thousands of years pass on Earth.

What's more, like speed, gravity also has the ability to affect our

THE PATHWAY OF PERCEPTION

perception of time. For instance, in the center of a black hole the gravity is so strong that not even light can accelerate fast enough to escape. This means that for someone unfortunate enough to be sucked into its dark belly, time is at an eternal standstill.

The practical consequences of extreme speed and gravity is the surprising fact that time does not flow from past to present to future like a Newtonian arrow shot from a bow. The Great Clockmaker in the sky does not wind his watch and set time ticking mechanically forward. Time may appear to flow consistently in one direction towards the future, but that is just an appearance. It is not objective fact but subjective distortion. Just as a distant object appears taller or shorter relative to our position in three-dimensional space, so time appears "taller" or "shorter" (or in temporal terminology: quick, slow, absent, static) relative to our changing position in three-dimensional space.

Einstein's equations, in fact, reveal that one-dimensional time and three-dimensional space are intricately connected in a four-dimensional static "lump" of space-time. Time and space are one entity, one continuum—like electricity and magnetism, they are the same thing at a deeper level—and what appears to take the form of time is just an illusory perception of that four-dimensional lump determined by our relatively changing position to it.

In other words, the rate of time experienced by any individual is simply a measurement of change of that individual's relative position in three-dimensional space to the rest of the universe. (A word of explanation: nobody is ever absolutely stationary—the earth is spinning and orbiting, the Milky Way is shifting and swirling, the universe is expanding and stretching—our positions are always changing relative to everything else in the universe even though it may appear otherwise.)

Einstein's "lump" of space-time also means that the past, present and future are one and the same thing, only this one and the same thing is not technically static. It is constantly changing, constantly renewing, giving the impression of movement, a flow of time, much as stop-motion animation gives the impression that cartoon characters can run, jump and talk. Interestingly, it also means that you are already dead—you just don't know it yet. Your consciousness hasn't arrived at the point in which your death is already happening.

You are also being born. You are also a child. You are also being conceived. Your consciousness has already moved through these points in space-time and documented them as being in the past. But the future and the past are nonetheless part of the four-dimensional space-time "lump" which is every bit as real as what is occurring right now in the present.

This may bring some comfort to those whose loved ones have passed on, knowing that, in some form, they still exist.

The Illusion of Time

Consider sitting in an unanchored boat far from land, bobbing up and down with the swell of the ocean. Watch as a wave approaches from the distant horizon, passes beneath the boat, and then moves on toward dry land. The movement of the wave that you see, however, is an illusion. Water does not move in waveform from the distant horizon to the shore like a flowing river, nor do ripples on a lake move across its surface. The water that constitutes the wave only moves up and down, not forward, which is why the boat in which you are sitting remains just as far from land as it did before the wave passed beneath it. So, if the wave doesn't move, what does?

Energy.

The ocean is simply the conduit for the movement of energy to pass from one point to another. The wave may seem to flow from point A to point B, but this is only an appearance. It isn't really happening—only energy is moving forward.

THE PATHWAY OF PERCEPTION

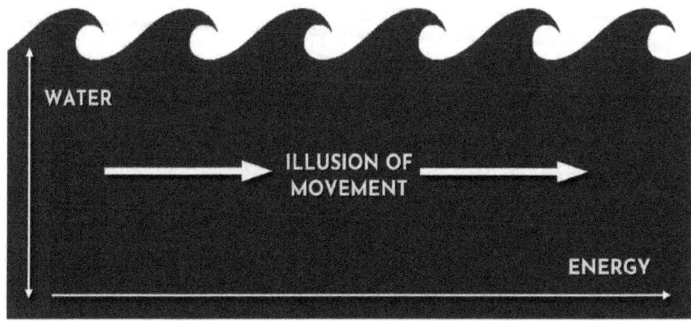

FIGURE 14:   Energy and the Illusion of Movement

Figure 14 can be used as a metaphor for time, where the ocean represents the fluidic spectrum of the space-time continuum, Einstein's "lump." Space-time is simply the conduit for the movement of life-energy, Consciousness, as it passes from one point to another in much the same way as energy moves through water, creating the impression of a "time-wave" which seems to flow forward from the past horizon to future shores.

The flow of this time-wave, however, is just as illusory as any wave on the ocean or ripple on a lake. The time-wave may appear to move forward, but in reality space-time is as static as a boat bobbing on the surface.

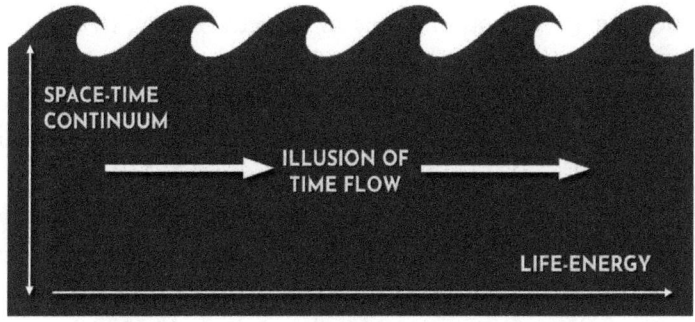

FIGURE 15:   Life-Energy and the Illusion of Time

Because the experience of time is a perceptual illusion, it can be altered, for instance, by modifying those factors which determine our physical position in three-dimensional space, such as our relative speed to one another and the strength of gravity in the space which we inhabit.

Furthermore, the experience of time can also be altered by modifying those factors which determine our perception of the space-time continuum. Such factors include our age, which happens subconsciously and naturally, and also, more importantly, our state of mind, which we have more control over.

The choices we make, and simply changing the way we look at things, can change the way we perceive the whole dimension of time itself.

PSYCHOLOGICAL TIME

The vagaries of the space-time continuum, however, are difficult concepts to fully grasp. But just as light can be considered as two differing but co-existent realities, as either a particle (photon) or as a waveform (probability), so too can time be considered existing in two states: as either a "lump", or as a probability or "energy field".

This alternative temporal state to Einstein's four-dimensional static lump is the consideration of time as a temporal field permeating in and around spatial objects, similar to the way a mind-field permeates in and around the body (see *Figure 12*).

As previously discussed, when life-energy flows through the body it generates a mind-field or sphere of individual awareness. Similarly, when life-energy flows through the dimensions of space it generates a temporal field or sphere of time awareness. Furthermore, in this field analogy, similar to the human mind-field's two functioning levels of basic awareness, sub-conscious and conscious, there can be considered two basic kinds of temporal fields, general and focal.

The spatial matter of the universe as a whole can be thought of as having a general temporal field permeating in and around it operating at a low, sub-conscious or subliminal level. This field maintains the general flow of time throughout the basic physical matter of the entire universe—synchronizing the orbits of the planets and the moons, the movements of the galaxies, the expansion of the universe, even including such things as the flow of water, the weather patterns, the flight of a golf ball, and so forth—much like the sub-conscious mind-field maintains the synchronization of the body's organs and reflexes on a subliminal level.

This general temporal field is more like Newton's directly flowing arrow of time than Einstein's individually experienced relative time. It is the flow of time we experience collectively as a whole—what keeps us "in sync" with everything else.

In comparison, the second kind of time-field is a specific field of temporal awareness that exists for each individual, a personalized time-field that has been created within the basic collective or general field of time. Like the concentrated mind-field generated by the cells of the brain, this relative time-field is a field of temporal awareness permeating each living organism as a direct result of the flow of life-energy through the organism's cells, a kind of containment field of time that localizes a focus of temporal awareness unique to that specific individual organism. (In this respect, humans can be considered the brain cells of the living universe.)

This focal temporal field is what gives us our awareness of time being fast, slow or stationary independently of anyone else. It is what allows any individual to become "out of sync" with everything around them, why an astronaut on a lightship is a virtual time-traveler to the future, remaining ageless while thousands of years pass on Earth, and why a grandmother never seems to have the time to prepare for dinner while her grandson seems to be waiting interminably to be fed.

It also goes some way to explain why different animal species experience different variations of time. For example, mammals with higher brain function tend to have longer life spans on the whole than those with lesser brain function, such as insects and reptiles (although some bird species seem to be the exception to this rule, having the ability to live to one hundred years or more!).

Individually, on a fundamental level, the awareness of time and the awareness of our mind are the result of the same ongoing process of supra-conscious life-energy flowing through our three-dimensional bodies. The process of one is the process of the other:

Mind and time are the same process.

Just as our own individual and unique mind-field is a focus for our own personal thoughts, words and actions, our temporal-field is also a focus for our own personal flow of time from birth, through to childhood, to adulthood and death.

In essence, the flow of life-energy through our spatial bodies generates a relative experience of temporal reality. As already discussed, this experience is dependent on factors unique to our personal individuality, factors such as our age and biological species, as well as environmental factors such as speed and gravity. We cannot escape the relativity of time and the fact that we determine the experience of it, quick, slow, static, or non-existent.

The perception of time, like spatial objects, is a uniquely psychological experience.

No Mind, No Time

Step 4 in the pathway of perception consequently gives us a glimpse into the mechanics of how the mind covers or misrepresents the perception of Spirit, how it distorts or warps the awareness of our Source. It also gives us a glimpse into the method required to clarify our vision of Spirit and to finally SEE the Uncreated Light, the Infinite Life and Eternal Love:

THE PATHWAY OF PERCEPTION

Lose or escape the influence of the mind (or ego) and you lose psychological time.

More precisely, lose or escape the influence of the mind and you gain no-time, the transcendent experience of eternity, which is none other than the transcendent experience of Spirit, our Source.

As a young teenager sitting in the rear passenger seat with my friend one day after high school, I experienced firsthand this timeless nature of eternity while watching the hood of the car crumple against the chassis of another sedan at 60 km/h. It was a hot afternoon and the driver of the sedan simply didn't see us coming around the bend. I, however, saw it all in slow motion. (The cliché of watching a movie frame-by-frame exactly describes the slowing down of time to almost a standstill.) I saw the sedan pull onto the road directly ahead. I saw my friend's father slam on the brakes. I smelled burning rubber. I heard the sickening *crunch*! of metal on metal. I saw the hood of the car crumple like a tin can. I saw the gaping shock of the other driver as his sedan was rammed and thrown sideways.

From brakes locking, to impact, to deathly stillness, the accident lasted no more than two or three seconds. For me, it seemed to last a year. But during it all I felt an amazing sense of peace and calm. There was no fear of injury or death, just a sense that no matter what happened, everything was going to be all right. I felt immortal.

Thankfully, nobody was seriously hurt or required hospital treatment. Surprisingly, reflecting back on that moment all those years ago, I can still feel the sense of timelessness and peace that overwhelmed me during those few eternal seconds. Putting it into perspective, the surge of adrenaline that flooded my body when I saw the sedan pull onto the road ahead had caused me to fixate purely on what was happening at that very moment, pushing all other thoughts out of my mind, even the thought of death.

This heightened concentration momentarily released the

shackles of my mind from psychological time. Although I wasn't aware of what was happening back then, I had transcended thought and entered into the Realm of No Mind, a place of peace and calm, a place of no fear and no-time.

This is the experience of detachment enjoyed by spiritual masters. Not detachment from the happenings of this world, as it could be interpreted, but detachment from the small, egoic self. Detachment means we see our mind and body from the position of a third person—we literally watch our self from a distance, like watching our self on television. We are then in a position to choose our thoughts and behaviors with greater clarity and peace instead of getting carried away with the moment (which we are free to do at any time, if we so desire).

But who is doing the watching? What part of the self is watching the other parts of the self?

Your True Self, the Silent Witness, your Higher State of Being. You are, in fact, watching from the position of your Source, where imagination and relativity are seen from the level of the Absolute. This is what is referred to as "second attention". Detachment from the thoughts and desires of our ego means all barriers to our Source are removed, and from this perspective we get a glimpse into the Eternal Moment from which our four-dimensional universe of space and time is created

We get a glimpse of the world beyond duality.

SUBJECTIVE PERCEPTION

To recap, Step 4 in the pathway of perception involves the creation of a mental image of what the mind thinks is external to it, a virtual reconstruction or imaginary picture of objective reality, including time. It is a complex creative process we do not yet fully understand or can replicate in a scientific model.

THE PATHWAY OF PERCEPTION

It is also a process that is not exclusive to humanity. Even animals, especially mammals, have this level of awareness to some extent. They have cognition and they have memory, re-cognition. They have the ability to create virtual images from the sensory data collected by their brains and the ability to communicate what they have seen or observed to other members of their species, albeit on a limited scale.

What they seem to lack, or are barely able to achieve, however, is Step 5.

Step 5: Image Naming and Labeling

In Step 5, the penultimate step in human perception, the mind attaches a label or judgment to the perceived object. Step 5 is essentially the laying down of what we like and dislike about the things we encounter. In other words, thought. It is the process of naming what we see and it differs from the first four steps of perception in that it occurs entirely in the realm of the mind—it is the mind's reactions to its own images.

This step in the process of perception is therefore subject to the influence of our moods, emotions and personalities, which means that we are intricately involved in the creation of our own individualized and subjective experience of reality. Our heaven today can easily be a living hell tomorrow.

Step 5 is also behavioral. Judgmental and labeling behavior is learned though the personal experience of pain and pleasure, or, as is most often the case, from our parents, peers and culture. The subjective judgment and labeling of an object or event as good or bad is also hugely influenced by our beliefs, which we have discussed in Chapter 1 and will shortly be recapping and summarizing. These personalized points of view range from extremes such as racism, sexism and ageism to what political party we vote for, to the most simplistic things such as what kind of food we like to eat.

Jesus was referring to the proclivity of the human mind to judge and label when he remarked,[2]

> *How can you say to your brother, 'Let me take the speck out of your eye,' when all the time there is a plank in your own eye? . . . first take the plank out of your own eye, and then you will see clearly to remove the speck from your brother's eye.*

Our perception is determined by who we think we are, a subjective re-creation based just as much on our previous experiences and future expectations as it is based on the object being observed. The vision of our mother's face, the voice of a teacher, the smell of aftershave, all are tainted by our psychological state of mind. Even Spirit. What deity we perceive is only a reflection of reality, an image in a mirror clouded by our murky past and foggy future. We see our desires, our needs, our addictions. We see our self.

Removing the plank from our eyes—becoming aware of our judgmental and labeling behavior and then developing the will to transcend it—is a vital prerequisite if we are ever to SEE clearly our Source of Goodness, Truth, and Beauty, if we are ever to find salvation in this life.

Alas, for the majority of humanity, what we see—the image we finally perceive—is blurred or obstructed by the plank in our eye. The plank—thinking—dulls perception. Everything becomes viewed through the same conditions, or lens, or set of experiences, which, after time, gives the impression that we've seen everything and heard it all.

Indeed, when we sieve our experiences through the same filter every second of the day, life is pretty much the same day in, day out, from the time of our teenage years, when we seem to solidify our personal choices into a set personality, to when we die. Drudgery sets in. Boredom becomes us. The months and years pass and before we know it we're eighty years old and wondering what's happened to our life. Perhaps this is why we crave newness, freshness and creativity to release us from our prison of perception.

Perhaps this is why the fifty-year-old husband suddenly runs off with his twenty-something secretary. Perhaps this is why the retired wife turns to the grapes of Chardonnay, Riesling, Shiraz, and Champagne for comfort. Perhaps this is why a sea change is so appealing.

But, in the end, all attempts at revitalizing our life with newness, freshness and creativity is nothing less than the intrinsic search for our True Self in the outside world. The question is, is this realistic?

Can you really find yourself out there? Can you really find yourself outside yourself?

MIND RECEIVER

As with its role as a receiver of data from the body, the brain's reception of the mind's interpretation and judgment of its own images in Step 6 completes the brain's functioning as an interface or go-between. Communication between the brain and the mind is not just one-way traffic: it is a two-way highway.

But how does the mind communicate with the brain?

Step 6: Relay of Image Response from Mind to Body

Imagine the mechanism of communication from the mind-field to the brain occurring in much the same way as a magnetic field aligning and manipulating iron filings into patterns and shapes. Because the mind-field works at the most fundamental level of existence, the level of energy, it is able to align the stocks or "filings" of neurochemicals already stored in the cerebrum into codes and patterns that physically represent its desired will or intention (just as the neurochemical patterns of the brain in Step 3 are able to physically represent images of the outside world to the mind).

In this way, mental messages or thoughts become physically encapsulated within the brain as neurochemical fingerprints, where each fingerprint represents a specific instruction, such as walking, talking, eating, and sleeping, which is then transmitted in a matter of microseconds to the relevant parts of the body via the descending neurological pathways.

To a limited degree, this process can actually be simulated in the laboratory. Neuroscientists have mapped the entire motor cortex of the brain (the area of the brain responsible for the functional movements of the legs, arms, head, neck, hands, feet, and so forth) by opening the skulls of patients and stimulating the exposed brains with electrical probes. Stimulating part of the motor cortex involved in upper limb movement causes the arm to twitch. Stimulating yet another part of the motor cortex makes the leg kick. Scientists know what part of the brain is responsible for every kind of bodily movement. They can even see hotspots of brain activity associated with the body's motor function using imaging devices such as CT and MRI scanners. But what they don't know is how these parts of the brain are triggered into sending its messages to the rest of the body.

At the underlying level of base energy, the neurochemicals are somehow manipulated into patterns that are packaged by the brain and relayed via the nervous system to the relevant organs or limbs. But the intelligence behind the mechanism remains undetectable and out of reach. Scientists and doctors cannot capture the god in the machine.

This is not surprising. Just as our TV set is not the source of the programs it screens, the brain is not the source of our dreams or ideas or motivations, only its physical display center. Dismantle the TV and you won't find little people reading the news or chasing a football. Break the TV into pieces and you'll only find scraps of metal and wire and the chemical components of its plasma, LCD or phosphorescent screen. It is the TV station, the mind-field, that provides the content and the TV set, the brain, which receives its transmission, displaying them as patterns of neurochemicals on the organic interface of grey matter for the benefit of the rest of the body.

If our TV set in the lounge room is working properly, it receives the station transmission and gives a clear picture. When something is broken or malfunctioning with the TV receiver or tuner, however, things start to go wrong. No matter how good the TV station transmission is, our faulty TV set can only display a broken or partial picture. The screen may flicker. The sound could go. We can bang the TV and get angry with it, but only fixing or replacing the broken tuner will ensure a clearer picture.

Sometimes things go wrong with our internal receiver, our brain, and the reception of images and thoughts from our mind becomes obscured and faulty. In strokes, where large parts of the brain's internal mechanisms for reception of the mind are destroyed, along with its myriad of neural connections with the rest of the body, victims find that although the will of the mind is still strong and vibrant, the brain simply doesn't respond to it. Instructions to move the fingers or toes go unheeded. Messages to control the bladder and bowel go missing. The brain can no longer tune into the Action Channel. Whilst other channels in the brain are working fine—the History Channel, the Memory Channel, the Comedy Channel, the Sex Channel—the Action Channel has been destroyed and the body's motor functions severely affected in the process.

The brain needs its tuner fixed. Intensive physiotherapy is required to re-learn simple activities of daily life—eating, walking, bathing—as new cerebral connections are gradually laid down in an attempt to bypass the devastated area. More often than not, only a partial repair of the brain (internal tuner) is achieved and clear reception of the mind and its will remains forever impaired.

Other diseases such as Parkinson's Disease cause patients to suffer different but no less devastating problems of reception interference or "channel blockage". A patient with Parkinson's Disease suffers from depleted stores of dopamine in the neuronal cells. The result is poor reception of the mind's thoughts, especially thoughts or instructions to the body to move or remain still. For example, instructions to get dressed lead to a stuttering gait that can result in a severe fall, and a hand that trembles so much it can no longer fasten or undo a shirt button. Not to mention the associated frustration and despair at failing to achieve such a simple task of daily living.

Treatment is invariably aimed at alleviation of symptoms, as a total cure is often unobtainable and unrealistic. It consists of attempting to replace the depleted dopamine stores in the brain with drugs such as L-Dopa and re-educating the patient to control unwanted bodily movements whilst helping to increase the efficiency of desired, practical movements.

Another, more extreme, example of channel blockage is a condition known as Locked-In Syndrome, where the patient for whatever reason (such as a stroke or head injury) suffers a complete breakdown of mind to body communication. The mind is alert and aware, yet there is no transmission of its instructions by the brain.

Although the mind is functioning normally, the quality of its reception is not; all the channels of the brain are malfunctioning and the patient is locked into a body that will not respond to any commands whatsoever. This is not a loss of consciousness or coma, a cognitive problem of Step 3 and 4, but a problem further along the pathway of perception, a problem of Step 6. The brain simply doesn't respond to the mind. It will talk to the mind (transmit sensory information), but it won't listen.

Communication, in this instance, is only in one direction.

EVOLVING PERCEPTION

For many, sadly, Step 6 represents the end of human perception. We observe things, we recognize them, we label and judge them, and then finally we react to them. That's it. Day in, day out, from the moment we arrive in this world to the moment we leave it.

The Jesuits, in fact, have a saying that highlights this point: "Give me the boy until age seven, and I will give you the man."

The most formative years of the human psyche are the early years, when beliefs and behavior patterns are naïve and ripe for manipulation. After that, not much seems to change in our conduct or personality from the day we enter the classroom to the day we receive the golden handshake. Given similar events or occurrences over our lifetime, it is highly likely that we will interpret and react the same way to them as we did when we were a child or teenager:

We will come to the same conclusions about what has happened, we will have the same things to say about it and we will respond in the same manner as we have always done.

The purpose of our life eventually deserts us and we are led inexorably down the path of nihilism. Perception becomes bundled into a belief of existential meaninglessness. And because beliefs determine our interpretation, we literally get lost in the translation of life.

Yet this reflexive, robotic life needn't be the be all and end all of existence. As we have seen, communication of the mind's reactions and desires to external stimuli occurs at the level of awareness we know as thought. But awareness doesn't end at thought. There is a level of awareness beyond the thinking mind, a level of awareness that perceives thought itself, and this occurs on the level of supra-consciousness—the level of the soul.

As previously discussed, this is the level from which you can watch yourself as a third person, like on TV, the level of the silent witness or second attention. Whatever term we like to use, this level of awareness is the key to perceiving the Light, Life and Love of our Source, the key to living every moment with The Five Pillars of our Natural State of Being.

Maintaining this level of awareness means actively participating in the evolution of perception beyond our normal day-to-day robotic existence, an evolution that will open the doorway to another world.

POINTS OF REMEMBRANCE #12

- Your brain is a highly developed interface between the rest of the body and the mind-field.

- Chastity is the deliberate renunciation of the senses in order to obtain spiritual purification.

- Perception is as much a creative process as it is a scientific one.

- Psychotic events and memory loss reveal the imaginary nature of perception.

- The appearance of objects is determined by your relative position to them in three-dimensional space.

- Any image of God is a lesser God.

- Time appears quick, slow, absent, or static relative to your changing position in three-dimensional space.

- There are two kinds of temporal fields, general and focal.

- Mind and time are the same process: lose or escape the influence of your mind and you lose psychological time.

- You are intricately involved in the creation of your own individualized and subjective experience of reality.

- Your perception is determined by who you think you are.
- At the level of energy, your mind aligns neurochemicals into fingerprints that represent its will or intention.
- Second attention is the level at which you perceive your Natural State of Being.

12 ANOTHER WORLD

PERCEPTION OF SOURCE

THE PERCEPTION OF our Source has the power to transform our experience of life from one of addictive need to one of immense fulfillment, a joyous, secure, important, peaceful and liberated existence. It can mean the difference between feeling like a grubby caterpillar crawling in the grime and dirt and feeling like a beautiful butterfly fluttering amongst the lilies.

But what if we simply don't believe in a Higher Being? What if we just can't SEE the Uncreated Light, the Infinite Life and Eternal Love?

Spirit cannot be perceived with the normal everyday senses of sight, sound, taste, touch, and smell. It cannot be seen in the everyday sense of the word; if it were possible to do so, scientists would have already invented ways to measure and observe our Source with machines and equipment much as they can already measure and observe supernovas and distant galaxies with telescopes and radar.

The perception of our Source requires measurement and observation of a kind we are hitherto unused to.

As we have just discussed, the six steps along the pathway of perception can actually work against our better intentions and inhibit our awareness of Spirit's Presence. Our senses can, in fact, make us blind to it.

First, Spirit is not an external object of observation that can impinge upon our five "fleshy" sense receptors (Step 1). As such, Spirit does not trigger or stimulate the eyes, ears, nose, tongue, or skin into sending messages along the ascending neurological pathway to the brain (Step 2) to collect as packets of neurochemicals in the cerebrum (Step 3) for the mind to analyze and interpret (Step 4) as an image to be labeled and judged (Step 5). Consequently, any thoughts or mental reactions (Step 6) to such a perception are inherently misinformed; they are simply reactions to pain and pleasure.

What, then, are we to make of historical and contemporary figures that claimed to have seen God and to have lived in union with him? Are they false prophets? Are they dubious charlatans? Can their claims be believed?

Knock, and the Door Shall Be Opened

When Moses demanded that God reveal Himself atop Mount Sinai, he was awestruck at the vision that he beheld, unprepared for the Reality that was shown to him. The experience was of such overwhelming immensity that he could not comprehend its vastness in its totality. Moses, if we are to believe the scriptures, saw God as God sees Himself.

Yet this kind of awareness and perception is not the exclusive monopoly of saints or prophets, nor is it impossible to achieve. The ability to perceive our Source is embedded as a latent power in every person and readily accessible to all humanity. What distinguishes saints and prophets from the majority of us is the will to make it happen. They have the intent and the desire to go through with it, even (and especially) when the going gets tough. God, their experience tells us, wants us to see and commune with Him. God wants all His children to come home. All that's required is for us to fulfill our end of the bargain, to meet halfway. The will to SEE the Uncreated Light, the Infinite Life and Eternal Love is therefore one of the most important attributes you need to succeed.

To reiterate the stated premise in the introduction of this book, we must want to find salvation and an end to our suffering, for it is a fundamental truth that those who lack the will to commune with God, to reconnect with our Source, will simply not do so.

This is one of the reasons why Jesus warned his followers that it is easier for a camel to fit through the eye of a needle than for a rich man to get into heaven.[2] Not because God punishes rich men or women, but because money has a habit of precluding God from our thoughts and activities, of edging Him out of our life. The cherished belief that money provides everything we need and want prevents our search for any other form of permanent salvation. If we believe the misconception that money will fulfill our desires and wishes, where is the will or inspiration to search for anything beyond our checkbook or savings account? God becomes superfluous to anyone with a strong love of money, and this is as valid today as it was to the rich men in Jesus' parable.

But Jesus was trying to tell us more than that:

If we knock, the door shall be opened. If we seek, we shall find.

In other words, there is reward for those who take the time to look—to the victor the spoils. But without the initial effort on our behalf, there can be no victory. We must, of our own free will, make the first move.

Without desire or intent we will not have the enthusiasm to seek communion with God, our Source, and without enthusiasm or genuine effort the qualities of Goodness, Truth and Beauty will not be revealed to us—our Natural State of Being will forever be out of reach.

Not because God is a reprimanding pedagogue or a miserly scrooge withholding these things from our reach, but because it is simply logical that we cannot SEE the Uncreated Light, the Infinite Life and Eternal Love if we don't even use the perceptive powers we have been given to take a look. We must have the will to do it. If we can't be bothered walking down the driveway to the letterbox, how can we know if there is a parcel waiting to be collected?

Intent gives direction. Desire gives enthusiasm.

Together, intent and desire—will—orientates and motivates the seeker upon the path to Goodness, Truth and Beauty. What we seek we shall find, and what we find gives us the proof and surety of the Divine Being we have been seeking all along.

PROOF OF GOD

It bears repeating that without a belief in the existence of God, or Big Mind, or Spirit, it is extremely difficult to heal the broken connection with our Source. The trend in Western secular society is to refute God's importance in the greater scheme of things, that He either doesn't exist or, if He does, is of limited value in our day-to-day affairs. Like a trash bin, God has been put in a distant corner of the universe where He is far-removed and won't impinge on our delicate disposition.

This point of view is understandable in a society that prefers to educate its youth in the value of material wealth at the expense of spiritual worth. Simon E. is a friend and colleague who steadfastly holds to the secular philosophy of Western culture. He refuses to acknowledge in any way, shape or form the existence of God or a Higher Being.

"Show me the proof," he tells anyone that dares to mention Jesus, Jehovah, Allah, or Buddha in his presence. "If you can show me physical evidence that God exists, then I will believe it."

To Simon's way of thinking, life begins at birth and ends at death. Full stop. Period. Nothing exists before we are born and nothing exists after we die. We came from nothing and we return to nothing. Life is what we see, and it isn't pretty.

Furthermore, Simon E. believes that any faith contrary to nihilism is just a psychological defense mechanism to perpetuate the misconception that we are immortal. Belief in the soul, or God, or life after death is a fantasy, a delusion, created by our ego because it can't accept the fact that we are going to die at some point in time and cease to exist. In essence, humans need to create an omnipotent deity and to believe in an eternal life to prevent a catastrophic collapse into insanity.

"God is a crutch," he is fond of saying.

There are many people in the world believing the same philosophy as Simon, and I suspect that they too require physical proof or something similar (a photograph perhaps?) for the existence of God or a soul before they can believe in it. To many, seeing is believing.

Over one hundred years ago at the end of the 19th Century, an English doctor based in London set out to end speculation once and for all and provide proof of the existence of the soul the atheists of his time were demanding. He intended to extract scientific evidence of the human spirit by conducting experiments on several of his terminally ill patients that had hours, if not minutes, to live. He placed the dying patients onto a table that doubled as a set of scales, measured their weight, and proceeded to wait until they died. At the exact moment of death he took another measurement and recorded it in a logbook.

After recording several "before and after" weights, a pattern began to emerge that he believed showed conclusive proof of the existence of the soul. He managed to demonstrate that at the very moment of death the weight of the body decreased by a minute fraction, something in the order of twenty or so grams, indicating that something had been removed from or had departed the body at that precise moment. As the soul was the only thing that could theoretically leave the body, surely this was undeniable proof of its existence.

To say the least, his discoveries aroused immense interest. But they could, and were eventually, refuted by other experimenters. Over the course of years, just as many researchers confirmed his results as those that invalidated them. What one proved, another disproved. As such, the original findings were not accepted as valid scientific evidence and the experiment eventually faded into obscurity until Hollywood producers resurrected it in 2003 as an interesting tagline for a movie, *21 Grams*.

One problem the doctor overlooked, and was unaware of at the time, was the problem of observer influence. As discussed at various times throughout this book, scientists now know that the simple act of observing can influence an experiment's outcome:

> *The investigator or researcher, whether he or she is aware of it or not, plays a role in determining the results that are eventually observed.*

The observed and observer are interconnected. At the most fundamental level of existence, there is no separation between that which witnesses and that which is witnessed.

Stumped by this unwanted effect of observer influence, scientists have attempted to counter-act it by developing experiments that are double-blind. For example, in an experiment designed to research the effect of two different drugs on the body, the subject taking the drug and the observing researcher are both unaware of what drug has been administered. That is, both are deliberately in the dark or "blind" to the medication being ingested.

But if scientists are going to be honest with themselves, double-blind studies are actually an admission by the scientific community that there is no such thing as a truly independent and objective experiment. They are actually agreeing that there will always be a degree of subjectivity.

In other words, there is scientific recognition that what we see is what we want to see. More so, as this book has been suggesting all along, we see what we believe. In the experiment of the observed soul leaving the body, the London doctor wanted to see evidence for the existence of the soul, such as a fall in weight of the patient at the moment of death. It is no surprise then, that is what his experiments revealed. Later, those experiments that were designed to repudiate his claims achieved exactly that, a failure to deliver the same results.

Any provision of proof of God or the soul must therefore counter-act the phenomenon of observer influence and exploit the interconnectedness of subject and object. Proof of God or the soul then boils down to this: to simply experience it.

Anyone seeking or demanding proof of the spiritual realm must ultimately perform his or her own experiment. Ineffable experience far outweighs theoretical knowledge. This doesn't mean that we should all go out to the nearest hospital and ask if we can weigh people before they die. Rather, we need to perform our own internal experiment and document the results over an extended period of time.

We need to accumulate our own inner evidence.

THE EYE OF CONTEMPLATION

Individual and personal experimentation has in fact been the mainstay of accumulating human knowledge throughout history. The vast stores of knowledge that have been collected on life and the universe fall into three main categories: physical, mental and spiritual. Physical knowledge is accumulated from scientific experiments, the five bodily senses, investigative research, and so forth. Mental knowledge is accumulated from reason, ideas, logic, and thought experimentation. Spiritual knowledge is accumulated from intuition, insight, inspiration, and wisdom.

In *Paths Beyond Ego*,[15] Ken Wilbur reminds us that the Christian saint, St. Bonaventure, taught us to use our "three eyes" to assimilate knowledge, these being:

-> The eye of the flesh.
-> The eye of reason.
-> The eye of contemplation.

"The eye of the flesh" perceives the physical, objective realm of space and time, providing the cold hard facts so loved by scientists and contemporary society.

"The eye of reason" perceives the realm of the mind, where knowledge of philosophy and logic are taught and learned.

The third eye, "the eye of contemplation," is the forgotten eye of Western society. It perceives the realm of our Source, the realm that transcends all others.

A balanced assimilation of knowledge must therefore include all three realms of flesh, reason and contemplation. As such, we must not only focus on science and reason but access or connect with the Higher Knowledge that lies dormant in our self.

Wilbur makes the observation that there are three essential steps to gaining knowledge, whether it is physical (flesh), mental (reason), or spiritual (contemplative) in nature. First, we must follow a set of instructions, usually from people who have already acquired the knowledge that we wish to gain. Second, we must use these instructions and see with the particular "eye" (flesh, reason or contemplative) the very thing we seek to know or understand. Finally, when we have seen or been illuminated, our observations can be compared with what others have observed using the same techniques.

If our newfound knowledge has been compared with and agreed by the knowledgeable community, we can then share our understandings with those who wish to know what we now know and instruct them to see what we have now seen.

Following this strategy of attaining knowledge, a community of "knowledgeable folk" begins to grow (for example, a community of atomic physicists, or mathematicians, or spiritual leaders).

Complications arise, however, when the wrong eye is used to ascertain knowledge in another domain, such as using the eye of the flesh to gain knowledge of the spiritual realm. This most basic of mistakes has been made countless times in the past, especially since the time of Newton when the great split between religion and science was made. Consequently, mistakes will continue to be repeated until it is more widely recognized that the eye of the flesh simply cannot see what the eye of contemplation sees.

In Wilbur's own words,[15]

> ... for whatever type of knowledge, the appropriate eye must be trained until it can be adequate to its illumination. This is true in art, in science, in philosophy, in contemplation. This is true, in fact, for all valid forms of knowledge.

A physicist cannot give an opinion on Einstein's General Theory of Relativity until he or she has opened their eye of reason. Until we train the appropriate eye for whatever realm we wish to investigate, we are not sufficiently empowered to become a member of the knowledgeable community that we wish to join.

This is particularly valid in the realm of ascertaining Higher Self or spiritual knowledge. Source Knowledge is revealed in the realm of contemplation but cannot be understood or explained in fleshy terminology. Therefore, those who seek proof of God or the soul's existence must first develop and train their eye of contemplation to such maturity that they are able to fully SEE the Uncreated Light, the Infinite Life and Eternal Love of Spirit, to adequately fathom the Truth, Goodness and Beauty of our Source.

The choice, as it has always been, is whether or not we actively develop the will to open our eye of contemplation or we actively decide to live a life ignoring the Realm of Spirit.

POINTS OF REMEMBRANCE #13

- The perception of our Source requires measurement and observation of a kind we are hitherto unused to.

- Will orientates and motivates the seeker upon the path to Goodness, Truth and Beauty.

- Proof of God requires inner experimentation.

- A balanced assimilation of knowledge includes all three realms of flesh, reason and contemplation.

- The appropriate eye must be trained until it can be adequate to its illumination.

THE LAST WORD

BELIEF & PERCEPTION

A DISCUSSION ON perception is not complete without a word on belief. Although belief has been mentioned repeatedly throughout the chapters, it is worth our while spending the last few pages of this book recapping and summarizing the major points of belief, especially in relation to perceiving Spirit, our Source.

Beliefs are the eyes through which we see the world and our self. Belief is paramount to perception: without it we are blind.

> *First we believe, then we perceive. First we open our eye of contemplation, then we SEE the Goodness, Truth and Beauty of our Source.*

Belief in Spirit is the prerequisite for seeing Spirit, for without a belief in miracles there are no miracles. As Jesus taught, even faith as small as a mustard seed has the power to move mountains.[2]

Because beliefs also set the boundaries and borders of what we see, beliefs grant us the power to see beyond the horizon of the five senses. Problems or blockages occur in the perception of our Source, however, when our belief in darkness overwhelms our belief in the Light. But, as we now know, the Light is never switched off; it is permanent and abiding. Rather, it is the belief that it has been switched off that results in a life lived in the shadows, which is none other than the concept institutionalized religions preach as original sin.

Yet despite the negative connotations that have evolved over the decades toward the word sin, to also recap our discussions on ego consciousness, sin is just the belief that we have been separated from our Source, the Infinite and Eternal Being we describe as God, and cast into damnation.

What may arise from sin may be classed as evil but sin is not evil in its intent, just a mistaken belief that our life is somehow detached and independently functioning from Life itself, that the umbilical cord of our consciousness (small mind) has been surgically severed from the Higher Consciousness (Big Mind) that gave birth to it. Sin is just forgetfulness, although it can lead to all kinds of suffering.

In other words, the point is not so much that God has expelled us from the Garden of Eden and driven us away, but that we believe that we have been. In truth, there is actually nowhere else to go; we are still there, although we don't see it or feel it. Instead, we see war and rape and torture, we see death and cancer and disease and then declare that Eden has been lost. The sad reality is, through the perpetuation of original sin, we turn paradise into hell every moment of the day, year in, year out, over and over again for millennia. When we believe that we are separated from our Source, we see the world through disconnected eyes.

We see innocent children die of hunger and ask, "How can there be a loving God?"

We see valued members of the community brutally murdered and say, "A just God wouldn't allow such a thing to happen."

We see what we believe and our daily observations reaffirm the original sin. The illusion perpetuates the illusion.

Like Adam and Eve, eating fruit from the Tree of Knowledge has had the effect of turning the reality of Oneness in Eden into the duality of good and bad. Eating the apple has changed our belief of Absolute Unity to a belief of relative disunity, and there we have stayed.

Moreover, eating the apple has set us upon the lonely road as an isolated pilgrim; it has forced us to experience what it is like to be divorced from Love—the experience of suffering and evil.

Yet evil exists not so that we should succumb to it but that it should demonstrate Ultimate Reality, that there is only Love, that there is only Goodness, Truth and Beauty.

We see this, in fact, every day. We see good arising from the ashes of suffering like the mythical Phoenix everywhere we look. The problem is, like any miracle, we see it but don't believe it. We see the cycle of existence—life sprouting from death, something manifesting from nothing—but fail to see that there is no such thing as death, only Life reabsorbing itself, that there is no such thing as nothing, only the Formless reforming itself, because our belief is in separation from our Source, and we see what we believe.

> *We choose to see the negative, the bad, the evil, because that's where our core belief lies.*

What we sometimes fail to appreciate is that the act of affirming our separateness only serves to set our self in opposition to That Which Is, the Infinite and Eternal All, the Alpha and Omega, the Absolute Oneness of Being. It is akin to fighting the heavyweight champion of the world round after round, bout after bout, day in day out. We don't stand a chance.

To remove the suffering in our life and the world, to witness the Peace of our Source in everything, to experience a more joyful and fulfilling existence (if in fact that is what we want to do), we must first change our original belief. We must first acknowledge the seed from which our otherwise mistaken belief of separation grows, *forgetfulness*, then root it out and plant in its place a new seed from which a whole new belief system arises, one that encompasses the notion that absolutely nothing can affect the deep inner abundance of our Natural State of Being.

A new belief in our Natural State of Joy will cultivate a deep appreciation and enjoyment of life, even with all its ups and downs.

A new belief in our Natural State of Security will build confidence and strength, even in the midst of worry and fear.

A new belief in our Natural State of Acceptance will nurture worthiness and belonging, even in the most degrading of circumstances.

A new belief in our Natural State of Peace will bring tranquility and calm, even in our wildest storms.

A new belief in our Natural State of Freedom will endow us with an abiding love and forgiveness of all humanity, even if we are locked behind bars or nailed to a cross.

Changing our core belief is therefore extremely powerful. It has the power to change our perception of our self in the world, to SEE and experience directly our True Nature. It is the first step on the path toward experiencing a new way of life, a new way of being.

It is also the first step on the pilgrimage toward communion with our Source, which is merely the experience or realization of Oneness, that there is no separation from paradise, that we need not start from scratch and thereby accumulate material wealth to make up for the shortfall.

Changing our core belief has the power to change our perception and experience of Reality.

LIES & TRUTH

As we have learned throughout the course of this book, problems and suffering arise or continue to beset our life when we fall into the trap that our very own ego has set, which is to continue to believe in our separation from everything else, to believe in our banishment from Eden—to blind us from seeing the movement of life as one thing.

We have also learned that the ego, our small mind, is terrified of communion with Big Mind because it associates Unity or Oneness with its own death. Caught in the fear of annihilation, the ego wants us to believe that God has rejected us, to believe that every single one of us is on our own, that it's us against the world. It needs to believe in isolation, or so it thinks, to maintain its very own sense of identity, indeed its very own existence. This is the essence of original sin, the acorn from which a myriad of mistaken beliefs grow. It is forgetfulness. In the words of a little known saint: [8]

> *Thine existence is a sin wherewith no other sin may be compared.*

There is also an apt saying in the medical profession, "A little knowledge is dangerous." When we think we know a little about an illness or disease, we can fall into the trap of thinking we know everything there is to know about it. Doctors and nurses who act from this level of thinking unwittingly put patient's lives at risk, even though they believe they are doing the right thing by them. The ego is like that. It will have us believe that we know all there is to know, or if we don't know everything at this moment we soon will. Ego says all knowledge can be ours. It says all power can be ours. It says our life is ours.

These beliefs of the ego are designed to preserve the illusion of separateness. The reality is that all Knowledge, all Power, and all Life are the possessions of our Source. Do ink and letter together make two?

Ironically, once we give up the illusion of isolated separateness and then surrender everything we have to Spirit (in other words, when we acknowledge the Oneness of Being), all Knowledge, all Power and all Life is given to us. The ego, though, will fight the belief in Unity to the bitter end. It has a vested interest in perpetuating the original sin: its own survival.

Like a secret agent, the ego's control is subtle, working unnoticed from the inside and getting us to do all the hard labor. It chains us to our self and it does this simply by reaffirming our original belief of separateness.

"You don't believe in all that mumbo-jumbo nonsense, do you?" it whispers in our ear. "How can we be united with everything when it's so obvious that we're not? Our eyes don't lie, do they?"

We look around and see those with different colored skin, different colored hair and eyes. We hear others speak in different languages. We see the differences and we concur: we are not like them, we are different. The ego then smiles for the experience of disconnection from Spirit has been affirmed, the illusion of its separate identity has been strengthened, and it has tightened its control over us.

Unfortunately, an awareness rooted in original sin forces us to concentrate on our differences and leads to the assumption that we cannot be interconnected with our Source, that we must be separate from everyone and everything. The ego equates the experience of communion with Spirit—Oneness—with a loss of individual identity, with being the same as everyone else. But this is not true. It is an illusion. It is forgetfulness.

Goebels, the propaganda minister for Hitler's Nazi regime, used to brag: "Tell a lie often enough and the people will believe it."

He knew and manipulated to his advantage the basic psychology of humanity, that people see what they believe. Even if it is a lie, when we believe something with our whole heart, it becomes our reality.

Likewise, the same can be said of the truth: remind yourself of it often enough—remember it frequently—and you will begin to believe it. And once believed, it will be seen:

We are One with Consciousness. We are One with Life.
We are One with Love. We are One.

It must be said, however, that the reiteration of truth, unlike the lies and misrepresentations of Goebels, isn't brainwashing. Brainwashing confines us to a prison of distorted reality for the benefit of those perpetuating the lies. From little white lies to grand propaganda, the motive of lying is to control what we see, to control how we behave. It is the tenet of some marketing executives and advertising gurus.

The truth, in direct contrast, wants nothing to do with chains or control. The truth aims to let us walk our own path, to journey at our own pace, to arrive in our own time. The truth sets us free.

For there is one truth I hold to be self-evident, my motto, motivation and intention for life, as it were:

> *If everyone on this planet believed with the utmost conviction that we are born with the connection to our Source still intact within our hearts, that banishment from paradise is an illusion, forgetfulness, created by the limited perception of our ego, then the collective behavior of the world would be infused with the abundance of joy, security, acceptance, peace and freedom that humanity has been seeking since the beginning of time; we would know in our own experience the Bountiful Plenitude of our Natural State of Being, and we would know that we have everything we need right in this moment.*

And if this were to occur, there would be no more wars, no more hunger, no more sexual or physical abuse of women and children, no more torture, no more horrors perpetuated on other human beings or animals or the environment. We would sing in our hearts the words of John Newton,

> *How precious did that grace appear*
> *The hour I first believed!*

Paradise lost would once again be found. There would be heaven on earth, a New Jerusalem.

POINTS OF REMEMBRANCE #14

♦ Without a belief in miracles there are no miracles.

BIBLIOGRAPHY

1. Eckhart Tolle. The Power of Now. Namaste Publishing, 1997. ISBN: 978-1-57731-152-2
2. The NIV Student Bible, Revised. Zondervan, 2002. First published 1986. Library of Congress Catalog Card No: 2002101309. First published 1999. ISBN: 0-340-73350-0 2.
3. Kahlil Gibran. The Prophet. Penguin Arkana, 1998. First published 1923. ISBN: 0-14-019561-0
4. George Fowler. Learning to Dance Inside: Getting to the Heart of Meditation. Perseus Books, 1996. ISBN: 0201410397
5. W. M. Jr Thackston. Signs of the Unseen: The Discourses of Jalaluddin Rumi. Shambhala Publications Inc., 1994. ISBN: 1-57062-532-8
6. M. Scott Peck. People of the Lie. Arrow Books, 1990. First published 1983. ISBN: 0-09-972860-5
7. Evelyn Underhill. Mysticism: A Study in the Nature and Development of Spiritual Consciousness. Dover Publications, 2002. Unabridged, unaltered republication of the twelfth edition (1930) by Dutton and Co. ISBN: 0-486-42238-0
8. Martin Lings. A Sufi Saint of the Twentieth Century. Second edition. George Allen & Unwin Ltd, 1971. First published 1961. ISBN: 0-04-297023-7
9. Deepak Chopra. How To Know God. Rider (Ebury Press imprint), 2000. ISBN: 0-7126-7035-1

10. T. S. Suzuki. An Introduction to Zen Buddhism. 1st Grove Weidenfeld edition, 1991. ISBN: 0802130550

11. Fritjof Capra. The Tao of Physics: An Exploration of the Parallels Between Modern Physics and Eastern Mysticism. Flamingo: 3rd Revised Edition, 1992. ISBN: 0006544894

12. Tulku Thondup. The Healing Power of Mind. Shambhala Publications, Inc., 1996. ISBN: 1-57062-330-9

13. Anjam Khursheed. The Universe Within: An Exploration of the Human Spirit. Oneworld Publications, 1995. ISBN: 1851680756

14. Deepak Chopra. Ageless Body, Timeless Mind. Rider, 1998. ISBN: 0-7126-7129-3

15. R. Walsh, F. Vaughan. Paths Beyond Ego: The Transpersonal Vision. Penguin/Putnam Inc., 1993. ISBN: 0-87477-678-3

16. M. Scott Peck. The Road Less Traveled: A New Psychology of Love, Traditional Values and Spiritual Growth. Touchstone, 1998. ISBN: 0-684-84724-8

17. Paulo Coelho. The Witch of Portobello. Harper Collins Publishers, 2007. ISBN: 073228596-8

AN INVITATION

If the content of this book contributes to your spiritual development and enlightenment, I am delighted to have had some positive impact and I am grateful for the opportunity to help. If you would like to accelerate your journey, I'd be honoured to help you further. I have devoted myself to making the world a better place by helping others fulfil their immense potential and to make themselves better people.

Your Natural State of Being starts with you. If accessing your innate sense of joy, security, acceptance, peace and freedom is how you perceive yourself, then action is how you manifest it. I invite you now to reach out to me and join the growing community of Life Leaders who are committed to helping all of us become who we were born to be. Don't let life pass by you—let life pass through you.

It's now up to you to help make this world a better place by being a better you.

That's your Natural State of Being.

Connect with DoctorZed

Facebook: YNSOB.by.Dr.Scott.Zarcinas
LinkedIn: dr-scott-zarcinas-6572399
Instagram: doctorzed_motivational_speaker
Twitter: @DrScottZarcinas
Website: scottzarcinas.com

Growing great people is how you grow a great business!

Are you a leader of a team, involved in a team environment, a business owner, or entrepreneur looking to grow your business?

Ask me how I can help your business grow by growing your people.

E: scott.zarcinas@doctorzed.com
W: scottzarcinas.com/contact

The Life You Want, the Way You Want, How You Want!

Looking for a coach or mentor to help you get direction and take your life to the next level?

Ask me how I can help you maximise your capabilities and reach your fullest potential.

E: scott.zarcinas@doctorzed.com
W: scottzarcinas.com/contact

Book DoctorZed for Your Next Function!
Keynotes • MC • Presentations

scottzarcinas.com/book-doctorzed/

Other Titles by Scott Zarcinas

The Power of YOU! How to Manifest the Life You Want
by Scott Zarcinas M.D.

ISBN: 978-0-6456384-5-5
eISBN: 978-0-6456384-6-2

DoctorZed Publishing

Available in print and ebook.

Featuring 4 Power Habits of Success.

Self-Belief, Courage & Conviction!

For every 20 babies that are born, only one of them will be deemed 'successful' at the age of 65—only 5% of the population.

But those in The 5% Club are no different from anyone else. They have just learned the secret of success, which you can too.

The secret is this: Success is merely a habit. A habit of right thinking. A habit of right being. A habit of right doing.

When you get your habits right, your membership to The 5% Club is guaranteed.

www.scottzarcinas.com/books/the-power-of-you

It's Up to YOU! Why Most People Fail to Live the Life they Want and How to Change It
by Scott Zarcinas M.D.

ISBN: 978-0-6485726-4-0
eISBN: 978-0-6485726-3-3

DoctorZed Publishing

Available in print and ebook.

Featuring 9 Life Leadership Strategies to Live the Life You Want, the Way You Want, How You Want.

Do you feel stuck in a rut and your life is on hold? Are you looking for new direction but don't know which way to turn?

We all want to do more than just survive; we want to thrive. But if you're trapped in the same old routine, now is the time to start living the life you were born to live—with abundance.

This book is your go-to manual if:

- You need a break from the old and to take a new direction.
- You desire greater success and fulfillment.
- You seek the confidence to be yourself and not what others expect you to be.

www.scottzarcinas.com/books/its-up-to-you

The Banana Trap: How to Escape a Life of Stress and Finally Break Free
by Scott Zarcinas M.D.

ISBN: 978-0-6485726-1-9
eISBN: 978-0-6487107-9-0

DoctorZed Publishing

Available in print and ebook.

Science-based Stress Management Strategies to De-Stress & Prosper

Do you feel overwhelmed and over-stressed? Are you trapped in recurring cycles of worry and frustration? Do you crumble in stressful moments?

Don't worry, everybody has moments of high stress and overwhelm! This guidebook will help you to:

- Feel less overwhelmed and more confident
- Escape The Banana Trap and reclaim your life
- Identify and overcome the different types of stress
- Eliminate stressful habits and increase happiness
- Deal with high-pressure situations and be in control

PLUS develop a long-term strategy to prevent high stress before it occurs.

www.scottzarcinas.com/books/the-banana-trap

www.ingramcontent.com/pod-product-compliance
Lightning Source LLC
LaVergne TN
LVHW041611070426
835507LV00008B/188